Raspberry Pi for Arduino Users

Building IoT and Network Applications and Devices

D0555605

James R. Strickland

Apress®

Raspberry Pi for Arduino Users: Building IoT and Network Applications and Devices

James R. Strickland
Highlands Ranch, Colorado, USA

ISBN-13 (pbk): 978-1-4842-3413-6   ISBN-13 (electronic): 978-1-4842-3414-3
https://doi.org/10.1007/978-1-4842-3414-3

Library of Congress Control Number: 2018946559

Managing Director, Apress Media LLC: Welmoed Spahr
Acquisitions Editor: Aaron Black
Development Editor: James Markham
Coordinating Editor: Jessica Vakili

Cover designed by eStudioCalamar

Cover image designed by Freepik (www.freepik.com)

Distributed to the book trade worldwide by Springer Science+Business Media New York, 233 Spring Street, 6th Floor, New York, NY 10013. Phone 1-800-SPRINGER, fax (201) 348-4505, e-mail orders-ny@springer-sbm.com, or visit www.springeronline.com. Apress Media, LLC is a California LLC and the sole member (owner) is Springer Science + Business Media Finance Inc (SSBM Finance Inc). SSBM Finance Inc is a Delaware corporation.

For information on translations, please e-mail rights@apress.com, or visit http://www.apress.com/rights-permissions.

Apress titles may be purchased in bulk for academic, corporate, or promotional use. eBook versions and licenses are also available for most titles. For more information, reference our Print and eBook Bulk Sales web page at http://www.apress.com/bulk-sales.

Any source code or other supplementary material referenced by the author in this book is available to readers on GitHub via the book's product page, located at www.apress.com/978-1-4842-3413-6. For more detailed information, please visit http://www.apress.com/source-code.

Printed on acid-free paper

Table of Contents

iii

About the Author

 **James R. Strickland** is a professional nerd who writes steampunk, science fiction, technical books, and technical video. When that doesn't fill his time, he tinkers with his 3D printer, ebike, retrocomputer(s), code, and antique radios. He is still known to play role playing games occasionally. He lives in the Denver metro area with his wife, Marcia, and a variable number of cats. He can be found online at http://www.jamesrstrickland.com. He is also the author of another Apress book called *Junk Box Arduino, Ten Projects in Upcycled Electronics,* ISBN-13 (electronic) 978-1-4842-1425-1 and (paperback) 978-1-4842-1426-8.

About the Technical Reviewers

 **Massimo Nardone** has more than 22 years of experience in security, web/mobile development, and cloud and IT architecture. His true IT passions are security and Android. He has been programming and teaching people how to program with Android, Perl, PHP, Java, VB, Python, C/C++, and MySQL for more than 20 years. He has worked as a project manager, software engineer, research engineer, chief security architect, information security manager, PCI/SCADA auditor, and senior lead IT security/cloud/SCADA architect for many years.

His technical skills include security, android, cloud, Java, MySQL, Drupal, Cobol, Perl, web and mobile development, MongoDB, D3, Joomla, Couchbase, C/C++, WebGL, Python, Pro Rails, Django CMS, Jekyll, Scratch, etc. He currently works as a Chief Information Security Officer (CISO) for Cargotec Oyj. He worked as visiting lecturer and supervisor for exercises at the Networking Laboratory of the Helsinki University of Technology (Aalto University). He holds four international patents (PKI, SIP, SAML, and Proxy areas). He holds a Master of Science degree in computing science from the University of Salerno, Italy.

Sai Yamanoor is an IoT applications engineer working for an industrial gases company in Buffalo, NY. He completed his graduate studies in mechanical engineering at Carnegie Mellon University, Pittsburgh PA. His interests, deeply rooted in DIY and open source hardware, include developing gadgets that aid behavior modification. In his spare time, he tinkers with his Raspberry Pi and Arduino. You can find his project portfolio at `http://saiyamanoor.com`.

Introduction

Pre-Introduction Introduction

If you're in your favorite hobbiest electronics store with this book in hand (thank you!), and you're looking for all the parts you need, stop. Skip ahead to Chapter 1, called "Your Shopping List." The information you're looking for is there. The rest of this introduction will be here when you get back.

A Little Background

Once upon a time, real computing was done on mainframes, which could fill whole buildings, and minicomputers, which might be the size of a few file cabinets. Those machines had serious (for their time) computing power, and you were charged by the minute to use them. That began to change in 1971 with the invention of the Intel 4004, the first civilian microprocessor. The microprocessor, in turn, spawned two distinct families of computer.

Microcomputers

If you wanted a microcomputer—because you worked with computers during the day, or you were a computer science student perhaps, and wanted to experiment without paying for computer time—you bought a kit like the Altair 8800 (or its clone, the Imsai 8080), a Heathkit H8, or perhaps a Cosmac Elf if you were on a budget. If you were skilled and fortunate enough to get the kit soldered together and working properly, you had a computer. It was yours, and you could do what you wanted with it.

By late 1982, microcomputers had become a fad. You could go to Kmart and buy a Vic 20 or Commodore 64, or to Radio Shack for any of the vast TRS-80 family of computers. One thing was common to all of them, though. Software was expensive. Sooner or later, unless you were only using the machine as a glorified Atari (as in the Atari 2600, a video game console of the day), you were going to have to write some code. For a lot of us, this was the real attraction. The computer did what we wanted, even though some of us were kids. The more electronically astute added circuitry, just as their IMSAI forbearers had. You explored this machine all the way through to see what it was capable of, what you could make it do. Our IMSAI forebears and exceptional Apple II/TRS-80/Commodore 64 tinkerers developed deep understandings of their machines, pushed their limits, and learned computing all the way down to the logic gate level and beyond.

Microcontrollers

Back in the mid-to-late 1970s, it became obvious that computerizing traffic lights, your car, your toaster, and so on was still too expensive. A microcomputer had to have the CPU, the clock, the RAM, logic to control the RAM, and ROM to boot from. You had to build a complete computer to do simple tasks, and then it was too big, took too much power, and cost too much for volume production. Engineers at Texas Instruments and Intel addressed this problem first, with the TMS 1000 and the Intel 8048 and 8051 microcontrollers, respectively. These contained RAM and ROM on the IC, and in the case of the TMS 1000, also included the system clock. You programmed them like ROMs or EPROMs—placed the IC in a specially designed programmer and burned the program into the device, connected power and whatever peripheral circuitry they needed to do their jobs, and away they went. Today, when you compare desktop microcomputers to microcontrollers, like the bacteria in your digestive system verses the number of your cells in your body, they outnumber desktop computers by thousands to one. Um. You did know about the intestinal bacteria thing, right? Sorry.

The Decline

By the 2000s, thanks to the explosion of the Internet and computers that access it, home computers had become like the family car, packaged as consumer devices with no user serviceable parts inside, like my Mac Mini or my iPhone today. Sealed up, opening the case voids the warrantee, and I can't even load my own software on my iPhone. Just like today, microcontroller devices weren't user modifiable at all, and if you bought new, blank microcontrollers, you had to make a substantial investment in equipment, software, and licenses. The result was that fewer people had the kind of deep understanding of computers that built the industry in the first place, at a time when literally everything was—and is—becoming computerized. Could the Internet, which had produced the Linux operating system, not produce tools to allow new generations of tinkerers that same access? It could.

The New Beginning

There were always hobbyists. The 8051, and later the MicroChip PIC and Parallax BASIC Stamp platforms, have and still retain a hard core of enthusiasts, but these platforms required complex, often expensive, software tools and a great deal of study of individual ICs to learn how to control their specific peripherals. As his master's thesis project, Hernando Barragán set out to simplify the learning and programming of microcontrollers and to make the tools free and open source. His project gave each pin a standard name and a standard set of functions to control it, and to call its special functions, if any. He called it Wiring. He soon retargeted it to Atmel's less expensive AVR microcontrollers.

Wiring evolved to include an IDE and incorporated Brian Dean's AVRDUDE, which allowed users to upload programs to their microcontroller board easily. It was open source from the start. If all of this sounds familiar, it should. Wiring boards ran about $50 US each. According to Barragán, Massimo Banzi, originally his advisor on the Wiring project, developed a much cheaper board using the ATmega8 family of chips, forked Wiring to support it, and renamed the whole thing Arduino. The rest is history. Today, there's a whole family of microcontroller-based systems that use the Wiring/Arduino development environment.

On the microcomputer side, on February 29, 2012 came the Raspberry Pi. Faced with the problem of declining skills and lack of applicants to the St. John's College computing department, Eben Upton set out to provide a hackable computer, like the ones we had in the 1980s, for today's generations of students.

The Pi was originally a single core, 32-bit ARM CPU running with 256MiB of RAM, a socket for an SD card, and connectors for commodity monitors, keyboards, mice, and wired Ethernet. In sharp contrast to Wiring, it ran and still runs the quintessential open source operating system, Linux, descendant of UNIX, which in turn is the foundation of nearly all operating systems currently in use today that don't come from Microsoft. (It should be mentioned that Microsoft does have a version of Windows for the Pi, although what the advantage of that would be, I'm the wrong person to ask.)

The Raspberry Pi foundation controls development of devices called Raspberry Pi much more tightly, but there is still a family of Raspberry Pi products today, ranging from the Raspberry Pi Zero, the smallest and cheapest Pi, nominally priced at $5 US, to the Raspberry Pi 3, Model B, a 1.2GHz quad-core 64-bit ARM with 1GiB of RAM.

Two different approaches to essentially the same problem. One (Arduino) designed for university students, the other (Raspberry Pi) designed for home tinkerers, particularly kids. The game changer, once again, was the Internet.

Internet of Things and Raspberry Pi

As the Internet emerged, in the 1980s and beyond, it slowly but surely made those old 8-bit microcomputers unusable. The overhead for TCP/IP, the Internet protocol, was more than those computers could easily handle, to say nothing of the graphically and structurally complex web documents, video, and so forth that were to come.

Microcontrollers, for their part, rarely communicated in anything but serial protocols, like RS-232 (now properly called TIA-232-F, to reflect the revised standard). Today, by contrast, even microcontroller-driven gadgets are connected to the Internet. As I write this, my home thermostat and my home sprinkler controller are network accessible from anywhere in the world. So are the house laser printers, scanner, and all the TVs. Even my watch has a microcontroller that is networked to my phone. It's a networked world. Microcontroller or microcomputer, your gadget probably needs to communicate with the Internet.

You can get there with Arduino. You can add an Arduino Ethernet Shield 2, from the Arduino foundation, for less than $25 US. You can get tiny ARM devices with built-in Bluetooth and WiFi like the ESP8266. They are now supported by the Arduino IDE, and can be had for less than $10 US. Theoretically, all you need to do is add another library and write code.

Or you could switch to the Raspberry Pi. A Raspberry Pi 3 Model B will cost about $35 US, not including a microSD card. It has Ethernet, USB, WiFi, and Bluetooth built-in, and if you need to, you can plug in any commodity USB keyboard, mouse, and monitor. More intriguing is the Raspberry Pi Zero W, which costs about $10 US. It comes with USB, Bluetooth, and WiFi. The Raspberry Pis are price competitive. They offer orders of magnitude more compute power, a full-blown Linux-based operating system (called Raspbian), and like Arduino, they have an extensive community supporting them. There's a lot more complexity in a Pi, no matter what flavor you get, and there's a huge cultural gulf between the two. This book is about bridging that gulf. It's about leveraging the skills you've learned writing sketches for Arduino into writing Linux programs for Raspberry Pi. You'll know about the strengths and weaknesses of the Pi versus the Arduino. You'll know how to keep Linux alive, and what it can do for you. You won't have to learn any Python (I promise). When all is said and done, you'll be able to knowledgeably pick the platform that best suits the problem you're trying to solve.

How to Use This Book

Read This Book

There's a lot of theory sneaking around here, mostly about Linux, so that when you're done, you'll have more than some flashing LEDs and speakers making sounds, and stuff like that. You'll have the basics you need to operate the Raspberry Pi and to make it do what you want as easily as you do with Arduino. That's what this book is for.

Read the projects all the way through before you start, particularly the "Stuff You Need" sections. When a project doesn't turn out for me, it's usually because I was trying to work around a missing part, or I didn't have the right tool and tried to make do with my scout knife, or I didn't really understand what I was doing. The projects in this book are more than step-by-step instructions to make something fun. You're an Arduino user. You've done that. The projects are here to teach some important concept about the Pi, Linux, and the differences from what you're used to in the Arduino world. Each one assumes you not only did the previous project, but also thought about it, understood it, read the theory chapters, and that you're hungry for more.

Be Safe

Raspberry Pi hacking isn't a dangerous sport. Most of the risks are to the Pi and not you. There are exceptions. Double-check electrolytic capacitors. Some of them are polarized and can explode like firecrackers if connected backwards. (We're not using any like that in these projects.) When you fry an electronic component, the smoke isn't good for you, and they can get hot enough to start fires. Small parts can be swallowed by your small relatives or pets. The Pi can drive earbuds loudly enough to damage your hearing. The Pi, despite its name, is not edible. Finally, there is soldering involved in this book. If you don't already know how to solder and own the appropriate tools, I strongly recommend Dave Jones' EEV blog, and his soldering tutorial videos. You can find them on his YouTube channel here: `https://www.youtube.com/watch?v=J5Sb21qbpEQ`. Or just search on EEV Blog Soldering Tutorial. I will mention one thing about soldering, or using any power tool for that matter. Wear safety goggles every time. You only get one set of eyeballs in this life, and they're fragile. Protect them. Likewise, soldering fumes are vaporized flux, which is a strong acid. Not good for your lungs. Good ventilation is a good idea.

Be Fearless

Sooner or later, your Pi will crash. A program won't run. Your SD card will get corrupted. Your GPIO project won't work, or the Pi won't boot with it connected. Eventually you'll burn up a resistor, smoke a chip, maybe even fry your Raspberry Pi. This hobby can be frustrating some days. It's okay. Cut yourself some slack. Once you're calm again, find out why it happened.

A few years ago, I soldered a small computer up from bare chips and a circuit board. When I powered it up, nothing happened. I checked the voltages to all the chips and discovered that I'd missed soldering a bunch of pins. Once that was fixed, it would send a startup message to its serial port but then it would just sit there, ignoring any input from me. I dug out my logic analyzer, read up on how to use it, and slowly worked my way through that computer. The CPU clock worked. The CPU requested data from memory. Memory worked. The boot flash worked. So far as I could tell, the computer actually was booting, right up to the point where it needed me to tell it what to do next. It just wasn't getting my commands. That smelled like a communications problem. Finally, I used my multimeter to see if somehow one of the circuits between the connector and the serial chip was bad. The mystery unraveled. The input pins were wired wrong. The pin that should have taken my commands to the computer was connected to an entirely different part of the communications chip. It was wrong because I'd soldered the wrong gender of serial port to my board, and the pins were reversed. Simple error? Yes. Was fixing it a nuisance? Yes. But I learned how the whole computer worked, down to a level I'd never touched before. Those skills are mine to keep. All of that in exchange for some salty language, time, and replacing a $3 connector. Failure is part of learning. It's okay. That computer still works today. I wrote part of the conclusion of this book on it.

CHAPTER 1

Your Shopping List

This chapter is a shopping list. It's not very long. There aren't very many hardware projects in this book, really, and many of the software projects use the same hardware setup. If you're coming to this book from the Arduino world, I figure you *have* projects you want to connect. How many more "Light the Seven Segment LED" tutorials are really necessary? You may have some of these parts already—the ATmega328P, the 74LVC245, the LED arrays, resistors, hookup wire, and so on—they're staples of the Arduino world too. I'm going to assume you do already have the tools—digital multimeter, wire cutters and strippers, temperature controlled soldering station, and so on.

If your Arduino experience has mostly been about plugging in shields, you may want to look at my previous book with Apress: *Junk Box Arduino, Ten Projects in Upcycled Electronics,* as long as you're shopping. Blatant plug? You bet. That book is designed, among other things, to cover the ground between the online Arduino tutorials and knowing your way around electronics. In this book, I assume you know all that already.

The Raspberry Pi is a family of low-cost, high-performance 32- and 64-bit single board computer systems. They run a distribution of Linux called Raspbian, up to and including a full desktop suite and modern web browser (Chromium). This book covers the Raspberry Pi 3 Model B+, the quad-core 64-bit version running at 1.4GHz, and the Raspberry Pi Zero W, the single-core 32-bit version running at 1GHz. They feature connectivity with modern peripherals via USB, HDMI, and 802.3 Ethernet, as well as Bluetooth and WiFi.

© James R. Strickland 2018
J. R. Strickland, *Raspberry Pi for Arduino Users,*
https://doi.org/10.1007/978-1-4842-3414-3_1

Raspberry Pi

You'll need a Raspberry Pi. In this book, I'm going to assume you have one of only two models, for sanity's sake: the Raspberry Pi 3 Model B+, or the Raspberry Pi Zero W. The Raspberry Pi 3 Model B will also work.

Raspberry Pi 3 Model B+

The Raspberry Pi 3 Model B+ is the most powerful Raspberry Pi in existence. (It's shown in Figure 1-1.)

Figure 1-1. *Raspberry Pi 3 Model B+*

The Raspberry Pi 3 Model B+ is a quad-core, 64-bit Arm Cortex A53-based system running at 1.4GHz. It has 1GiB (*gibibyte*, discussed shortly) of RAM running at 900MHz, with 1000BASE-T 802.3 Ethernet (running at 300Mbps), 2.4GHz 802.11ac, and Bluetooth 4.2. It stores its data on a microSD card. It has an HDMI port, a 3.5mm analog audio-video jack, four USB 2.0 ports, a 1000BASE-T Ethernet jack, a 40-pin GPIO header (with the pins already soldered in), and camera and display serial interfaces.

Wow. Jargon. Let's break that down.

Quad Core

Essentially, there are four CPUs built into the Raspberry Pi 3 Model B+'s Broadcom 2837B0 chip. These can execute four threads or processes (we'll cover those later) at a time. Typically, multicore CPUs share level2 (L2) cache, but have their own level 1(L1) caches, which means that instead of talking to external memory directly, each core has its own small, fast memory space for its own use (L1 cache), which is updated to and from the L2 cache, which in turn updates and is updated by the system RAM.

What's the cache for? The short answer to the question is *speed*. Main memory is farther away (a few millimeters) and has to go through more electronics, each stage of which adds a little delay. Having RAM inside the core means the core does not have to wait for system RAM to catch up. Memory caching also lets the core read its next instruction while it's busy executing the one it has. This gets very complicated when programs branch (jump to instructions out of order), and these considerations as well as all the *other* interesting things you can do with cached memory are the bread and butter of a CPU architect's job.

64 Bit

Every register (an area inside the CPU where it can store data during processing) is at least a 64-bit word, or eight bytes, wide. (A word is simply the number of bits of width. In ancient times—the 1970s and 1980s—you might have heard computer scientists talk about 12-bit bytes and 16-bit bytes, but the word byte has become standardized to mean 8 bits,—no more, no less.) Technically, this is all that's required, although it's likely the interface to system RAM is also 64 bits wide.

The upshot? Each core can execute single instructions on 64-bit words. If the instruction is moving words to and from RAM, you can move 8 potentially unrelated bytes at a time. The real value-add of 64-bit words is doing number crunching on 64-bit values. If your core can't process 64-bit values and it needs to, you have to write a lot of extra code to break the value down into 32-bit words, or even 8-bit words, and then put it all back together after you've done the math. Instructions take time. Instructions that act on 64-bit values save time.

ARM Cortex-A53

This is the type of core. ARM is a family of core definitions, all descended from the ARM (Acorn RISC Machine) chip designed for the Acorn Archimedes personal computer by Acorn Computers, of Cambridge, England. Today they are designed by ARM Holdings, also of Cambridge and licensed to a bewildering variety of chip manufacturers, including Broadcom, maker of the Raspberry Pi's system chip. To come full circle with Arduino, Atmel (now Microchip), maker of the ATmega microcontrollers used in Arduinos, also manufactures ARM-based products.

ARM cores are used in nearly every consumer tablet and phone, as well as a huge variety of embedded devices. They're reasonably powerful and electrically efficient, which is important for battery life. The ARM core comes in a huge number of varieties. The A53 is one to four cores of the ARM v8-A architecture, backward compatible with the ARM v7, 32-bit cores, which is undoubtedly why the Raspberry Pi foundation chose it. It has better floating-point math, and more compute power than the previous versions. It's designed for tablets and phones, primarily. The BCM2837B0 in the Raspberry Pi 3 Model B+ also comes with the Broadcom VideoCore IV GPU, and in fact more of the space on the chip is GPU than ARM. This does exactly the same thing as the GPU in your desktop: it accelerates graphics and decodes video streams.

Networking

802.3 1000BASE-T Ethernet is wired Ethernet in its most common form today. It's capable of up to 300 megabits per second on the Pi and uses two pairs of copper wire in the usual Category 5 (Cat 5) cable. If you've used Ethernet in the last 10 years, you've probably dealt with this type of wiring, and with 1000BASE-T. (There are older standards. Trust me when I say that 10BASE-T and its descendants, 100BASE-Tx and 1000BASE-T, are vast improvements. 10BASE-2 was awful.)

802.11ac is the current standard for WiFi. If you happen to have an 802.11ac Wireless Access Point (WAP), it's theoretically capable of up to 1.3 gigabits per second, although the real world performance for the Pi is more along the lines of 75-100 megabits per second. I don't have such a WAP, so I can't comment on the speed from personal experience, except to say that it's fast enough.

GPIO Header

These have many of the same functions as the GPIO pins on an Arduino, although they are strictly 3.3v pins. If you apply five volts on a Pi's GPIO header, you will destroy that line (and possibly more) within the chip itself. They are not protected or current limited in any way. The Raspberry Pi 3 Model B+ has pins soldered into the GPIO header. This is important if you don't feel comfortable soldering on crowded printed circuit boards.

Camera and Display Serial Interfaces

The camera and display serial interfaces take a fine ribbon cable and connect to the official Pi digital camera and the official Pi display.

Gibibyte versus Gigabyte

Once upon a time, a kilobyte (KB) was 1024 bytes, a megabyte (MB) was 1024KB, and a gigabyte (GB) was 1024 megabytes. These numbers were, and are, defined by the JEDEC standard used for memory. In the 1990s, hard drive makers cheated on these numbers using decimal gigabytes (1000 megabytes) for binary storage, resulting in lawsuits. In response, in ISO80000-13, the IEC/ISO standardized an explicitly binary (if unpronounceable) set of units: kibibyte (KiB), mebibyte (MiB), gibibyte (GiB), and so on. Your microSD cards will be sold in decimal gigabytes, which is cheating you a little, but your RAM (thanks to JEDEC) will be sold in binary gigabytes. I'll use the ISO/IEC standard notation throughout.

Why Buy This Pi?

If you're planning to do much development on the Raspberry Pi, and it fits in the budget, this is the Pi to have, even if you plan to run the project on a Pi Zero W. The Raspberry Pi 3 Model B+ was released during the writing of this book, so most of the code prototyping was actually done on its predecessor, which is only slightly slower. Even then, the extra speed and RAM made compiling much more pleasant.

Note   If you're shopping online for the Raspberry Pi 3 Model B+, pay careful attention to your search results. A lot of search engines like to eat + signs, which will give you the Raspberry Pi 3 Model B (the old, pre-B+ version). The older version will work, but since they're the same price, why not get the faster one?

Suppliers

Adafruit: `https://www.adafruit.com/product/3775`

Microcenter: `http://www.microcenter.com/`
`product/505170/Raspberry_Pi_3_Model_B`

Newark: `http://www.newark.com/raspberrypi-`
`boards#mk-pi-3-model-b+`

Sparkfun: `https://www.sparkfun.com/products/14643`

Raspberry Pi Zero W

If your budget is *that* tight, or you don't want to spend about US $35 on a Pi
until you're sure you like them, you can do all the projects in this book on
the Raspberry Pi Zero W, (shown in Figure 1-2), for less than half the price
(about US $10). I've tested all the projects in this book and included any
changes you need to make to get them to work on the Pi Zero W.

Figure 1-2. *Raspberry Pi Zero W and adapters*

The Raspberry Pi Zero W is the least expensive Raspberry Pi model with built-in Bluetooth and 802.11n WiFi. It runs the Broadcom BCM2835 chip, which is the same one used on the original Raspberry Pi. This is a single, 32-bit ARM core with the Video IV GPU, running at 1GHz. It has 512MiB of RAM probably running at 600MHz, essentially stable overclock settings from the original Raspberry Pi. It has an earlier ARM core version, the ARM11, with the ARMv6 architecture instead of ARMv8-A.

Its peripherals are the same as the Raspberry Pi 3 Model B+'s, except that it does not have the 1000BASE-T Ethernet jack or IC, and has only one USB Micro-B socket for USB.

The Pi Zero W's GPIO header is not populated from the factory. This means that if you want normal GPIO pins, the holes are there, but you'll have to solder the pins in yourself. You can use this to your advantage. I knew that for the photographs, I was going to be plugging my Pi Zero W into a breakout board. I soldered in a 2x20 pin stackable header like the one on the bottom-left of Figure 1-2 (I got mine from Adafruit at `https://www.adafruit.com/product/1979`). Since the holes are plated through and double sided, I put the stackable header underneath and soldered on the topside of the board. This lets me put the Pi Zero into the breakout board's socket directly, without a ribbon cable. It photographs better this way.

Note   The Pi Zero W is different from the less expensive Pi Zero in one crucial respect: it has a WiFi interface and antenna built in. Since the Pi Zero and Zero W have only one USB port (USB Micro-B, to be exact), it's really not practical to plug a USB WiFi dongle into them.

Why Buy This Pi?

Above all, the Raspberry Pi Zero W is inexpensive. If you came to this book looking for an effective, inexpensive way to connect your gadget to the net, the Pi Zero W is as cheap as you can get, in the Pi world.

If you go the Raspberry Pi Zero W route, you will need a few things that the Pi 3 Model B+ crowd does not. We'll cover this in "Adapters," later in this section.

Suppliers

Adafruit: `https://www.adafruit.com/product/3400`

Microcenter: `http://www.microcenter.com/product/475267/raspberry_pi_zero_wireless`

Sparkfun: `https://www.sparkfun.com/products/14277`

Newark: Incredibly, Newark doesn't seem to carry the Raspberry Pi Zero W. You might check anyway. They could just be out.

Adapters

In Figure 1-2, you can also see the adapters you need for the Raspberry Pi Zero W in order to use it with a keyboard, mouse, and monitor. At the top is a mini-HDMI to HDMI adapter. This lets you plug a standard HDMI cable from your monitor into the Pi Zero W.

Below that is a USB OTG host cable. It goes from the Micro-B OTG socket on your Pi Zero W to a standard USB A female socket, so you can plug in your keyboard. Make sure you get an OTG cable and not a mini-USB cable. They're not the same connector. I plugged my keyboard into the OTG cable, and my mouse into the keyboard.

If you want to do the project in Chapter 11, you'll also need a powered USB hub and a microSD to USB adapter. These are common items. You might already have them.

Suppliers

Adafruit: `https://www.adafruit.com/product/1099` (OTG cable)

`https://www.adafruit.com/product/1358` (Micro-HDMI to HDMI)

`https://www.adafruit.com/product/939` (microSD-USB adapter)

`https://www.adafruit.com/product/961` (powered USB hub)

Microcenter: `http://www.microcenter.com/product/458736/Micro_USB_OTG_Cable` (OTG cable)

`http://www.microcenter.com/product/391044/10_inch_Digital_A-V_HDMI_Female_to_Mini-HDMI_Male_HD_Camcorder_Conversion_Cable` (Mini-HDMI to HDMI female; needs regular HDMI cable to connect to monitor)

`http://www.microcenter.com/product/467960/SuperSpeed_USB_30_SD_-_MicroSD_Card_Reader_-_Writer` (microSD to USB card adapter)

Mouser: http://www.mouser.com/ProductDetail/
Terasic-Technologies/FCB-3086-JMS/?qs=sGAEpi
MZZMs1xdPSgahjwjGC642QpXDf6ZIMhL6zKyc%3d (No
hard specs, but it looks like the right cable)

http://www.mouser.com/ProductDetail/Adafrui
t/1358/?qs=sGAEpiMZZMsMyYRRhGMFNmO2zoVxdpam
RD2wuqh6ijw%3d (This is the Adafruit cable again, so
despite the lack of specs on the Mouser page, it's the
right one)

Newark: http://www.newark.com/startech/
uusbotgadap/usb-otg-adapter-usb-a-micro-usb/
dp/26Y8300 (OTG cable)

http://www.newark.com/adafruit/1322/cable-
assembly-micro-hdmi-plug/dp/88W4554 (Mini-
HDMI to HDMI Male. Plugs into a monitor)

Sparkfun: https://www.sparkfun.com/
products/11604 (OTG cable)

https://www.sparkfun.com/products/14274
(Mini-HDMI to HDMI Male. Plugs into a monitor)

Other Raspberry Pis

The older Raspberry Pi 3 Model B (without the plus) definitely works for all
these projects. Other Raspberry Pis may work. Should work. Theoretically,
if you plugged a WiFi dongle into an original 2012 Raspberry Pi, you could
do all the projects in this book, and in theory, you'd have the equivalent of
a slower Pi Zero W. The system chip on the Pi Zero W is the same model
as the original Pi, albeit running faster, and with twice the RAM as the very
first Pis. It *should* work.

I don't claim that it *will* work because I didn't test any of the projects with the larger family of Raspberry Pis. My assumption with this book is that you're coming to the Pi world from the Arduino world, and in so doing, you'll be buying new Pis. Also, the first generation Pis had some issues particularly with the on-board power supply and SD card corruption, that make them a little more painful to work with at times. The Pi has gotten a lot better over the last five years (as of this writing, in Autumn of 2017). Gone are the days when plugging in a USB device would crash the Pi from power line fluctuations, and I, for one, don't miss them.

There's also the larger concern: Raspberry Pis before the Raspberry Pi 2 had a 26-pin GPIO header. The pin numbers are different, and different pins of the system chip are brought out on them. If you use one of those, my circuit diagrams won't work for you, and a lot of modern Pi peripherals (including all HATs) won't connect to them. Unless your budget really is that tight, and I know it gets that way, I recommend springing for at least the modern Pi Zero W.

Raspberry Pi GPIO Breakout Board

You'll also need a Raspberry Pi GPIO breakout board, as shown in Figure 1-3. You could do without this board in favor of female-to-male premade jumpers. I don't recommend it. We'll be using nearly all the pins on the Pi, and flakey connections can ruin your whole day.

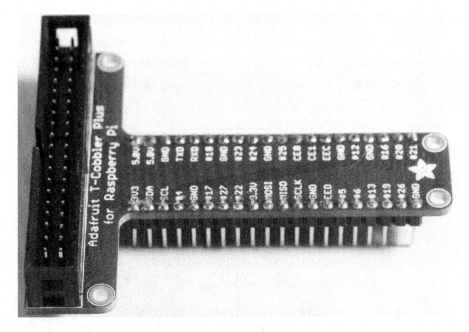

Figure 1-3. *Raspberry Pi GPIO breakout board*

These are Raspberry Pi specialty items. They let you break the GPIO pins of the Raspberry Pi to your breadboard easily. Normally, this is connected to your Pi via a 40-pin ribbon cable (included but not shown).

You might be tempted, as I was, to use an old PATA 40-pin cable and some pin headers for this job. Unfortunately, it doesn't work. PATA's pin #20 is usually plugged and often not connected, and we need pin 20. Alas. There's no good substitution for this part, although with the proliferation of the Pi it's not exactly uncommon either.

Breakout boards come in several flavors. The straight kind are, to my mind, awkward, since they put the ribbon cable over one side or the other of your breadboard, and are constantly in the way when breadboarding. I used one in the R&D phase of this book. Trust me on this. I recommend the T kind, as shown in Figure 1-3. You can also get them assembled or unassembled. You'll have to solder the socket and the pin headers into

13

the unassembled kind, obviously, so if soldering 80 pins relatively close together isn't something you want to do, get the assembled kind.

There is one important consideration. For modern Pis like the Raspberry Pi 3 Model B+ and the Raspberry Pi Zero W, you need the 40-pin version, not the 26-pin one. Make sure it says so in the documentation. All the schematics assume a 40-pin breakout.

Suppliers

Adafruit: `https://www.adafruit.com/product/2028` (Assembled)

`https://www.adafruit.com/product/1989` (Unassembled, requires soldering)

Microcenter: `http://www.microcenter.com/product/455628/assembled_pi_t-cobbler_plus_-_gpio_breakout_for_raspberry_pi` (The assembled Adafruit board again)

Mouser: `http://www.mouser.com/ProductDetail/Adafruit/1754/?qs=sGAEpiMZZMu%252bmKbOcEVhFQfi8wYXkauJUOoyVV9ZEOsL91c53Z%2fj5Q%3d%3d` (Adafruit board, assembled)

`http://www.mouser.com/ProductDetail/Adafruit/1105/?qs=sGAEpiMZZMu%252bmKbOcEVhFQfi8wYXkauJVgSSysK9ZXSr%252b2jvqA4dxA%3d%3d` (Adafruit board, unassembled)

Newark: `http://www.newark.com/piface/shim/gpio-duplication-board-raspberry/dp/83X9199` (An inline, unassembled board. About as simple as it gets)

Sparkfun: `https://www.sparkfun.com/` `products/13717` (A slightly different board with some decoupling caps and a separate breakout for TTL level RS232. Fully Assembled)

5-Volt USB Micro Power Supply

Figure 1-4 shows a 5-volt USB micro power supply designed for Raspberry Pi. I recommend these, to the exclusion of all other solutions, at least for development.

Figure 1-4. *5v USB micro power supply*

I've used phone chargers, and USB hubs, and all kinds of other power supplies for the Pi. These have been the most reliable. Gone are the bad old days when plugging the wrong keyboard in would get you mysterious keyboard jittering. Gone are the days when a power sag might corrupt your microSD card, and the first time you know about it is when the system either freezes or spews filesystem warnings at boot time. A good power supply is worth the investment.

Other Power Supply Options

You might be tempted to use your benchtop power supply, should you have one. If you make up a power supply to Micro-BM (aka MicroUSB) power connector to plug into the Pi, this should work. I don't recommend connecting your power supply to the breadboard and then connecting the Pi's 5v rail to the breadboard. Last time I tried it, the Pi would boot and run okay, but you've bypassed the fuses and other power protection built into the Pi's onboard power supply. My benchtop power supply is one of those modified PC ATX power supplies, producing well over 10 amps on its 5v rail. Nothing in the Pi can handle that kind of current if a short occurs, once you're past the on-board power supply. I hate that connector too. Please. Use it anyway.

You might also be tempted to power your Pi from your desktop computer or a powered USB hub. Adafruit even sells powered USB hubs with this in mind. It *should* work. USB 1.0 and 2.0 ports can provide a maximum of 500mA, if they're built according to the spec, and they're wired correctly. For a Pi Zero W, it might suffice. Or it might not. Most USB cables weren't designed to carry heavy currents, and their resistance is pretty high. A high-resistance cable with a heavy load on it will let the voltage sag below 5v, and your Pi will complain. (Older Pis didn't complain. They just crashed.)

You might also be tempted to use that powerful charger for your iPad with a standard USB cable to power your Pi. I was. Then I discovered, by putting my multimeter across the 5v rail of the Pi, that between the cable's resistance and the charger's output voltage, I was getting a bit less than 4.5 volts on the Pi end of things. The Pi complained.

All these solutions may work for you. I recommend getting a dedicated Pi power supply because I know that it *will* work. A flakey Pi is no fun to develop projects on.

Suppliers

Adafruit: https://www.adafruit.com/product/1995

Microcenter: http://www.microcenter.com/
product/465196/Power_Supply_for_Raspberry_
Pi_2-3_with_Built-in_4ft_Micro_USB_Cable

Mouser: http://www.mouser.com/ProductDetail/
Adafruit/1995/?qs=sGAEpiMZZMu%252bmKbOcEVhFQf
i8wYXkauJ4nPu9ATFGEqzMfarTlOtrg%3d%3d

Sparkfun: https://www.sparkfun.com/
products/13831

Newark: http://www.newark.com/stontronics/
t5989dv/psu-rpi-5v-2-5a-multi-plug-blk/
dp/81Y7474

Integrated Circuits (ICs)

ATmega328P-PU

Coming from the Arduino world, you probably recognize the heart of the Arduino Uno in Figure 1-5. It's an ATmega328P-PU. We'll be making an Arduino-compatible with it that's attached to the Pi's GPIO port later in the book.

Figure 1-5. *ATmega328P*

17

Tip   Don't buy an ATmega328 PU. It's not the right microcontroller. The PU tells you about the package the IC is in (28 leads, plastic inline DIP package). The microcontroller you want is the ATmega328P-PU. The leading P indicates the version with Pico-power (a power saving feature.) It wouldn't make a difference—the two are code-—compatible—except that the device IDs are different, so AVRDUDE won't upload to the ATmega328 PU with normal Arduino configurations.

It's interesting to compare the specs between the ATmega328P-PU to the Pis. The ATmega is an 8-bit AVR RISC microcontroller, capable of running at 20MHz. (We'll run it at 16, as is standard for Arduinos.) It can execute about one instruction per clock cycle, and has SPI, I2C, analog-to-digital converters, and a programmable USART. It has 32KiB of flash memory, and 2KiB of RAM. Compared to the Pi, as we've seen before, it's a much, much smaller, less powerful computer.

Suppliers

Adafruit: https://www.adafruit.com/product/123
(Note that these come from Adafruit pre-programmed with a bootloader that we don't actually need)

Mouser: http://www.mouser.com/ProductDetail/
Microchip/ATMEGA328P-PU/?qs=%2fha2pyFadujcrAc
owhVCzjOvtgCenYitTBfrdeSNJnmn1EI7EVhhFw%3d%3d

Newark: http://www.newark.com/atmel/
atmega328p-pu/ic-8bit-mcu-avr-mega-20mhz-28/
dp/68T2944?rd=atmega328p-pu&searchView=table
&ddkey=http%3Aen-US%2FElement14_US%2Fsearch

Sparkfun: https://www.sparkfun.com/products/9061

Datasheet

Atmel was recently purchased by Microchip, so I've included both links, in case they consolidate their web presence at a later date. It's the same datasheet.

Microchip: `http://ww1.microchip.com/downloads/en/DeviceDoc/Atmel-42735-8-bit-AVR-Microcontroller-ATmega328-328P_Datasheet.pdf`

Atmel: `http://www.atmel.com/Images/Atmel-42735-8-bit-AVR-Microcontroller-ATmega328-328P_Datasheet.pdf`

16MHz TTL Clock Oscillator

The 16MHz TTL clock oscillator, shown in Figure 1-6, is a complete oscillator in a package, requiring no external components other than power. It will give our Arduino-on-the-breadboard project its clock signal.

Figure 1-6. *16MHz TTL clock oscillator*

While most Arduinos use the traditional capacitors+crystal approach to generate their clocks, we'll use this all-in-one package to do that job. The solderless breadboard we'll be using will add a certain amount of capacitance to the circuit, and with the variables of wire length, breadboard manufacturer, corrosion on the tie points on the breadboard, and so on, we don't really know how much capacitance it adds. A TTL clock removes all those uncertainties and guarantees a 16MHz clean signal for the ATmega to run on.

Figure 1-6 shows the "full can" 14-pin DIP size, and that's the one in the schematic. These parts are pretty much generic. I fished a 16MHz 14-pin DIP size TTL oscillator out of my big-bag-of-oscillators, and it works fine. The datasheet listed next is an example.

Note   The datasheet lists a dip 8 "half can" size as well, which is electrically identical to the full can. It should work, but the pinout is necessarily different. Make sure you get the 5v version. "Half can" models come in 3.3v versions as well.

Suppliers

Alltronics: `http://www.alltronics.com/cgi-bin/item/OSC_16/search/16-MHz-Oscillator` (Listed here because the oscillator I used came from one of their grab bags)

Digikey: `https://www.digikey.com/product-detail/en/abracon-llc/ACO-16.000MHZ-EK/535-9207-5-ND/675402`

Mouser: `http://www.mouser.com/ProductDetail/CTS-Electronic-Components/MXO45-3C-16M0000/?qs=sGAEpiMZZMt8zWNA7msRCrC1jWmTwM81pk7U9Kk%252bb8M%3d`

Newark: `http://www.newark.com/raltron/co12100-16-000mhz/oscillator-16mhz-dip-8-hcmos-ttl/dp/21M6840`

Datasheet

`http://www.mouser.com/ds/2/96/008-0258-0-786357.pdf`

74LVC245A Octal Bus Transceiver

The 74LVC245A octal bus transceiver (see Figure 1-7) is an IC normally used to drive electronic busses. In the Arduino world, we're accustomed to plugging pretty much whatever we want into the Arduino's pins. The ATmega microcontrollers are robust, and their pins are internally protected and have strong driver electronics. Not all ICs are like that. The Pi's GPIO pins are not well protected at all, so any noise, any overload, any over-voltage, is sent right back to the system chip, and if you damage the pin's driving electronics in the system chip, they're not repairable.

Figure 1-7. 74LVC245A octal bus transceiver

The 74LVC245 has the additional property of being the low voltage version of the part. This means it operates on a maximum voltage of 3.3v, and its logic high outputs will be a large percentage of this voltage at maximum. Its inputs, however, are capable of handling up to 6.5v, well above old fashioned 5v TTL levels.

We're going to use the 74LVC245 as a level shifter. That's how we'll get 5v TTL signals into the Pi safely, by reducing them with this IC to 3.3v or so. You might wonder how the 3.3v or so outputs of the 74LVC245 are going to drive 5v TTL logic (in this case the ATmega328P-PU). It's a good question, and I'll answer it in Chapter 12. I will give you a hint. The answer is also on page 386 of the ATmega datasheet. That's where I got it.

Note   Make sure you get the LVC part. The 74LS245 is the logically identical part, but it requires at least 4.5v to operate, and its output voltages are typically 3.4v, and may be higher (the datasheet isn't clear), which is too high for the Raspberry Pi's GPIO pins.

Suppliers

Adafruit: `https://www.adafruit.com/product/735`

Digikey: `https://www.digikey.com/product-detail/en/texas-instruments/SN74LVC245AN/296-8503-5-ND/377483`

Mouser: `http://www.mouser.com/ProductDetail/Texas-Instruments/SN74LVC245AN/?qs=sGAEpiMZZMs9F6aVvY09btkPv7nrVS6TnubCUzQAbVc%3d`

Newark: `http://www.newark.com/texas-instruments/sn74lvc245ane4/non-inverting-bus-transceiver/dp/37K3467`

Datasheet

`http://www.ti.com/lit/ds/symlink/sn74lvc245a.pdf`

LEDs

There's nothing special about the LEDs in the projects in this book. You can use literally any normal (not high brightness, high current types) LEDs, but you might have to change the schematic slightly to hook them up.

10-Segment Bar Graphs

I used a pair of the Kingbright DC10GWA 10-segment bar graph display (see Figure 1-8) because I had them from previous projects. They're the ones I show in the schematics.

Figure 1-8. *Kingbright DC10GWA*

You can use just about any 10-segment LED bar graphs, so long as their current demands aren't more than what the Pi can deliver (we'll get to that in Chapter 5), but watch out. Some larger bar graphs are wired with the expectation that you'll multiplex your pins rather than use one pin per LED, as we're going to do here for clarity. Multiplexing is interesting and fun, but I'm not covering it in this book. The Kingbright LEDs also have an adequate, easy-to-read datasheet, which can't be said for many other types. I got these from Mouser, but most electronic supply places will have them or something like them.

Datasheet

```
http://www.us.kingbright.com/images/catalog/
SPEC/DC10GWA.pdf
```

Generic LED

I also used a generic yellow LED that's been kicking around in my parts drawer for years, perhaps decades from the look of those leads (see Figure 1-9).

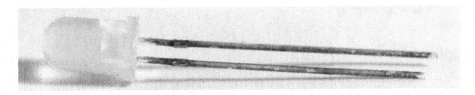

Figure 1-9. *Generic LED*

I don't even know where my LED came from. We'll use it as an activity light in Chapter 12. I've included a generic LED datasheet from Vishay, but there's no way for me to know who made mine. I guessed its forward voltage drop was about 2v and picked a conservative resistor value for it—bright enough to see reliably. With common LEDs you can get away with that. High brightness, multicolored, and other more advanced types, not so much. Got an LED in your parts drawer? Use that. It'll probably be fine.

I'm not listing suppliers for LEDs. Most electronic and hobby stores will have them.

Datasheet

http://www.vishay.com/docs/83030/tllg540.pdf

microSD Cards

Both Raspberry Pis supported by this book use the same microSD format SDHC/SDXC cards, as shown in the middle of Figure 1-10. They're the small kind, not the larger kind most often used in digital SLRs, where photographers might need to change cards quickly or with gloves on.

Figure 1-10. *microSD card*

Jargon Breakdown

microSD is the physical format of the card. SDHC and SDXC are the electronic specifications for communicating with these cards. SDHC stands for Secure Digital High Capacity, and indicates a card between 4GiB and 32GiB. These are the ones I recommend for your Pi. The Pi can communicate with SDXC cards (or so I read), but in most cases you won't need that much capacity. If you do need that much capacity, you'd really be better off plugging a USB-SATA adapter in to the Pi and hanging a small hard drive or SSD off of it. SD cards are *slow*, and they really weren't designed to be the filesystems for Linux computers.

Get an 8GiB card for the Pi. You can make do with 4GiB, but not for very long. Linux likes drive space, and it does not like running with the filesystem nearly full. Class 10 is as fast as they come, but I haven't seen that big a difference on the Pi between class 10s and other classes. I recommend going with a name brand, rather than generics. This wouldn't have been true a month ago, but I had two generic cards from the same store fail within a week of each other during development for this book, and I've learned to buy better.

USB Flash Device

A USB Flash Key, any size of at least 1GiB, or a card adapter and another microSD card will work. We'll use them in Chapter 11 for writing files on. You almost certainly have something that will work. I used a USB-microSD card adapter. Some examples are shown in Figure 1-11.

Figure 1-11. *USB Flash devices*

Resistors

We're only using two resistors in this whole project. That's right, even with 20LEDs, only two resistors. They are shown in Figures 1-12 and 1-13.

Figure 1-12. *The 220Ω resistor*

Figure 1-13. *The 10kΩ resistor*

Figure 1-12 shows the 220Ω, 1-watt resistor. It will keep the current in the LED down to 10mA. Wattage-wise, it's total overkill. A ¼-watt resistor is still overkill, but it's about as small as I can read. Since this resistor needs to show up in photos, I went with the 1-watt unit for most of the builds, and a ¼-watt in Chapters 11 and 12.

You'll also need a 10kΩ resistor, shown in Figure 1-13 It's the reset pull-up resistor for Chapter 12. Again, a ¼-watt resistor is fine, and it's what I used in the build, but the big ones photograph better. Any electronics store should have ¼-watt resistors. I probably got my 1-watt resistors from a vacuum tube (valve) supply house, but I don't really recall.

Hookup Wire

Hookup wire is your friend. Hookup wire is what makes these projects go. Coming from the Arduino world as you do, you probably have a favorite roll of the stuff. If you want to, you can use that. I have this box, shown in Figure 1-14. It has one important advantage: multiple colors. (And you can see where I've reloaded one of the slots in this box. That's why the slot is marked "Yellow" but the wire sticking out of it is purple.)

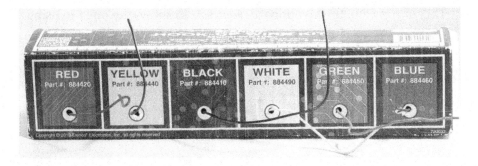

Figure 1-14. *Hookup wire multicolor pack*

The manufacturer of your hookup wire doesn't matter much, nor do the actual colors, so long as you can keep track of which wire goes where. Mine came from Elenco, via Microcenter. The only important qualities of the wire are that it must be 22 gauge (0.35mm) so it fits in the tie-points of your breadboard, and it must be a solid copper conductor, not stranded, Also, for sanity's sake, I really do recommend you get more than one color. At least three colors—one for ground, one for Vcc, and one for data. Preferably more.

Pre-Made Jumpers

I know a lot of places sell pre-made jumpers. I have bunches, but I don't use them. I've found that with repeated use/abuse (I do tend to pull them out by the root instead of the pin connector), the conductors break off from the pin connector fairly quickly. Sometimes, insidiously, they do it without breaking the insulation, so you can't tell. I've chased my tail for hours trying to find out why a circuit stopped working, most often with a chapter deadline rapidly approaching. I am also photographing my work, and multiple colors of hookup wire make that look much better. Do I waste a lot of wire this way? Well, yes. If that bothers you, you can get pre-made jumpers. But don't say I didn't warn you.

This brings us to the breadboard. Figure 1-15 shows the one I'm using in the photos.

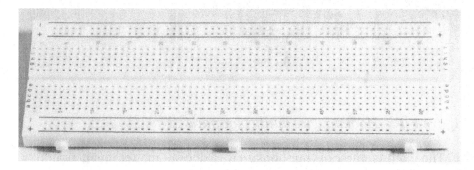

Figure 1-15. *Solderless breadboard*

There's nothing special about this breadboard, except that it's new. I've found that particularly inexpensive breadboards wear out quickly. Remember how I chased my tail with broken jumpers? I've also had it happen when the tie-points in cheap breadboards wear out. If a circuit stops working inexplicably, or doesn't work at all, you might want to use your multimeter (I just assume you have one at this point) to check and make sure your tie-point is good, and that your components and hookup wire are, in fact, connected together.

A word about breadboard quality. You can tell by the price whether you've got a cheap "hobbiest" breadboard or a professional grade one. The professional ones start at about US $20 and go up fairly steeply. They usually have a metal base, too, which helps keep them at a comfortable angle. The one in the photos is a hobbiest breadboard, so I'm taking my chances with it. I prototyped the circuits we're going to use in this book on an older, higher quality breadboard. The plastic is yellowed, it's scratched up, and it looks terrible in photos, but it works absolutely reliably. If you've been in the Arduino world long, you may have a better quality breadboard than the one shown in the photos in this book. If you don't, you might think about getting one.

Tactile Switch

You'll need a button, a normally open, momentary tactile switch. These close the circuit only when you're pushing on them. The one I used is shown in Figure 1-16.

Figure 1-16. *Tactile switch*

I've found it easier to get these into a breadboard by straightening their leads with pliers, although they pop out easily. Again, any electronics store should have these, or something similar enough to do the job.

Soldering Tools and Knowhow

It's very likely you're going to need soldering tools and the skills to use them. You *can* do all the projects without soldering, assuming you can find a Raspberry Pi breakout board, and a Raspberry Pi that already have their pins soldered in for you, but if you're going to move forward in electronics, soldering is a required skill sooner or later. Get good tools for it. I'll talk briefly about these in Chapter 11. They make all the difference in the world when combined with good instruction.

Some Words About Suppliers

You've probably noticed that I've included a list of suppliers for each component discussed in this chapter. This is by no means an exhaustive list. These are suppliers that I've used recently, who've done the job.

I'm an American, so most of the suppliers are in the continental United States, Newark being the exception for my British readers. I've listed a variety of suppliers, so ideally so you can order all the parts you need in one or two orders. Often (at least in the United States) it's more expensive to ship the part than to purchase it. Even if you have to pay a few dollars more to get a Raspberry Pi from Mouser, if you're already ordering the LEDs, resistor(s), and what-not there, the savings in shipping will probably more than make up the difference. Check your shipping. Finding parts and getting good deals on them is at least part of the fun.

Some Words on Parts Cost

A year or so ago, when my last book with Apress came out, I got an email from a gentleman in India, asking if he could substitute the ATmega328P-PU for the ATmega1284P-PU I called for in that book. I forget the exact conversion, but the upshot was that for him to buy an ATmega1284P-PU would be the equivalent of me buying an IC for between US $50-100. I cringed, because part of my advice in that book was to "Buy a spare. They're cheap." I know that where you are, the economics of the projects in this book may be very, very different than where I am.

This is a different book. Many of the projects in it are software-oriented. That's where the big differences between the Pi and the Arduino are, anyway. But in that gentleman's name, I've tried to keep my parts cost low and to use the most commonly available parts I could.

All the Parts, All Together

Here's the short version of the list, for those who find it easier that way.

- 1 Raspberry Pi, preferably the Raspberry Pi 3 Model B+, although a Raspberry Pi Zero W will work for most of the projects

- 1 Raspberry Pi GPIO breakout board

- 1 5v USB micro power supply

- 1 ATmega328P-PU microcontroller

- 1 16MHz TTL clock oscillator

- 1 74LVC245 octal bus transceiver (level shifter)

- 2 10-segment LED bar graphs displays

- 1 generic LED

- 1 microSD card

- 220Ω resistor, at least ¼ watt

- 1 10kΩ resistor, at least ¼ watt

- Hookup wire

- 1 solderless breadboard

- 1 tactile switch (button), momentary, normally open

- 1 microSD to USB adapter, or nearly any USB Flash Key of 1GiB or larger

- Optional: 1 powered USB hub

CHAPTER 2

Meet the Raspberry Pi

Introduction

In this chapter, we'll hook the Pi up so we can work with it, download the NOOBS installer, put it on the SD card for your Pi, and boot the Pi for the first time. I'll cover how to do this for Windows, MacOS X, and Linux.

Windows

These procedures were developed with Windows 10 and should work on any subsequent version. Windows 7 might also work, but I haven't tried it. I should mention that I'm not a Windows user by preference, so these procedures were developed in a virtual machine. It shouldn't make a difference.

MacOS X

These procedures should work with any version. Underneath the pretty graphics layer, MacOS X is a reasonably competent UNIX-style operating system, although Apple does sometimes randomly break things. Especially when they're trying to increase the security. These procedures were developed with and tested on 10.12.6, aka Sierra.

© James R. Strickland 2018
J. R. Strickland, *Raspberry Pi for Arduino Users*,
https://doi.org/10.1007/978-1-4842-3414-3_2

Linux

Linux users, your procedures were developed with Raspbian 4.9 and Xubuntu 16.04LTS, but it should work on any version of Linux capable of mounting SD cards.

As you may already be aware, Raspbian, the Raspberry Pi operating system, *is* Linux, of the Debian persuasion, like many of the most popular distributions. In answer to the obvious question, yes, you could use a friend's Raspberry Pi for the installation on your own microSD card, if your friend's Pi has a good sized card of its own and the optional USB microSD card adapter listed in "The Stuff You Need."

The Stuff You Need

- A Raspberry Pi, set up with a keyboard, monitor, and power as discussed in Chapter 1, "Your Shopping List."

- A microSD card, at least 4 GiB, preferably 8GiB or larger.

- Some other computer, even if it's a friend's working Raspberry Pi, hereafter referred to as your desktop computer.

- A microSD card reader. This can be built in to your desktop computer, or it can be a USB add-on.

- Broadband Internet access for your desktop computer and your Pi. We'll be assuming WiFi availability with all the Pi projects.

- You may also need your administrator/root/system password.

- MacOS X users: You'll need to go to `https://www.sdcard.org/downloads` and download the SD Memory Card Formatter for Mac.

- Linux users: You'll need GParted and dosfstools. The GParted application is a standard part of most Linux distributions, and dosfstools is often installed by default.

- NOOBS, from the Raspberry Pi Foundation. Download it at `https://www.raspberrypi.org/downloads/noobs/`.

Hardware Setup

Here's how you set up your Pi. If you're sharing a keyboard and monitor with your regular computer, you'll need to do these steps after you prepare the Pi's microSD card.

Raspberry Pi 3 Model B+

In Figure 2-1, I've labeled the various ports on the Raspberry Pi 3 Model B+.

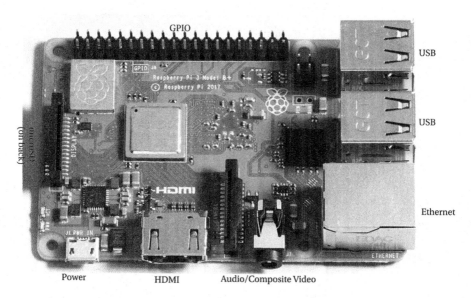

Figure 2-1. *Raspberry Pi 3 Model B+ with labeled ports*

Hardware setup is pretty straightforward. Plug your USB keyboard and mouse into one or more of the USB connectors. (I plug my mouse into the USB socket on my keyboard, to save sockets.) Connect the HDMI cable to the Pi and your monitor.

Raspberry Pi Zero W

The Raspberry Pi Zero W is a little more complicated to set up, but only a little. In Figure 2-2, I've labeled the various connectors.

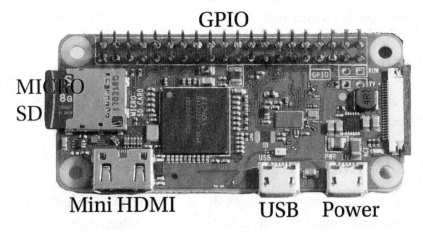

Figure 2-2. *Raspberry Pi Zero W with labeled ports*

Connect your OTG host cable to the USB Micro B port. While this is the same kind of connector as the power port, the two are not interchangeable. You can't power the Pi from the USB port, nor will the power port give you USB connectivity. Early versions of the Pi would actually let power from a USB connection onto the 5v rail, but this was a defect in the design and has been fixed since. Plug your keyboard into the USB-A end of the OTG cable and plug your mouse into the USB-A connector on your keyboard.

Connect your mini-HDMI connector to the mini-HDMI socket on the Pi. If you have the mini-HDMI to HDMI adapter like I have, you plug the HDMI cable from your monitor into the adapter. If you have a mini-HDMI to HDMI cable, you plug the HDMI end of the cable into the monitor directly.

Unplug the power supply from the wall and plug its Micro-B plug into the power socket on the Pi.

Both Pis

Unplug the power supply from the wall socket and plug it into the power socket on the Raspberry Pi. The Pi won't boot or do anything useful without the microSD card installed, but we can't do that until we load an operating system on the card.

Install Raspbian with NOOBS

We're going to install Raspbian on our Raspberry Pis using the NOOBS installer. First, let's break down the jargon a bit.

What Is NOOBS?

NOOBS stands for New Out Of Box Software. It's a software installer from the Raspberry Pi foundation. It removes some complicated (and in the case of Windows, poorly supported) steps in putting an operating system on your microSD card.

Here's the problem. Operating systems typically know how to read only one "disk" format at boot time. The Pi knows only FAT32, the standard since the days of MS-DOS, and conveniently, what microSD cards are normally formatted in from the factory. Linux (including Raspbian) will usually boot from a Linux filesystem. If you're using Windows or MacOS X, there's no easy way to create one by hand. Since a partition (I'll talk about these more shortly) is just a series of bytes on the raw storage device (the microSD card, in our case here), we used to have to download an image file of the SD card and write it out, byte by byte, to the card. Linux, of course, does this easily enough, although the tool (dd) is powerful and dumb, so you have to be careful with it. MacOS X has dd as well, but you have to know the secret name for the actual raw device, or MacOS X will severely degrade the performance of the card, by a factor of ten if memory serves. Windows, as usual, can't do it without adding another program.

NOOBS handles this process for you. You pick the operating system you want (Raspbian, in our case), click on it, and wait. It unpacks the partitions it needs, already loaded with the operating system.

NOOBS is also the boot manager. Once it's installed, when you boot your Pi, it will come up, offer you the chance to go into recovery mode, and if you don't tell it otherwise, it will then go ahead and boot your default operating system. If your default operating system doesn't work and you select recovery mode, it will give you some options and tools.

If you want a little more of your microSD card's space, and you don't care about recovery mode or other Pi operating systems, you can download Raspbian from the foundation's website and install it the way we had to in the bad old days. Full instructions are found at https://www. raspberrypi.org/documentation/installation/installing-images/ README.md.

For this book, we'll stick with NOOBS.

What Is Raspbian?

One thing that's very different between the Arduino world and the Raspberry Pi world is that the Arduino world assumes you have a desktop computer, and the Raspberry Pi essentially *is* one. Raspbian is Linux. We'll do all our coding for the projects in this book on the Pi itself, in its desktop Linux environment.

For the Linux-savvy reader, it's Debian 9 (Stretch) built for the Pi, with a custom desktop called Pixel, made by the foundation. Debian is also what Ubuntu is based on, so if you're used to Ubuntu Linux, Raspbian will feel very familiar. In fact, when I went back to Linux after a long hiatus, I went from Raspbian to Ubuntu. Both use the apt package manager and take .deb files to install things.

Raspbian comes with the Chromium web browser, which is the open source version of Google Chrome. It's a little slow, even on the mighty (by comparison) Raspberry Pi 3 Model B+, and it's *very* slow on a Raspberry Pi Zero W. It does work, however, and it's more compatible with the modern web than other solutions were in the past.

Format Your microSD Card

Your microSD card came from the factory formatted. If your card is fresh out of the box, you could skip this step, but it won't hurt to do it. All others, you need to format.

For our purposes, the device is the microSD card reader with the card in it. A partition is a chunk of the available storage space on a microSD card, set up to behave like it's a separate device. We'll only be making one, but your card may have several on it if it's used. A filesystem lives inside the partition. It contains all the logical structures your operating system needs to actually use the space. Directories live inside the filesystem (Windows and MacOS X call these folders, but they're the same thing). There's always at least one directory in a filesystem. Your files go inside directories. There can be other directories inside directories, but every filesystem will have at least one directory. All this is universal for desktop operating systems, but the names and organization can be different depending on which one you use.

Windows

Windows calls a partition with a filesystem a volume. Mounted volumes get drive letters. A disk, in Windows, is a physical device, like your microSD card and reader, and will have a disk number. For example, if I put my microSD card into a Windows machine and look for it using diskpart, it will show up as Disk 1. If I open File Explorer, the partition and filesystem on that card show up as USB Drive (E:).

When you plug your microSD card reader (with the microSD card already in it) into your computer, you may get a message that Windows is (trying to) install a new driver for the USB mass storage device. Go ahead and let it. You'll need that driver.

Once it's done, go to the Start menu and type Disk Management.

The Disk Management window will open, and you should get something like the window shown on the top-left side of Figure 2-3.

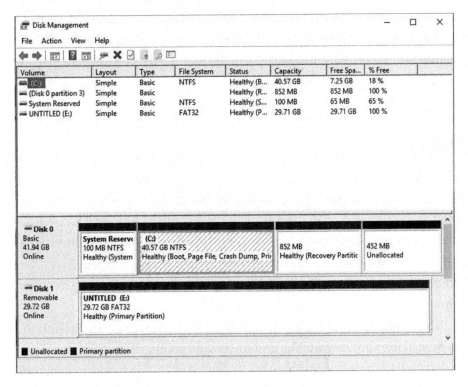

Figure 2-3. *Disk Management window*

Disk Management will list all the volumes that are available in the upper half of its window. Choose the volume that looks most like your SD card, by size, and so forth. If your SD card is new, it may be called

UNTITLED. If you've already had NOOBS on this card, it may be called RECOVERY, and be about 783MB in size.

In the lower section of the Disk Management window, you'll find that same disk (Disk 1 Removable, in my case). You'll see the correct size for your SD card when you're looking at the right device, and to the right of that it will list all the partitions on your SD card. We need to get rid of them. Right-click on each partition and select Delete Volume to delete it.

When you're done, the entire disk should be listed as unallocated. That means none of its space is being used for anything else. Right-click on the unallocated space and pick New Simple Volume. A wizard will open. The defaults should be okay, but make sure the filesystem is FAT32, and give it the Volume Label NOOBS. Note that your drive letter will have changed, but the disk number will not. The volume should re-mount automatically.

MacOS X

In UNIX-style operating systems like MacOS X, everything is a file. Every device gets a special device file, and every partition, mounted or not, is listed as a separate device—the original device plus a number. The UNIX-style directory system, however, is one big tree that often spans filesystems and devices. So, when your formatted microSD card is mounted, it's mounted to an existing directory. Whether that directory is empty or not, it is mapped to the top-level directory of the device.

So, for example, if I put my microSD card (in an adapter) in the slot on my Mac, if the card is readable, and the partitions are filesystems the Mac understands, it gets the device name (/dev/disk2). The partition becomes /dev/disk2s1, and the filesystem on it is mounted to the directory /Volumes/NO NAME. These paths and devices may be different on your Mac.

Note   MacOS X is completely ignorant of Linux filesystems. Worse, its disk utility tool can't reliably format SD/microSD cards with the required FAT32 format. If you know how to use virtual machines, I suggest setting up a small Linux VM and formatting the microSD card as needed. If you go this route, use the Linux instructions.

If, for some reason, the microSD card doesn't mount, it won't show up on the desktop. You'll be able to find it anyway with Disk Utility. Go to the Applications folder and click on the Utilities folder. The Disk Utility app is in there. When you kick it off, it should look something like Figure 2-4.

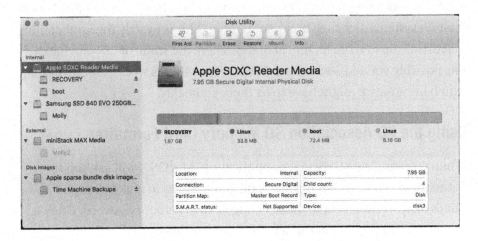

Figure 2-4. *Disk Utility showing a used NOOBS microSD*

This microSD card has been used with Raspbian/NOOBS before. The partition is named RECOVERY, the one below it is marked boot, and the fact that the rest of the microSD card's space is just marked as Linux gives it away. You might only have one partition, possibly called NO NAME, if the card hasn't been used, or has only been used in a digital camera. Go ahead and close Disk Utility. We're done with it. We just wanted to make sure we have the right microSD card.

Did you download the SD Memory Card Formatter software from
`https://www.sdcard.org/downloads` like it said in "The Stuff You Need"
section? Good. It's provided by the people who write (and sell) the SD card
specs. It's not a good tool on the Mac. It's slow, but it gets the job done.
When it's done, you'll have a card with one FAT32 partition, called `NOOBS`.
That partition will be formatted with the FAT32 filesystem. That's what
NOOBS expects, and that's what we want.

A Short Rant

You used to be able to do this job with the Disk Utility application, but in
recent years this application has had its functionality severely reduced.
Apple, it would seem, doesn't want pesky users to have much control over
their filesystems, lest they break something. This is exactly the kind of thing
that drives me to write technical books. There are some of us—obviously
me, possibly you too—who want to know how things work, not the least of
which because we might have to fix them some day.

Using the SD Association SD Memory Card Formatter

When you start the SDFormatter application, MacOS X will ask you to
authenticate yourself, saying the application wants to make changes.
That's okay. We do want to make changes. Give it your password. Once it
accepts it, you should get the screen shown in Figure 2-5.

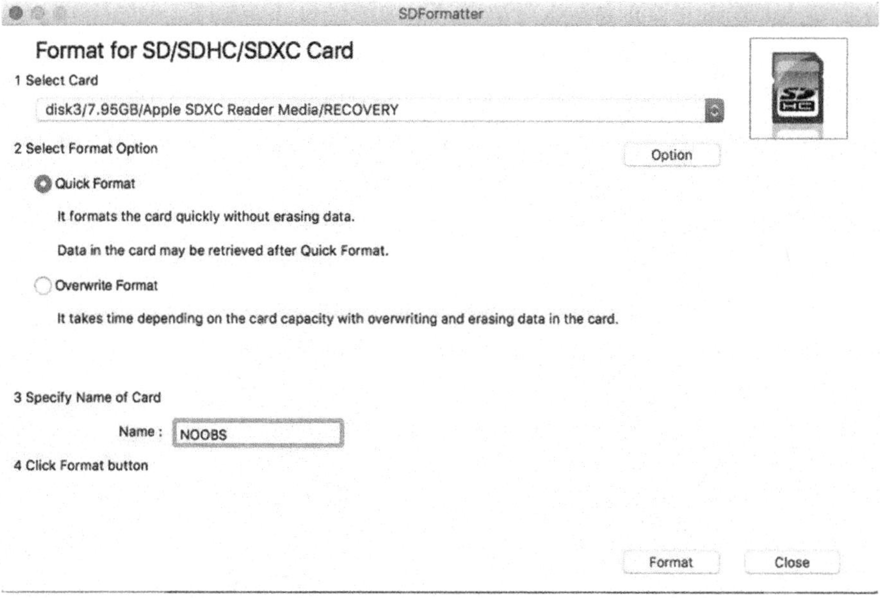

Figure 2-5. *SDFormatter application*

We don't care about whatever data is on the card, if any. We don't care about its partition table either. Go ahead and select Quick Format. You can use Overwrite Format if you need to, but it's going to take a whole lot longer. Possibly hours longer. Either way, the name of the card doesn't actually matter, but we'll call it NOOBS for convenience. Fill that in and click on Format.

Linux

In Linux, the mounting process is the same as in MacOS X, except that the card is called /dev/sdc, the partition is /dev/sdc1, and its point on the directory tree is /media/jim/3764-3231. Depending on the filesystem and how your groups are set up, you may need to use sudo or gksudo to access it.

Make sure you have GParted, the disk formatter, installed. On Ubuntu and Raspbian, open a terminal window (xterm, uxterm, LXTerminal, etc.) and type sudo apt-get install gparted Then press Return. Linux will

47

ask for your system password. Give it. You also need to make sure that dosfstools are installed. Using sudo apt-get install dosfstools will do the job in Raspbian or any other Debian-derived Linux, like Ubuntu.

If your desktop Linux doesn't use the Debian-style apt-get command to add software, you'll have to look up the correct one for your system. Likewise, on some Linux systems, sudo is not installed by default. Use su on those.

Once everything is installed, type sudo gparted to start it up. You should get a screen that looks like the one in Figure 2-6.

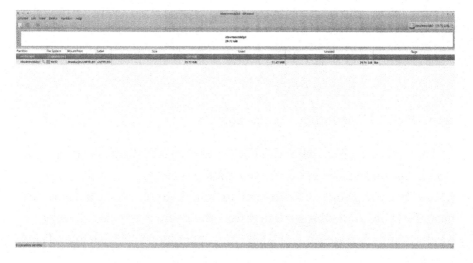

Figure 2-6. *GParted screen*

We need to tell GParted what device we want to work on. By default, it will mangle your Linux system's boot partition. Not a good choice. So in the GParted window, at the top left, choose GParted ➤ Devices and look over the list for one that most looks like your card, based on size. If you know you have a 16GB card, look for that in the device list.

Raspbian users: Be especially careful here. Your card and your friend's card may look a lot alike. If your SD card doesn't show up in the devices list, choose on GParted ➤ Refresh Devices.

Once you've selected the device, the window will change. Toward the middle of the window will be a bar that marks the columns: Partition, File System, Label, Size, Used, Unused, and Flags. What it lists in there really doesn't matter, so long as it doesn't look like the wrong drive or filesystem. Click one of the partitions.

We can't do deep work on the SD card while any of its partitions are mounted, so click on one of the partitions, then choose Partition ➤ Unmount. Do this for all the partitions on the SD card. If they aren't mounted, the option to unmount them won't be in the dropdown.

Choose Device ➤ Create Partition Table. You'll get a warning that everything on the entire drive (physical device) is going to be erased, and that it will create an MS-DOS partition table by default. Both of these are what we want. GParted will go to work immediately, and the SD card will, indeed, be empty, showing only unallocated space.

Choose Partition ➤ New. The default values in the Create New Partition popup are fine, except we want the FAT32 (MS-DOS) filesystem instead of ext2. This is in the right column of the Create New Partition window toward the bottom. Select File System ➤ FAT32. Label the partition NOOBS, or whatever you want. You want it to look like Figure 2-7.

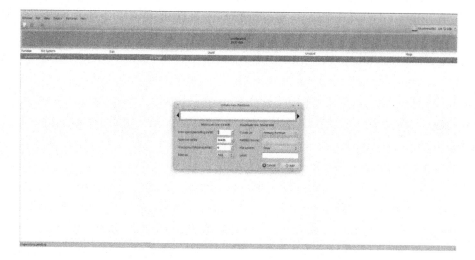

Figure 2-7. *Creating a FAT32 partition with GParted*

Nothing has actually happened yet. GParted, in an effort to save us from ourselves, makes us take an extra step. Go to Edit ➤ Apply All Operations. When it asks if you really, truly want to do this, click Apply Changes. The microSD card may or may not be remounted. Click on it on the desktop to make sure.

Download NOOBS

If you're used to downloading and unzipping large files, that's what we're doing here. If you're not, read on.

All Operating Systems Except Raspbian

Point your web browser at http://www.raspberrypi.org/downloads/, look for NOOBS Offline Network and Install, and select Download Zip. Wait. It's a big download, over 1.5GiB as of this writing. If you know what torrents are and how to use them, the torrent may be significantly faster, but the ZIP download is the sure thing. Let your browser put the download wherever it usually does. If you can spare the drive space on your desktop computer, it's best to keep the NOOBS ZIP file around, at least until you get the Pi going. Sometimes bad things happen to SD cards. In my house, these may involve cats.

Raspbian

Before you download, check to make sure your friend's root filesystem has enough space to hold a GiB and a half of stuff. Open a terminal window and type df -h. One of the entries will be listed as being mounted on /. That's your root filesystem. If you have more than 2GiB available, you're probably good.

Note   The NOOBS installation gets bigger as time goes on. It was about a GiB and a half when this book was written, in the fall of 2017. It may well be larger. Adjust your free space requirements accordingly.

If you don't have enough room on the root filesystem for the download, you're not out of luck. If you took my advice and got at least an 8GB microSD card (slightly less than 8GiB) you've got more than enough space on your card to store the download. Just make sure to right-click on the icon marked Download Zip and click on Save Link As. Then choose your own card.

The Raspberry Pi 3 Model B+ might or might not have enough RAM to expand the NOOBS download using the GUI tools, and the Pi Zero almost certainly does not, so we'll have to do it by hand. Open a terminal window and type df -h.

The DF screen should list all the devices on your friend's Pi. One of these will be quite obviously your NOOBS card, even though it may not say so. It will be empty and most likely mounted at /media/pi.

Type `cd /media/pi/<whatever>`. This sets your default directory to your microSD card. Now type `unzip NOOBS*.zip`.

While we're waiting, I'll explain. Using an asterisk in the file name like that means "any file whose front is NOOBS and whose back is .zip." That way I don't have to type `NOOBS_v2_4_4.zip`, which will probably be out of date by the time you read this anyway. It takes a long time for a Pi to unzip the NOOBS ZIP file. Be patient. Maybe visit with family for a while. Maybe walk the dog.

Install NOOBS

Use your usual file manager—Explorer in Windows, Finder in MacOS X, Nautilus/Thunar/PCManFM/whatever in Linux—to drag and drop the files from your download directory (often called `Downloads`) to the SD card. Don't drag the whole directory, just its contents. Once the files are copied, you're ready to go.

Windows

Right-click on the NOOBS volume from Explorer and select unmount. Give it a couple of seconds to complete and remove the card from your SD card reader.

MacOS X

The MacOS X finder likes to leave files for its own use hidden in filesystems. They can sometimes confuse your Pi at boot time, so we need to get rid of them before we go. Start the terminal. The easiest way is to go to spotlight and type `terminal.app`. In the terminal window that opens, type `cd /Volumes/NOOBS`.

By the way, MacOS X, like Linux, is case sensitive in terminal windows. (If you called your partition something besides NOOBS, use that in place of NOOBS in the command.) The cd command tells MacOS X to change directories. /Volumes means go all the way to root (the bottom of the UNIX-style directory tree, remember?), then go to the Volumes directory (where filesystems are usually mounted), then go to the NOOBS subdirectory of that, which is, in fact, on your SD card. Type ls -a, which tells MacOS X to show you any hidden files, and Finder's mess becomes visible. Note that my Mac's system name is Molly.

```
.                                  ._riscos-boot.bin
..                                 .fseventsd
.Spotlight-V100                    BUILD-DATA
._BUILD-DATA                       INSTRUCTIONS-README.txt
._INSTRUCTIONS-README.txt          RECOVERY_FILES_DO_NOT_EDIT
._RECOVERY_FILES_DO_NOT_EDIT       bcm2708-rpi-0-w.dtb
._bcm2708-rpi-0-w.dtb              bcm2708-rpi-b-plus.dtb
._bcm2708-rpi-b-plus.dtb           bcm2708-rpi-b.dtb
._bcm2708-rpi-b.dtb                bcm2708-rpi-cm.dtb
._bcm2708-rpi-cm.dtb               bcm2709-rpi-2-b.dtb
._bcm2709-rpi-2-b.dtb              bcm2710-rpi-3-b.dtb
._bcm2710-rpi-3-b.dtb              bcm2710-rpi-cm3.dtb
._bcm2710-rpi-cm3.dtb              bootcode.bin
._bootcode.bin                     defaults
._defaults                   os
._os                         overlays
._overlays                   recovery.cmdline
._recovery.cmdline                 recovery.elf
._recovery.elf                     recovery.img
._recovery.img                     recovery.rfs
._recovery.rfs                     recovery7.img
._recovery7.img                    riscos-boot.bin
```

All that .Spotlight, .Trashes, and .fseventsd stuff? All the ._ prefixed stuff? That has to go. Just type rm -R .* to remove it.

```
jim@Molly /Volumes/NOOBS $ rm -R .*
rm: "." and ".." may not be removed
jim@Molly /Volumes/NOOBS $ ls -a
.                           bcm2710-rpi-cm3.dtb
..                          bootcode.bin
BUILD-DATA                  defaults
INSTRUCTIONS-README.txt         os
RECOVERY_FILES_DO_NOT_EDIT  overlays
bcm2708-rpi-0-w.dtb         recovery.cmdline
bcm2708-rpi-b-plus.dtb          recovery.elf
bcm2708-rpi-b.dtb           recovery.img
bcm2708-rpi-cm.dtb          recovery.rfs
bcm2709-rpi-2-b.dtb         recovery7.img
bcm2710-rpi-3-b.dtb         riscos-boot.bin
jim@Molly /Volumes/NOOBS $
```

This erases all the files in the current directory and below whose names start with . (which makes the file hidden). We'll cover rm and its flags along with wildcards (* signs) in Chapter 3, "Survival Linux."

Caution   The . (dot) before the asterisk in rm -R .* is critically important. Without it, this command will erase the whole microSD card.

Type cd ~ to go back to your home directory. The SD card will be busy and can't unmount otherwise.

Now drag the NOOBS icon from your desktop to the trash/eject button, give it a few second to complete, and remove the card from your SD card reader.

Linux

Using Nautilus/Thunar/PCManFM/whatever, right-click on the NOOBS SD card and select Unmount or Eject Removable Media. Give it a few second to finish, then remove it from your SD card reader.

Raspbian

We need to clean up a little before we're done with the card. Click on the mounted card on the desktop to open it. Then find the NOOBSv<whatever>.zip file, drag it to the trash, and *empty the trash*. Only when the trash is emptied will the file actually be removed from the SD card, and that's what we want.

Raspbian, Linux, and MacOS X

A lot of the commands we've used in the terminal may seem like Sanskrit to you right now. We'll get into almost all of them again in Chapter 3, "Survival Linux," and they'll seem like old friends when we're done.

Boot NOOBS

This is it. This is the moment of truth. Is your Pi all hooked up? Keyboard plugged in? Monitor connected? Power supply plugged into your Pi but not the wall outlet? Good. The Pi has no Off switch, so don't plug in the power supply just yet.

No matter which model/variant of the Raspberry Pi you're using (of the ones I recommended), if the Pi is right side up with all the components facing you, the microSD card goes in the slot upside down. Slide it in until it stops. Don't force it. It's designed to go in only one way.

Now plug the Pi's power cable into the Pi.

If you have a problem after this point, you'll be reformatting and reloading the SD card. Be aware that in addition to resizing the boot partition, NOOBS also renames all the partitions on the SD card, so if you have to reformat the SD card and reload it, it will no longer have the volume name NOOBS, nor will your single partition be the only one on the card.

Once NOOBS is done resizing the boot partition, which might be another good time to walk the dog, you'll get a popup window that says NOOBS v<some version>-Built:<some date.>. If you got something that looks like Figure 2-8, congratulations! It's working!

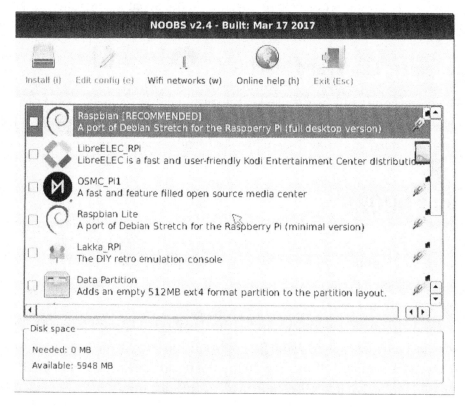

Figure 2-8. *NOOBS window*

Troubleshooting

If your Pi doesn't boot, there's some troubleshooting you can do.

- Is the Pi's power supply plugged in? If you're on a Pi Zero W, make sure it's in the power socket and not the USB socket. (Been there, done that.)

- Is the microSD card in? Disconnect power to the Pi, remove the microSD card, and reinsert it to check.

- Is your monitor on? (Been there, done that.)

- Is the monitor set to the input your Pi is using? Some monitors will automatically switch between inputs depending on which one they're getting a signal from. If your desktop computer is on the same monitor and it's running, you'll probably have to switch the monitor over to the Pi's input manually. If you have certain brands of ultra wide monitor that a support split screen, you should be aware that these rely on software on the desktop machine to switch automatically. The Pi doesn't have that software, so once again, you'll have to configure the monitor to do what you want manually.

- Is the Pi, in fact, working? The Raspberry Pi Zero W has exactly one LED to tell you what's going on, so sometimes it will sit there and look dead, but it's really running fine. It's just busy.

- Are there any lights on your keyboard? If the NUM-LOCK light is on and you can switch the CAPS LOCK light on and off with the caps lock key, it means the Linux kernel is running. Be patient.

- If all else fails, unplug the power, put the microSD card back in your desktop machine, and see if anything has happened.

Install Raspbian

When NOOBS is finished booting, you should get a screen something like
the one in Figure 2-9.

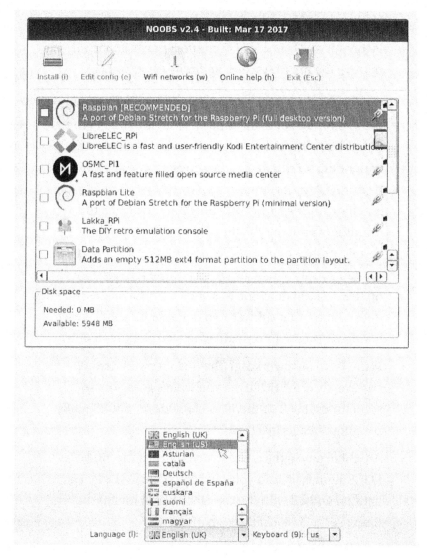

Figure 2-9. *NOOBS window with language popup*

At the bottom, where it says Language, click on it and set it to your regional language. It's important, if you're using a U.S. keyboard, to select English (U.S.), or some keys won't work right.

Next, in the menu in the middle of the NOOBS window, select Raspbian, as shown in Figure 2-10.

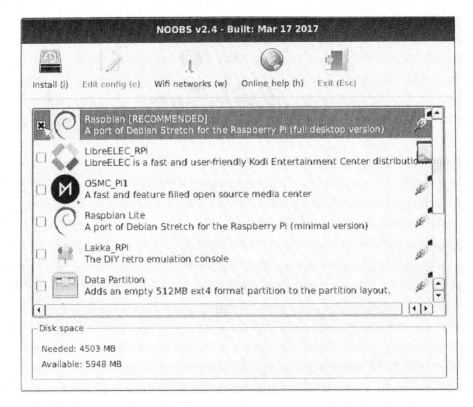

Figure 2-10. *Selecting Raspbian on NOOBS*

Next, click on the Install icon at the top left of the NOOBS window. You'll get a warning about erasing all other data on the drive (your microSD card), as shown. This is fine. Click Yes. NOOBS will begin the installation process for Raspbian. This might be another good point to walk the dog.

Eventually, NOOBS will give you a popup like the one shown in Figure 2-11. This tells you it's done.

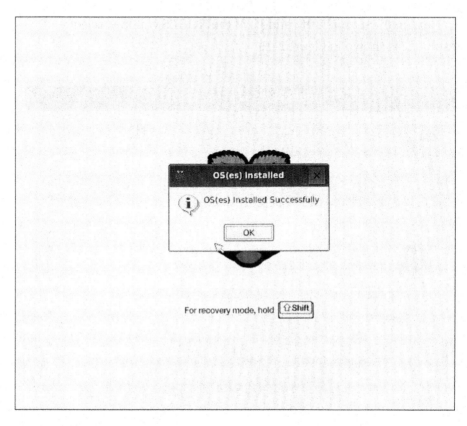

Figure 2-11. *OSes installed*

Now when you click OK, the system will reboot, a raspberry will appear at the top left (one for each core in the system), and Linux will boot. There are a lot of text messages involved in that. You don't have to try to read all the messages as they come out. There shouldn't be any red `Failed` messages, but really this information matters only if Pi completely fails to boot. Eventually, and be especially patient if you have a Pi Zero W, the screen will clear, and after an anxious few moments, the graphical user interface will come up, as shown in Figure 2-12.

Figure 2-12. *Raspbian desktop*

Congratulations. You're in.

Conclusion

The tl;dr version goes like this: Grab NOOBS from `https://www.`
`raspberrypi.org/downloads/` and install Raspbian. In the next chapter,
we get Raspbian set up for the projects and learn enough Linux to keep the
Pi going from project to project.

CHAPTER 3

Survival Linux

One of the big differences between a Raspberry Pi and an Arduino is the operating system. The Arduino's "operating system," if you want to call it that, is little more than some libraries that get added to your sketches, and a bootloader to make it easier to load them into the ATmega's flash memory. The Raspberry Pi, even the Pi Zero W, runs Raspbian, a full-blown Linux desktop installation.

An in-depth treatment of Linux/Raspbian could be a book by itself. Instead, I'm going to start with the basics: what you need to know *right now* so you don't wreck the hard work you've done putting Raspbian on your Pi in the first place. I call this Survival Linux. As we get deeper into doing projects with the Pi, I'll dig into the mechanisms that underlie what we're doing. It helps to know what's going on behind the curtain.

© James R. Strickland 2018
J. R. Strickland, *Raspberry Pi for Arduino Users*,
https://doi.org/10.1007/978-1-4842-3414-3_3

Orientation

When we left off in Chapter 2, you'd just reached the Raspbian desktop. Figure 3-1 shows a screenshot of it again.

Figure 3-1. Raspbian desktop

If you're looking for how to shut the Pi down safely, skip ahead to the "Rebooting and Shutting Down" section.

If you're a regular user of Linux, particularly of Ubuntu or other Debian-based distributions, this will look reasonably familiar. For everyone else, let's do a quick orientation.

The Desktop

The Raspberry Pi desktop is pretty straightforward. The top-left most raspberry icon has a list of applications, by type, that you can launch. The globe icon next to it is the web browser. The file folder icon next to that is PCManFM, the equivalent to Desktop Explorer on Windows, the finder on a Mac, and one of the many, many file managers (Thunar, Nautilus, etc.) used in various Linux distributions. Next to that is a terminal, and that's going to be our friend in coming chapters. We'll cover it in this chapter shortly. Next to that, the little sea urchin icon is for Sonic Pi, a sound effects tool, and next to that is Wolfram/Mathematica, which is somewhat similar to a search engine. We'll be removing those two applications to clear space on our SD card later, as they're not especially useful for the kinds of projects we're doing.

The trashcan is in the top-left corner under the menu (the Raspberry icon) and the Application Launch Bar in the top panel of your screen. (These are the Linux names for these desktop parts.) It's handled by PCManFM. We'll dig into PCManFM much more when we talk about creating and deleting files in the "Filesystem Navigation" section. To empty it, right-click on it and choose Empty. Then press Return.

MacOS X users, heads up. The trashcan does not automagically switch modes to become the eject button for mounted volumes. There's a proper eject button all the way on the right side of the topmost panel of your screen.

While we're over there, there are more icons. From right to left are the Bluetooth icon, the Wireless and Wired Network icon (looks like a WiFi icon), the CPU Usage Monitor, the Digital Clock, and as I said before, the volume eject button.

The Terminal App

For those too young to have ever seen an actual terminal, Figure 3-2 shows a classic Digital Equipment VT220, plugged in to a Raspberry Pi. When we talk about the terminal application, this is what it's emulating, in software.

Figure 3-2. *A physical terminal*

Before the widespread use of graphical user interfaces circa 1984, when the Apple Macintosh was released, terminals like this were how computing was done. UNIX, and by extension Linux, still remembers. So does MacOS X, as a UNIX-like platform. Windows likes to pretend the command line is gone, but some time click on the search icon and type command prompt, and you'll see something rather similar. Terminals are practically extinct now, but every mainstream operating system still finds the need for software emulation of them. Terminal commands are powerful.

Go ahead and click on the terminal icon in the top panel of your screen, or choose Raspberry Menu ➤ Accessories ➤ Terminal.

Type who in the terminal window. You'll get something that looks like this.

```
pi@Pi3plus:~$ who
pi        tty7         2017-09-21 16:15 (:0)
pi        tty1         2017-09-21 16:15
pi@Pi3plus:~$
```

Those are two users logged in as pi. Don't worry, they're both you. One is for the console (under the graphical desktop) and one is the desktop itself.

We'll use the terminal a lot in this book. Oftentimes it's easier, faster, and uses much less memory to do things via the terminal, and especially on the Pi Zero W, we don't have a lot of memory to spare.

The Web Browser

The default web browser on your Raspberry Pi is chromium, the open source version of Google Chrome. The biggest difference between Chrome and Chromium is that Chromium uses the Duck Duck Go search engine instead of Google. You can change that in Chromium's settings.

Behind the Curtain

Have you ever wondered what, exactly, your "desktop" in a computer is? Where it comes from? What software makes it go? For the Pi, I can answer this.

The desktop in the Raspberry Pi, as are most things in Linux, is a stack of software. Officially it's called PIXEL (Pi Improved Xwindows Environment Lightweight). It's derived from LXDE, a standard Lightweight

Linux desktop, and most of the LXDE components are still used. The bar across the top and the icons in it are generated by LXpanel. The wallpaper and the desktop file icons are managed by PCManFM, which is also the LXDE equivalent of Finder in MacOS X, Desktop Explorer in Windows, and Nautilus/Thunar/whatever that other distributions of Linux use. LXpanel started PCManFM for you. LXpanel was started by LXsession. As the name might suggest, LXsession is a session manager. This means that it keeps track of what apps should be running on your desktop and starts them when you log in. One of those apps is Xwindows, which is what draws all the windows on your screen.

LXsession was started by LightDM, which is a display manager. If Linux asks you for a login username and password, odds are you're talking to LightDM through one of its "greeter" programs. That's its whole job. It logs you in and kicks off your session manager.

By now you might be wondering why we weren't asked for a username and password to log in. The answer is that the Pi is configured to have LightDM automatically log the pi account in, without asking. We'll cover that when we get to the "Configuration" section, later in this chapter.

So okay. PCManFM was started by LXpanel. LXpanel was started by LXsession, which was started by LightDM. What started LightDM?

The answer is systemd, which is big and rolls a lot of functionality up into one big glob. Mostly it starts up services, makes sure they stay running, and generates log files when things happen. Linux, like its UNIX ancestor and all of its UNIX-like cousins, is made up of services. These are usually (but not always) programs running in the background called *daemons.* Like all daemons, systemd runs in the background, not talking to any user directly. You can send it commands if you have the right privileges (we'll get to that in this chapter), but so can other daemons, user programs, and so on.

systemd also started the server that gives us windowing in the first place, called Xorg.

What started `systemd`? It's one of three processes created by the kernel when it starts up.

The kernel is what lets Linux run multiple programs. It allocates memory and CPU time to each running program, along with moderating requests to use hardware, and a great many other functions. Where, in Arduino, the bootloader and the libraries that are silently added to your sketch are the operating system, such as it is, in Linux, the kernel really could be called the operating system. It does all the things those hidden libraries in Arduino do, plus a lot more so multiple programs can run at once.

What starts the kernel? The Pi has a bootloader. Before you ask, the bootloader is started from commands built into the system chip.

Whew. All that to get to a desktop.

Well, yes. You don't have to keep all this in your mind to use the Pi, but I wanted to make clear just how different things are from the Arduino where, as I've said, if the bootloader's not running, your sketch is. All these levels and daemons add functionality that ultimately gives us the desktop we're looking at.

Rebooting and Shutting Down

Like most modern desktop operating systems, (i.e., those designed since the 1980s), Rasbpian/Linux shouldn't be switched off without warning. It happens, and the filesystem is designed to recover from it, but in my experience, if you do it often enough, you'll make a mess on the microSD card from which Raspbian will not be able to recover. So now that we know what's where, let's talk about booting up and shutting down. We'll do it both ways—in the GUI/desktop and in the terminal window.

GUI/Desktop

If you click on the Raspberry icon at the top left of your screen, then go to the bottom of that menu and click Shutdown, you'll see the following menu pop up, shown in Figure 3-3.

Figure 3-3. *Shutdown Options menu*

- Clicking on Shutdown shuts the Pi down without further discussion.

- Clicking on Reboot reboots the Pi without further discussion.

- Clicking on Logout closes your session and exits you out to LightDM. You can log back in to the pi account with the password raspberry. We'll change the password shortly.

Terminal

All this can be done from the terminal window as well. Sometimes, when you're connecting to a Pi or other Linux computer from the network and you haven't got the GUI tools handy, knowing the terminal commands can be the difference between shutting down cleanly and just turning off the power, and risking filesystem damage.

Note   You can also get a terminal window by pressing Ctrl+Alt+T.

At the shell prompt (mine is pi@PiOw~$ on this particular Pi), type systemctl halt to shut down. Systemctl commands are all privileged, but systemctl is smart. Here's the process.

```
pi@PiOw:~$ systemctl halt
==== AUTHENTICATING FOR org.freedesktop.systemd1.manage-units ===
Authentication is required to start 'halt.target'.
Multiple identities can be used for authentication:
 1.  ,,, (pi)
 2.  root
Choose identity to authenticate as (1-2): 1
```

The pi account can do the job. It has sudo privileges. We'll cover sudo later. The password is still raspberry at this point.

```
Password:

==== AUTHENTICATION COMPLETE ===
```

At this point, the Pi will shut down. The halt command deserves some explanation. In the old days, when UNIX ran on minicomputers, halting the system did just that. It stopped execution of all programs. It did not, as the modern computers do, shut the system's power off. What we just did would have been a software halt, but most systems also had a hardware halt. The advantage to halt, in those days, was that often you could run diagnostic software to see what went wrong. With the advent of ATX power supplies in PCs, it's become possible and subsequently fashionable for halt to power the computer off completely. The Pi can't switch off its own power supply, but in all other ways it is powered down.

Note   As this book goes on, you'll notice that a lot of Linux terminal commands have their roots in the old days of UNIX, going back to the 1980s and before. Linux got a lot of its terminal environment from the GNU project. The GNU project, in the early days, was all about providing open source replacements for all the standard UNIX tools, and they weren't about to alienate the old-school UNIX users by changing all the commands.

To reboot the system from the terminal window, type `systemctl reboot` This reboots the system *right now*, without asking for a password, and without any further discussion.

Logging out...is more complicated. Here's the problem. Remember when we typed `who` and got two users logged in? One of those is your session, and the other is your terminal window. If, as we did in the old days, you type `exit` in the terminal window, the terminal will end its session and dutifully close. It doesn't log you out of your desktop though.

There are no really good solutions for this. Either exit from your terminal window and then use the GUI to log out, or shut the Pi down, or reboot it. For us, because our Pis are almost always set up for only one user (the `pi` account), logout isn't that necessary.

Oh, a quick hint. If you find you've sent a command you didn't really want to, or your command seems to get stuck, pressing Ctrl+C will sometimes stop the command. It's not terribly reliable, so it's best to either do this so often that your hands type the right command automatically, or think twice before pressing return. Or both.

Command Summary

TL;DR? Too long, didn't read? Okay. Here's a summary of the terminal commands we used in this section.

```
sudo systemctl halt
sudo systemctl reboot
```

Configuration

Now that we can shut the Pi down, reboot, and log out easily, we've seen another issue we really do need to address: the password. Every Raspbian installation on the planet starts out with `raspberry` as its password, and it basically gives you the keys to the kingdom on the Pi. Since one of the reasons to use a Pi instead of an Arduino is networking, we should lock that down. While we're at it, there are other configuration issues we should address. While there are command-line utilities for this, we have to do it only once (unless we reformat the microSD card), so we'll just go ahead and use the GUI versions. First, let's run the Raspberry Pi Configuration App.

Raspberry Pi Configuration App

Choose Raspberry-Menu ➤ Preferences ➤ Raspberry Pi Configuration.

You should get a menu that looks like Figure 3-4. This is the front tab of the configuration app.

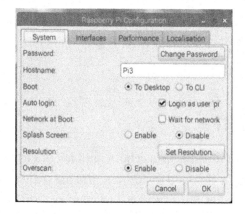

Figure 3-4. *Raspberry Pi Configuration menu*

System Tab

Password

The first thing we *must* do is change the password. Even if your Pi is not going to talk to the public Internet, it would still be nice to keep anyone who wanders by from breaking into your gadget.

Click on Change Password and enter your new password, and enter it again to confirm. As this is the only account on this system, it's a lot of work to reset the password if you forget it, so... don't.

Hostname

You may have noticed in some of the screenshots that the text prompt in my terminal window changes. Sometimes it's `pi@Pi3plus:~$` and sometimes it's `pi@PiOw:~$` In reality, my screenshots were taken on two different Pis. The hostname is where you set names like that, so you know which Pi you're talking to. It also helps with network names, which we'll get into later in this chapter. You want this name to be unique in your network.

Auto Login

The Auto Login configuration option controls something we talked about earlier in the section "Behind the Curtain." By default, the Pi is configured to log the user pi, without requiring a username or password. This is up to you.

It's handy to not have to log in every time you want to work on your Pi, and it's true that if you don't have physical security, you don't have security. You can always pull the Pi's microSD card out and put it in your (Linux) desktop computer and access whatever files you want.

On the other hand, someone could wipe out everything you've done on your Pi with only one keyboard command: rm -R *. This is why it's up to you. If you're keeping this Pi at home, and you trust the cat, leave it unlocked. Otherwise, disable Auto Login and type your username and password every time.

Note that Auto Login only applies to the console—the keyboard, mouse, and screen connected directly to the Pi.

Resolution and Overscan

Resolution and Overscan are video settings. If your Pi's desktop doesn't go to both the left and right edges, or to the top and bottom of your screen, you may need to enable overscan. Likewise, if you don't seem to be getting the kind of quality you expect from your monitor, check the resolution settings. Sometimes the Pi guesses wrong.

Interfaces Tab

The next tab at the top of the Raspberry Pi Configuration window is Interfaces. This one's easy. For now, the only one you want on is SSH. We're not going to use SSH in this book; it's just handy to have when you switch your keyboard, monitor, and mouse back to your desktop and then realize you forgot to shut the Pi down. You can SSH into the Pi (ssh pi@pi.local) and shut down with the terminal, as described previously. Assuming you have SSH turned on. And assuming your Pi is connected to the network, which we'll get to shortly.

Performance Tab

For the purposes of this book, we don't need to change the performance settings. If you're doing a lot of graphical work on the Pi and you find its video performance is poor, you can turn up the amount of system memory the video system gets. Likewise, if your Pi won't be running with a graphical console (you're going to ssh into it once you're done developing on it), you can reduce this to a minimum of 16MB. If your Pi offers the chance to overclock it, bear in mind that in times past, overclocked Pis have been known to mess up their SD/microSD card filesystems.

Localization Tab

The localization settings (see Figure 3-5) are quite important. They tell the Pi what kind of keyboard you have, where you are, what time zone you're in (so the Pi's automatic network time system can work correctly), and what country's WiFi bands to use.

Figure 3-5. *Localizations tab of the Configuration app*

You want to fill all of these settings in, most especially the keyboard. If you don't know what kind of keyboard you have, it will usually say in the info plate on the bottom, and if that won't tell you, searching on the model number online will. Keyboard layout is important because command-line Linux relies on certain punctuation—forward slash, tilde, exclamation points, at signs, dollar signs, and asterisks, all of which are frequently in different places on different kinds of keyboards.

You may be wondering, "didn't we set the localization on the NOOBS screen?" Well, yes. We did. The catch is, we set it up for the NOOBS system rather than the Raspbian system we installed.

When you're done with the localizations tab, go ahead and close the Raspberry Pi Configuration app. You'll be asked to reboot the Pi. It doesn't really give you a choice.

WiFi and Network Configuration

On the top panel of your screen at the right, there should be a cluster of icons. You can see them in Figure 3-6.

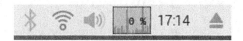

Figure 3-6. *Raspbian desktop right side icons*

The WiFi icon lets you turn WiFi on and off, and lets you determine which WiFi network you want to use. Click it, choose your WiFi network, and enter the network password as usual.

Your Pi is configured and ready to go. Well. Almost.

Installing and Updating Software

You know the drill. By the time you download an operating system installer, or worse, get the DVD of the software, it's out of date and you need to update it. The version of Raspbian packed with NOOBS is inevitably behind the times, so we'll need to update the system. Also, there are some big software packages we don't really need for this book, so I'll cover how to uninstall them, too.

The GUI Software Installer

Like most Linux GUI software install/upgrade systems, the Add/Remove software program (choose Raspberry menu ➤ Preferences ➤ Add/Remove Software) is nice for finding applications you might want. It's much less useful for maintaining the system itself. For that, we'll go to the terminal window. That's Raspberry Menu ➤ Accessories ➤ Terminal, in case the icon in the top panel of your desktop ever goes missing.

The Apt-Get Package Manager

The simplest package manager on Debian-derived systems like Raspbian is the command-line apt-get system.

Type this:

```
pi@Pi3plus:~$ sudo apt list --installed
```

The Pi will respond like this:

```
pi@PiOw:~$ apt list --installed
Listing... Done
adduser/stable,now 3.115 all [installed]
adwaita-icon-theme/stable,now 3.22.0-1+deb9u1 all [installed,automatic]
alacarte/stable,now 3.11.91-2+rpi5 all [installed]
```

Many dozens of packages later...

```
zenity-common/stable,now 3.22.0-1 all [installed,automatic]
zip/stable,now 3.0-11 armhf [installed,automatic]
zlib1g/stable,now 1:1.2.8.dfsg-5 armhf [installed]
zlib1g-dev/stable,now 1:1.2.8.dfsg-5 armhf [installed,automatic]
pi@Pi0w:~$
```

Those are all the packages installed on your Pi. In fact, all the software that comes in Raspbian is organized into packages, and all of them can be installed, updated, or removed with apt-get.

Wondering what sudo is? In short, it tells the system to do what you want with root privilege instead of normal user privilege. It lets you alter system files. We'll cover it in depth when we get to the section called "Permissions and Privileges".

Removing Packages

Here's an example of how to remove a package. We don't really need the Wolfram Mathematica and knowledge managing systems, and they use a considerable amount of space on the microSD card. Let's remove them.

```
pi@Pi3plus:~$ sudo apt-get remove wolfram-engine
```

The Pi will respond:

```
Reading package lists... Done
Building dependency tree
Reading state information... Done
The following packages were automatically installed and are no longer required:
  coinor-libipopt1v5 libexiv2-14 libgmime-2.6-0 libgpgme11 libmumps-seq-4.10.0
  libraw15 wolframscript
Use 'sudo apt autoremove' to remove them.
The following packages will be REMOVED:
  wolfram-engine
0 upgraded, 0 newly installed, 1 to remove and 0 not upgraded.
After this operation, 705 MB disk space will be freed.
Do you want to continue? [Y/n] y
```

We do want to continue, so type Y or y. It's not case sensitive here, but sometimes a script specifies Y/n, and it wants a capital Y to make sure you're paying attention.

```
Do you want to continue? [Y/n] Y
(Reading database ... 125651 files and directories currently installed.)
Removing wolfram-engine (11.2.0+2018011502) ...
Processing triggers for mime-support (3.60) ...
Processing triggers for desktop-file-utils (0.23-1) ...
Processing triggers for man-db (2.7.6.1-2) ...
Processing triggers for shared-mime-info (1.8-1) ...
Processing triggers for gnome-menus (3.13.3-9) ...
Processing triggers for hicolor-icon-theme (0.15-1) ...
pi@Pi3plus:~$
```

Let's also remove sonic-pi. It's not very big, but it's not useful for the kind of projects we're doing.

```
pi@pi3plus:~$ sudo apt-get remove sonic-pi
Reading package lists... Done
Building dependency tree
Reading state information... Done
The following packages were automatically installed and are no longer required:
  coinor-libipopt1v5 erlang-base erlang-crypto erlang-syntax-tools fonts-lato
  libboost-thread1.62.0 libexiv2-14 libgmime-2.6-0
```

Lots of other packages...

```
  rubygems-integration supercollider-server wolframscript
Use 'sudo apt autoremove' to remove them.
The following packages will be REMOVED:
  sonic-pi
0 upgraded, 0 newly installed, 1 to remove and 0 not upgraded.
After this operation, 512 kB disk space will be freed.
Do you want to continue? [Y/n] Y
(Reading database ... 115875 files and directories currently installed.)
Removing sonic-pi (1:3.0.1+1) ...
Processing triggers for mime-support (3.60) ...
Processing triggers for desktop-file-utils (0.23-1) ...
Processing triggers for gnome-menus (3.13.3-9) ...
pi@pi3plus:~$
```

See all those packages that are installed that are no longer required?

Apt-get handles these (they're called *dependencies*). We can tell it to remove any libraries that aren't known to be used by installed application packages.

Did you hear that gotcha as it went by?

If you're using a library that was installed with a package, but you're using it from software that wasn't installed with apt-get, apt-get will happily remove your library anyway. Something to watch out for. You can always reinstall the library manually.

We don't have anything like that, so let's go ahead and use the autoremove command for apt-get and have them all removed.

```
pi@pi3plus:~$ sudo apt-get autoremove
Reading package lists... Done
Building dependency tree
Reading state information... Done
The following packages will be REMOVED:
  coinor-libipopt1v5 erlang-base erlang-crypto erlang-syntax-tools fonts-lato
```

Lots of other packages...

```
  ruby-net-telnet ruby-power-assert ruby-test-unit ruby2.3
  rubygems-integration supercollider-server wolframscript
0 upgraded, 0 newly installed, 32 to remove and 0 not upgraded.
After this operation, 67.7 MB disk space will be freed.
Do you want to continue? [Y/n] Y
(Reading database ... 101452 files and directories currently installed.)
Removing coinor-libipopt1v5 (3.11.9-2.1) ...
Removing erlang-syntax-tools (1:19.2.1+dfsg-2+deb9u1) ...
```

Lots of packages being removed and triggers being processed...

```
Processing triggers for hicolor-icon-theme (0.15-1) ...
Processing triggers for fontconfig (2.11.0-6.7) ...
pi@pi3plus:~$
```

Installing Packages

Apt-get is not just a tool for removing packages. It's also good for installing them too, and as a side benefit, it will check to see if a package is already installed, rather than installing it twice. Before we start, we should make sure our package database is up to date. Type sudo apt-get update to do that. Be patient. This takes a few minutes.

```
pi@pi3plus:~$ sudo apt-get update
Get:1 http://archive.raspberrypi.org/debian stretch InRelease [25.3 kB]
Get:2 http://raspbian.raspberrypi.org/raspbian stretch InRelease [15.0 kB]
Get:3 http://archive.raspberrypi.org/debian stretch/main armhf Packages [144 kB]
Get:4 http://raspbian.raspberrypi.org/raspbian stretch/main armhf Packages
[11.7 MB]
Fetched 11.8 MB in 10s (1,092 kB/s)
Reading package lists... Done
pi@pi3plus:~$
```

Now that our package database is up to date, we'll try installing Geany, the programming environment we'll be using. It's installed by default, so apt-get should tell us so.

```
pi@pi3plus:~$ sudo apt-get install geany
Reading package lists... Done
Building dependency tree
Reading state information... Done
geany is already the newest version (1.29-1+rpt1).
0 upgraded, 0 newly installed, 0 to remove and 7 not upgraded.
pi@pi3plus:~$
```

As expected, the Geany package is already installed. Note, by the way, that package names are almost always in all lowercase.

Let's install something small so you can get the feel for how installation works without cluttering up the microSD card. Let's install that most classic of UNIX tools: the fortune command. This gives you a pithy saying on command.

```
pi@pi3plus:~$ sudo apt-get install fortune
Reading package lists... Done
Building dependency tree
Reading state information... Done
Note, selecting 'fortune-mod' instead of 'fortune'
```

Note what just happened. Apt-get is smart enough to know that the package we really want is fortune-mod. It'll tell us what packages it's actually going to install next.

```
The following additional packages will be installed:
  fortunes-min librecode0
Suggested packages:
  fortunes
```

It also recommended a library of additional fortunes. Not especially useful for this package, but if you're installing something to develop code with it, you may need libraries or additional data, and apt-get may recommend them here.

```
The following NEW packages will be installed:
  fortune-mod fortunes-min librecode0
0 upgraded, 3 newly installed, 0 to remove and 7 not upgraded.
Need to get 602 kB of archives.
After this operation, 1,588 kB of additional disk space will be used.
Do you want to continue? [Y/n] Y
Get:1 http://raspbian-us.ngc292.space/raspbian stretch/main armhf librecode0
armhf 3.6-23 [477 kB]
```

Apparently, fortune-mod depends on a lot of other packages. Apt-get installs those for us, too. Lots of stuff cut for brevity. Apt-get unpacks and sets up all the packages, and the triggers add them to menus, man pages, and things like that.

```
Fetched 602 kB in 1s (326 kB/s)
Selecting previously unselected package librecode0:armhf.
(Reading database ... 99603 files and directories currently installed.)
```

Shortened for brevity...

```
Unpacking fortunes-min (1:1.99.1-7) ...
Setting up fortunes-min (1:1.99.1-7) ...
Processing triggers for libc-bin (2.24-11+deb9u3) ...
```

Shortened for brevity again. Apt-get is very chatty, but it's nice to know what's going on.

```
Processing triggers for libc-bin (2.24-11+deb9u3) ...
pi@pi3plus:~$
```

Let's try our new prize.

```
pi@Pi3plus:~$ fortune
Today is the first day of the rest of your life.
pi@Pi3plus:~$
```

System Updates

Apt-get is also the go-to tool for doing system updates. To update the whole system, type sudo apt-get dist-upgrade, for distribution upgrade. Upgrading the distribution is Linux-speak for installing all the updated packages of the Raspbian (in this case) distribution, even if they include the kernel. This can sometimes be a problem for desktop Linux installations, since complex driver situations may mean that a kernel upgrade breaks the graphical interface completely (another good time to have terminal window skills), but Raspbian has the advantage of a very small, relatively fixed hardware set. It's safe to let the kernel be upgraded in most cases. As with all apt-get activities, it's a very good idea to update apt-get's database before updating the system.

```
pi@Pi3plus:~$ sudo apt-get update
```

You've seen update before. Let's skip over its output.

```
pi@pi3plus:~$ sudo apt-get dist-upgrade
Reading package lists... Done
Building dependency tree
Reading state information... Done
Calculating upgrade... Done
The following packages will be upgraded:
  libssl1.0.2 libssl1.1 openssl
3 upgraded, 0 newly installed, 0 to remove and 0 not upgraded.
Need to get 2,691 kB of archives.
After this operation, 6,144 B of additional disk space will be used.
Do you want to continue? [Y/n] Y
```

Apt-get proposes to update libssl, which is the secure socket layer used to encrypt communications that go over the Internet. That's fine. We want that kept up to date.

```
Get:1 http://raspbian-us.ngc292.space/raspbian stretch/main armhf libssl1.0.2
armhf 1.0.2l-2+deb9u3 [894 kB]
Get:2 http://mirrors.syringanetworks.net/raspbian/raspbian stretch/main armhf
libssl1.1 armhf 1.1.0f-3+deb9u2 [1,105 kB]
Get:3 http://mirror.us.leaseweb.net/raspbian/raspbian stretch/main armhf
openssl armhf 1.1.0f-3+deb9u2 [692 kB]
Fetched 2,691 kB in 2s (1,102 kB/s)
```

apt-get has downloaded all the updates.

```
Reading changelogs... Done
Preconfiguring packages ...
(Reading database ... 99096 files and directories currently installed.)
Preparing to unpack .../libssl1.0.2_1.0.2l-2+deb9u3_armhf.deb ...
Unpacking libssl1.0.2:armhf (1.0.2l-2+deb9u3) over (1.0.2l-2+deb9u2) ...
Preparing to unpack .../libssl1.1_1.1.0f-3+deb9u2_armhf.deb ...
Unpacking libssl1.1:armhf (1.1.0f-3+deb9u2) over (1.1.0f-3+deb9u1) ...
Preparing to unpack .../openssl_1.1.0f-3+deb9u2_armhf.deb ...
Unpacking openssl (1.1.0f-3+deb9u2) over (1.1.0f-3+deb9u1) ...
```

Some packages have scripts that need to run after installation to configure the new software. New packages will want to put icons in the Raspberry menu, and new or updated packages will want to update the man pages—the traditional UNIX/Linux help system. These are handled by triggers in the package.

```
Setting up libssl1.0.2:armhf (1.0.2l-2+deb9u3) ...
Processing triggers for libc-bin (2.24-11+deb9u3) ...
Setting up libssl1.1:armhf (1.1.0f-3+deb9u2) ...
Setting up openssl (1.1.0f-3+deb9u2) ...
Processing triggers for man-db (2.7.6.1-2) ...
Processing triggers for libc-bin (2.24-11+deb9u3) ...
```

Sometimes the system will require a reboot. More often than not, it won't. Typically, I reboot anyway

```
pi@Pi3plus:~$ sudo systemctl reboot
```

Command Summary

For those in the TL;DR crowd, here are the commands we used in this section. Anything enclosed in <<>> marks indicates a package name you have to fill in.

```
sudo apt-get update

sudo apt-get remove <<package name>>

sudo apt-get autoremove

sudo apt-get install <<package name>>

sudo apt-get dist-upgrade
```

Filesystem Navigation

Arduinos don't really have a filesystem. They just have flash space with stuff in it, and normally you can't even see what's there once you upload a sketch to the Arduino. Linux, of course, has them, and you need to be able to get around in them.

Navigating the filesystem gives the answers to a few basic questions.

- Where am I?

- What files are here?

It also gives you some capabilities.

- Creating files

- Creating directories

- Deleting files and directories.

We'll break down both methods of navigation—the GUI/desktop way and the terminal window way into these questions and capabilities.

By the way, if you're a dyed-in-the-wool Mac user, the idea of directories may be a little alien. Don't worry. A directory and a folder are two names for the same thing. Folders are typically talked about in the GUI world, and directories in the terminal window/command-line world, but in Linux the two are hopelessly muddled together. They're the same thing exactly when you look at the guts of the filesystem. Because I came up in the terminal/command-line world, I'll almost always call them directories.

GUI/Desktop

GUI/desktop filesystem navigation is handled by PCManFM. It's the file folder icon on the top panel of your desktop close to the Raspberry menu icon. Speaking of the Raspberry menu, PCManFM is in there, too. Choose Raspberry Menu ➤ Accessories ➤ File Manager to get it. You should see something like Figure 3-7.

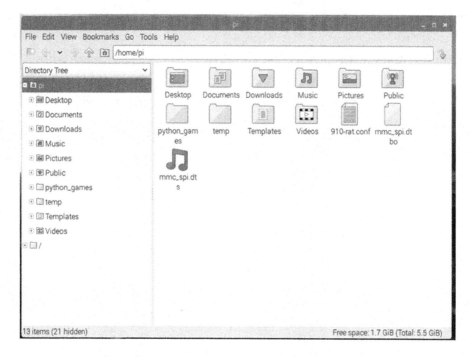

Figure 3-7. *The File Manager, aka PCManFM*

Where Am I?

On the top bar of PCManFM, you can see the word "pi". This is the directory you're in. It's also shown on the left bar labeled "Directory Tree". That's your home directory for the pi account (we'll cover accounts in the section "Accounts, Users, and Passwords"). When you log in as pi, which we're doing automatically, that's where the files go unless you tell them to go somewhere else.

What Files Are Here?

The directory tree is also telling us which directories are in the pi directory. In this case, you can see Desktop, Documents, Downloads, Music, etc. If you want to go to one of those directories, you can click on it in the directory tree bar.

The directory tree will not tell you about files in a given directory. The right-side bar of the PCManFM window will. It repeats the list of directories (represented as folders), but also shows regular files. So, for example, if I want to move the file in my `pi` directory called `910-rat.conf` (It's a copy of a configuration file for my weird, nonstandard mouse. You won't have this file.) to my `Downloads` directory, I can just click and drag the file either to the folder icon labeled `Downloads` near it, or to anywhere on the directory tree. Either one will work. Go ahead and try it.

Creating Files

Don't have a handy file to move around? We need to cover that anyway. PCManFM will let you create empty files. Just choose File ➤ Create ➤ Empty File. Done. What use is an empty file? Sometimes Linux needs to know a file is there even if it doesn't contain anything. These are sometimes used as lock files (which is far deeper than "survival Linux," so I won't go into it) or for programs that must have a configuration file or they crash on startup. In our case, it's useful for demonstration.

Special Directories

Go ahead and click on Downloads in the directory tree bar. If you haven't already created and moved a file there, go ahead and create one now. Here's where the directory tree bar becomes useful. Nested directories, that is, directories inside directories, are a way of life for UNIX-like operating systems such as Linux. The icon display tells you only what's in your current directory, but you can drag your file from there to any directory in your directory tree. Now drag your empty file to Desktop.

The desktop is a special directory. Two things just happened. First, when you dragged the file, it didn't move out of the `Downloads` directory as it did when we moved it to `Downloads` in the first place. Instead, we created a symbolic link to the file and stuck that link in the `Desktop` directory. Desktop is also special in that anything in the Desktop directory is displayed *on the desktop*. So that icon under the trash that looks like a page of text with a dog-eared corner? That's the link. You can access the file from there.

Links

It's important to understand that the symbolic link icon on the desktop isn't an actual file. It's an alias for the actual file. If you modify it, you'll modify the copy in your Downloads directory. If you delete the alias, it does not affect the original in the Downloads directory.

This gets fairly deeply into how Linux files are stored in the filesystem, but the upshot is, there's a file. It's pointed to by what's called an *inode*. The filename is stored separately, and it points to the inode that points to the file. The symbolic link is another filename that points to the first filename. If you delete the file, it goes away, its inode goes away, and its filename goes away. The symbolic link doesn't go away, but it's broken and won't work. This concept is used a lot in Windows and MacOS X.

Digression: Hard (Regular) Links

There's another type of link that isn't used much anymore called simply a link. It points not to the filename, but to the inode where the file data is. In UNIX-like operating systems, as long as the inode exists, the file exists. As long as at least one filename points to that inode (or any program has that inode marked in use), the inode and the file data won't be deleted. So what this means is if you link (as opposed to symbolically link, or symlink, for short) a second filename to the file data, and then delete the original file, your link will still work. If your link wasn't in the same directory as the link, the file will now magically be in the directory you put the link in.

Making Directories

So we know how to create files and move them around, and we know how to tell where we are and what files are there. Next up, let's make some directories. Make sure you're in the Downloads folder. Choose File ➤ Create New ➤ Folder (or right-click on Downloads and choose Create New ➤ Folder). You should get a window that looks like Figure 3-8.

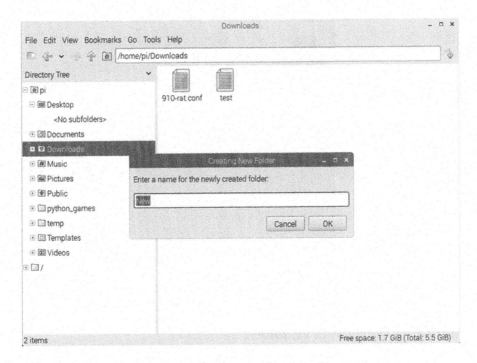

Figure 3-8. *Create folder in PCManFM*

91

New is a fine name for the folder (we'll get rid of it later anyway), but you can call it whatever you want. Unsurprisingly, you can see your new folder in the icons for the Downloads directory. If you click on the little + in the directory tree next to Downloads, you'll see that your new folder called New is now part of the directory tree, as shown in Figure 3-9.

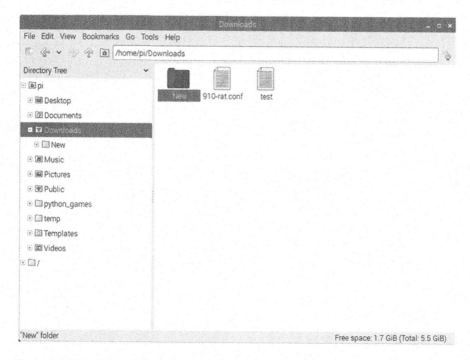

Figure 3-9. *Downloads, expanded*

That's what the + does; it expands the tree deeper on that branch. If there were any directories in our new directory, its + would not be grayed out, and we could expand it too.

Deleting Files and Directories

We've made a bit of a mess with new folders and copies of stuff. Let's clean up.

To delete any file or directory, you can drag and drop it in the trash. You can also right-click on it, either on the desktop or in the Desktop directory, and click Move to Trash. When PCManFM asks if you want to move it to the trash, choose Yes.

As with most GUIs, you can click a box around all three files and drag them to the trash. Make sure to empty the trash. The files are still taking up space until you do.

Terminal

It's that time again. Kick off the terminal. Choose Raspberry Menu ➤ Accessories ➤ Terminal, or once again, the icon is in the list of icons in the top panel of your screen on the left.

Terminal Mode Orientation

What you're looking at, with the green pi@Pi3plus:~$, is the text output of bash (*Bourne Again Shell*). Linux users and MacOS X users, it's exactly the same bash you're used to.

Bash is a shell program. CP/M had CCP, MS-DOS had COMMAND.COM., and VMS had DCL. UNIX and UNIX-style operating systems (including Linux) had (and have) a great multitude of shells. They all do the same job—interact with the user through text messages sent from the keyboard and to the screen and allow the user to run other programs by calling them by name. The programs we're going to call are all about manipulating files. But we need to talk a little more about what's on your terminal window first. The prompt is actually important.

The Prompt

This prompt is set up, among a great many other things, in your .profile script, which is called at login. You can edit that file some time if you want to change it. I leave mine stock, because the prompt it sets gives a lot of useful information.

```
pi@Pi3plus:~$
```

There are a lot of moving parts in that one little prompt. The leftmost part is pi. This tells you what account you're using. We're using the pi account, all lowercase.

@Pi3 is telling us which machine we're on. In a networked environment like the one we're using, it's very important to know what machine you're ordering around, particularly if you have multiple machines running the same operating system. I have half a dozen Pis of various types, all of which could be connected to the network at any given time. Because I'm lazy, each of those has only its pi account. See the problem? If you wondered why it's important to give your Pi a unique name, as we did in the "Configuration" section, this is where it pays off.

The next piece of the prompt is ~. This is telling you what directory you're in.

Where Am I?

As I mentioned briefly in Chapter 2, "Meet the Raspberry Pi," the UNIX-style directory system is one big tree that spans filesystems. It starts at root, or /. Any directory will have a name after that, so /bin, /boot, /dev, /home, and so on are all directories inside /. (For reference, again, directories and folders are two names for the same thing. A graphical folder on most, if not all, graphical operating systems is showing the contents of the directory it's named for.) Inside /home, for example, you'll find a directory for every user on the system. In this case there's only one: pi. If we write a file right now, without telling Raspbian someplace else to put it, it will show up wherever the shell *is* right now.

To see where the shell is, here's your first shell command: Type pwd. It stands for Print Working Directory, and it should give you /home/pi This is called a *pathname*. With a pathname you can specify any file in any directory in the entire directory tree, so /home is in the home directory, which is in the root (/) directory. The pi directory, in turn, is in /home. So /home/pi goes from root to home to pi.

Shouldn't that be in the prompt? Actually, it is. The ~ is a shortcut for your home directory, whatever it is. Most versions of Linux use the / home/<username> convention, but it's not universal in different UNIX-style operating systems. MacOS X, for example, puts user home directories in /Users/<username>. The ~ shorthand, by contrast, always points to your home directory, no matter what UNIX-style operating system you're using.

(Note: Should you pursue bash scripting, the ~ alias does not usually work in bash scripts. You must specify the full pathname.)

You can get a directory tree view, similar to the one in PCManFM, by typing tree. Try it. You'll see just how much stuff is really in your home directory. If you've used the Chromium browser at all, you'll find the answer is *lots*.

Changing Directories

Changing directories, as you probably expect by now, has yet another separate command. That command is cd, for change directory. If you type cd ~/Downloads, you'll enter the Downloads directory. Remember that ~ is shorthand for /home/pi, so we're now in /home/pi/Downloads. Also remember that directory and filenames are case sensitive.

```
pi@Pi3plus:~/Downloads$ ls -l
total 8
-rwxr-xr-x 1 pi pi  323 Sep 21 16:10 910-rat.conf
drwxr-xr-x 2 pi pi 4096 Sep 26 18:01 New
-rw-r--r-- 1 pi pi    0 Sep 26 17:34 test
pi@Pi3plus:~/Downloads$
```

Do any of these files look familiar? Does it look very much like I forgot to clean up after the GUI navigation section? That's what they are. Did you notice that the prompt changed to pi@Pi3plus:~/Downloads$? It's telling us we're in Download, which is one step below (away from the home directory) of the pi account. (That's what the ~ means. We'll cover that shortly.)

That 910-rat.conf file is the same one I mentioned before. I moved it to the Downloads directory to get it out of the way. New is a directory. Test is the test file we created. Your Downloads directory may not have anything in it. We'll get to that shortly. We'll use pwd to see where we are, and cd to go up one level toward the root of the directory tree. Another pwd will show where we are now, but you can also see it in the prompt.

```
pi@Pi3plus:~/Downloads$ pwd
/home/pi/Downloads
pi@Pi3plus:~/Downloads$ cd ..
pi@Pi3plus:~$ pwd
/home/pi
pi@Pi3plus:~$
```

Note the use of the .. shorthand. It takes you one level down in the directory structure, back to /home/pi. In this case, we could as easily have typed cd /home/pi or used the tilde shorthand cd ~. There are lots of ways to get around in the terminal window.

What's in This Directory?

Here's another, and probably the single most useful, shell command. Type
ls. As with pwd, ls stands for something, in this case *list*, or *list directory*
contents. It shows you all the files and directories in bash's current
directory. So pwd tells you where you are, and ls tells you what's there.
Here's what's in mine. Yours probably looks similar.

```
pi@Pi3plus:~$ ls
Desktop    Downloads  Pictures  python_games  Templates
Documents  Music      Public    temp          Videos
pi@Pi3plus:~$
```

These directories should ring a bell. They're exactly the same as the ones
you saw from PCManFM. If we had any files, they'd be in this list too. Want to
see which are directories and which are files? Type ls -l for *ls long*.

```
pi@Pi3plus:~$ ls -l
total 40
drwxr-xr-x 2 pi pi 4096 Sep 26 18:08 Desktop
drwxr-xr-x 6 pi pi 4096 Sep 27 17:44 Documents
drwxr-xr-x 3 pi pi 4096 Sep 26 18:01 Downloads
drwxr-xr-x 2 pi pi 4096 Aug 15 19:40 Music
drwxr-xr-x 2 pi pi 4096 Aug 15 19:40 Pictures
drwxr-xr-x 2 pi pi 4096 Aug 15 19:40 Public
drwxr-xr-x 2 pi pi 4096 Aug 15 19:11 python_games
drwxr-xr-x 2 pi pi 4096 Aug 18 17:32 temp
drwxr-xr-x 2 pi pi 4096 Aug 15 19:40 Templates
drwxr-xr-x 2 pi pi 4096 Aug 15 19:40 Videos
```

Right now, your home directory doesn't have much in it, just the
various directories that come with the pi account automatically. Because
we have bash set up to color-code file types, they show up as blue in any
color terminal. If your screen or your eyes don't do color, this doesn't help
you much, and it's nearly impossible to tell files from directories on sight
in ls. Fortunately, ls has options called *flags* that we can give it to get more
information. The three most useful flags are -l (lowercase L), -a, and -h.
The -l flag gives you a long format listing (that's what it stands for), which
tells you a lot more about each file. Type ls -l, and I'll explain.

```
pi@Pi3plus:~$ ls -l
total 40
drwxr-xr-x 2 pi pi 4096 Sep 26 18:08 Desktop
drwxr-xr-x 6 pi pi 4096 Sep 27 17:44 Documents
drwxr-xr-x 3 pi pi 4096 Sep 26 18:01 Downloads
drwxr-xr-x 2 pi pi 4096 Aug 15 19:40 Music
drwxr-xr-x 2 pi pi 4096 Aug 15 19:40 Pictures
drwxr-xr-x 2 pi pi 4096 Aug 15 19:40 Public
drwxr-xr-x 2 pi pi 4096 Aug 15 19:11 python_games
drwxr-xr-x 2 pi pi 4096 Aug 18 17:32 temp
drwxr-xr-x 2 pi pi 4096 Aug 15 19:40 Templates
drwxr-xr-x 2 pi pi 4096 Aug 15 19:40 Videos
```

We already know (because they're blue and I mentioned it earlier) that these are all directories. Now we can see it. The names are in the rightmost column. To the left of that are the modification dates and times.

Note   Modification, or "touch," dates will sometimes be stamped December 31, 1969. They were not, in fact, created the year I was two. UNIX-style operating systems keep time in seconds from December 31, 1969. When `ls -l` doesn't have a valid time stamp to show (it's most likely zero), it shows December 31, 1969: the beginning of time. They may also be different from the creation date, as you'll see in the "Creating Files" section.

To the left of the time column is how big the file is, in bytes. Note that this is the size of the directory file itself, not its contents. Even the root directory, /, which contains everything in the system, some two or three gigabytes of files, is itself only 4096 bytes. It helps to remember that a directory may be said to contain other directories and files, but to UNIX-style operating systems, it is a file with a list of filenames and pointers to inodes in it. Lists of names and inodes don't take much space, hence 4096 bytes.

To the left of the size column is the group name, and to the left of that is the owner name. There's a lot of complexity buried here. We'll get into it when we get to the "Accounts, Users, and Passwords" section.

On the far-left column is the most complicated part of ls -l. This is a series of 10 letters. The first (furthest left) is the type field. It will always be d for directories. If it's a -, it's blank and is an ordinary file. That's how you tell for sure.

The remaining nine letters are in groups of three from left to right owner permissions, group permissions, and world permissions, which we'll cover in the "Permissions and Privileges" section.

The -a flag, by contrast, is a lot simpler. Sometimes it's a good idea to hide files to discourage people from tampering with them and keep them out of the way. You can do this by having a filename with a . (dot) as the first character. Linux and MacOS X *love* hidden files, mostly for configuration of the desktop and/or applications.

They're not all that well hidden, as ls -a reveals them.

```
pi@Pi3plus:~$ ls -a
.                 .dbus       Music              python_games   .Wolfram
..                Desktop     .nano              .ssh           .WolframEngine
.bash_history     .dmrc       .oracle_jre_usage  temp           .Xauthority
.bash_logout      Documents   Pictures           Templates      .xsession-errors
.bashrc           Downloads   .pki               .themes        .xsession-
                                                                errors.old
.cache            .gnupg      .profile           .thumbnails
.config           .local      Public             Videos
pi@Pi3plus:~$
```

You may not have some of these files, and you may have others. The important thing is that now all the files in your home directory are visible, including .profile, which sets up how bash appears to you. The . and .. directories are more shortcuts: . always refers to the directory you're in, and .. always refers to one directory closer to the root (up) from the one you're in.

We can combine the flags too, so `ls -al` gives you all files, including hidden ones, in the long format. Try it with your Pi.

The `ls` command takes parameters in addition to flags. This means you can give it some value that tells it where you want to look. By default, if we don't tell it anything, it assumes we want the current directory. It doesn't have to be that way.

```
pi@Pi3plus:~$ ls .
Desktop     Downloads  Pictures  python_games  Templates
Documents   Music      Public    temp          Videos
pi@Pi3plus:~$ ls ..
pi
pi@Pi3plus:~$
```

See? Try it. Try `ls /usr/bin`. That's a lot of files. The dark blue ones are directories. The light blue ones are executable programs. If you'd like to see the ls program itself, type `ls -l /bin/ls`. Here's how mine looks.

```
pi@Pi3plus:~$ ls -l /bin/ls
-rwxr-xr-x 1 root root 108804 Feb 22  2017 /bin/ls
pi@Pi3plus:~$
```

It's not a directory, it doesn't have all its permissions turned on (we'll get to that, I promise), it's owned by root and in the group root (we'll get to that too), it's about 108,804 bytes long, and it was last modified on February 22nd, 2017. (This will probably be different for later versions of Raspbian.)

The `ls` command is one of those utilities that shows its age, listing everything in bytes. Today, it's like trying to measure a road map in millimeters. Fortunately there's a newer flag—`-h`—which converts file lengths to "human readable" units. `K` is for kilobytes, `M` is for megabytes, and `G` is for gigabytes. We can stack the `-h` flag with other flags (particularly `-l`) and type `ls -lh /bin/ls`.

```
pi@Pi3plus:~$ ls -lh /bin/ls

-rwxr-xr-x 1 root root 107K Feb 22  2017 /bin/ls
pi@Pi3plus:~$
```

About 107K, for kilobytes. (In most circumstances with Linux tools, these are equal to kibibytes.) That's human-readable.

If you pass a directory name to ls, you'll see the contents of the directory. Here's an example:

```
pi@Pi3plus:~$ ls -l Downloads
total 8
-rwxr-xr-x 1 pi pi  323 Sep 21 16:10 910-rat.conf
drwxr-xr-x 2 pi pi 4096 Sep 26 18:01 New
-rw-r--r-- 1 pi pi    0 Sep 26 17:34 test
pi@Pi3plus:~$
```

There is also a d flag for ls. This is most often useful for scripting, where you don't want a list of any files in that directory so much as whether the directory exists at all. Type ls -d Downloads, for example. It should return Downloads. Likewise, ls -d /bin/ls will tell you that the file /usr/bin/ls exists.

Want to see how much space all this is taking on your microSD card? Type du (for disk usage) -h (for human readable sizes). Again, if you've touched the Chromium browser, the answer will be... lots. 172MiB (mebibytes) in my case. It's also a very long printout that I won't make you wade through.

Creating Files

Creating empty test files in the terminal is shockingly easy. As with most things, there's a command for it that does that. It's called touch.

touch does two things. If the file exists, it changes the last-modified date in ls, without modifying the contents of the file. This is mostly used for scripting, when you want the file to seem new, often for testing purposes.

If the file doesn't exist, touch will create it.

Links

I already explained what a symbolic link is under the "Links" section in the GUI section. To create them in the terminal window, use the ln command. Its syntax can be a little confusing, so I'll spell it out here first.

```
ln -s <the filename that already exists> <the name of your link.>
```

Here, I cd into Videos (mostly because it's empty) and create a link to Downloads.

```
pi@Pi3plus:~$ ls
Desktop    Downloads  Pictures  python_games  Videos
Documents  Music      Public    Templates
pi@Pi3plus:~$ cd Videos
pi@Pi3plus:~/Videos$ ls -l
total 0
pi@Pi3plus:~/Videos$ ln -s ../Downloads my_link_to_downloads
pi@Pi3plus:~/Videos$ ls -l
total 0
pi@pi3plus:~/Videos$ ls -l
total 0
lrwxrwxrwx 1 pi pi 12 Apr  4 18:28 my_link_to_downloads -> ../Downloads
```

Yup. There's the link. Let's cd into it.

```
pi@Pi3plus:~/Videos$ cd my_link*
pi@Pi3plus:~/Videos/my_link_to_downloads$ pwd
/home/pi/Videos/my_link_to_downloads
```

We're there. How do we find out where we really are?

The answer is with a flag to pwd. The P flag tells pwd to ignore symlinks.

```
pi@Pi3plus:~/Videos/my_link_to_downloads$ pwd -P
/home/pi/Downloads
```

We're really in /home/pi/Downloads.

```
pi@Pi3plus:~/Videos/my_link_to_downloads$ cd ..
```

Although cd will follow the symlink back up to Videos.

```
pi@Pi3plus:~/Videos$ rm my_link_to_downloads
```

Note that my_link_to_downloads is not, itself, a directory, so we can just rm it. Modern implementations of rm seem to prevent rm -r running amok with symbolic links, but I wouldn't count on someone else's fail safes with my data, were I you.

Deleting Files

To delete a file in the terminal window, just type rm <filename>. Like this

```
pi@Pi3plus:~$ touch test-file1
pi@Pi3plus:~$
```

First, we'll create the file.

```
pi@Pi3plus:~$ ls
Desktop     Downloads   Pictures   python_games   test-file1
Documents   Music       Public     Templates      Videos
pi@Pi3plus:~$
```

Then we'll use ls to see if it's there.

```
pi@Pi3plus:~$ rm test-file1
pi@Pi3plus:~$ ls
Desktop     Downloads   Pictures   python_games   Videos
Documents   Music       Public     Templates
pi@Pi3plus:~$
```

Then we'll remove it with rm and use ls to see that it's gone.

As with ls and touch, you can pass rm a pathname—the full path from root or any shorthand—and access files in directories you're not currently "in." Here's a demonstration. We'll touch a file to create it in my Downloads directory, use ls it to see if it's there, and then rm it.

```
pi@Pi3plus:~$ touch ~/Downloads/test
pi@Pi3plus:~$ ls ~/Downloads/test
/home/pi/Downloads/test
pi@Pi3plus:~$ rm ~/Downloads/test
pi@Pi3plus:~$ ls ~/Downloads/test
ls: cannot access '/home/pi/Downloads/test': No such file or directory
pi@Pi3plus:~$
```

Creating Directories

Like creating files, creating directories in Raspbian is very straightforward. The command is mkdir. Like ls, touch, and rm (and indeed most commands that take a filename as a parameter), you aren't limited to creating directories in the current directory.

```
pi@Pi3plus:~$ ls
Desktop    Downloads  Pictures  python_games  Videos
Documents  Music      Public    Templates
pi@Pi3plus:~$ mkdir my_test
pi@Pi3plus:~$ ls
Desktop    Downloads  my_test   Public        Templates
Documents  Music      Pictures  python_games  Videos
```

Here, we've created the directory called my_test in the directory we're in, which happens to be the pi account's home directory. We don't have to do it that way. We can create directories anywhere by giving a path. Here, we'll use the full path from the root of the directory tree, /, to tell mkdir exactly where we want the new directory to be: in /home/pi/Documents. Then we'll check that it's there using the ~ shortcut for /home/pi.

```
pi@Pi3plus:~$ mkdir /home/pi/Documents/test_in_documents
pi@Pi3plus:~$ ls ~/Documents/test_in_documents
pi@Pi3plus:~$ ls -d ~/Documents/test_in_documents
/home/pi/Documents/test_in_documents
pi@Pi3plus:~$
```

Here's one of those times when ls -d is useful. You can see where I typed ls ~/Documents/test_in_documents and got nothing back. There's nothing in that directory, so ls returns nothing. When we hit it with ls -d ~/Documents/test_in_documents, we can see the directory itself.

Deleting Directories and Files

You won't be surprised to discover there's a rmdir command that removes directories. What might surprise you is that almost nobody uses it. The rmdir command simply fails if there's anything in a directory. To make it work, you'd have to go into the directory you want to remove, delete all its contents, then go into any directories inside it, delete all their contents, `rmdir` them, and so on. Most people use `rm`, the file remover, and pass it a flag, `r`, which tells it to recurse.

Imagine we have a directory tree three levels deep that looks like this:

```
pi@Pi3plus:~/Downloads$ tree
.
├── 910-rat.conf
└── directory_under_documents
    └── directory_two_levels_below_documents
```

We could just type `rm /home/pi/Downloads/directory_two_levels_below_documents/*` (where the `*` is a wildcard meaning "all files"), but we'd also have to get `directory_under_documents`. We could change directories into `directory_under_documents`, clean it out, then `cd` back out and `rmdir` it.

We could. But why? We can get them all in one command with the recursive flag. The `r` flag tells `rm` to go into any directories it finds and remove the selected files there. If there are any directories in *that* directory, go into those, and repeat the process. The `r` flag also allows `rm` to remove empty directories, which it won't do otherwise.

Note   Remember how I said `rm -r *` from your account's home directory could wipe out all the files in your account? Be careful with the `r` flag for `rm`. You can wind up with directories being removed that you actually need. It's a good idea, until you're used to using the terminal commands, to type `ls -R <whatever you were going to feed to rm>` to see what will really be destroyed. In `ls`, the `-r` has to be capitalized.

So let's try it from a directory we're in. We'll change to the Downloads directory, then see what a recursive rm would erase if we used it here.

```
pi@Pi3plus:~/Downloads$ ls
910-rat.conf  directory_under_documents
```

Okay, a regular ls shows the directory we want gone: directory_under_documents. Let's see what would happen if we used rm -r directory_under_documents.

```
pi@Pi3plus:~/Downloads$ ls -R directory_under_documents
directory_under_documents:
directory_two_levels_below_documents

directory_under_documents/directory_two_levels_below_documents:
pi@Pi3plus:~/Downloads$
```

The ls -R command shows us that there's a file inside directory_under_documents called directory_two_levels_below_documents. It then realizes that's another directory and *recurses* into it. It finds nothing inside that deeper directory.

Let's go ahead and remove them.

```
pi@Pi3plus:~/Downloads$ rm -r directory_under_documents
pi@Pi3plus:~/Downloads$ ls
910-rat.conf
pi@Pi3plus:~/Downloads$
```

Yep. The subsequent ls shows that they're gone.

Dealing with Spaces in Filenames

You may have noticed that all the directory names I've used or accessed from the terminal do not have spaces. This is by convention. Spaces have special meanings to bash and most other shells in UNIX-like operating systems. If you type mkdir directory with spaces what you'll get are three directories—one called directory, one called with, and one called spaces. Like this:

```
pi@Pi3plus:~$ ls
Desktop     Downloads   my_test    Public         Templates
Documents   Music       Pictures   python_games   Videos
pi@Pi3plus:~$ mkdir directory with spaces
pi@Pi3plus:~$ ls
Desktop     Documents   Music     Pictures   python_games   Templates   with
directory   Downloads   my_test   Public     spaces         Videos
pi@Pi3plus:~$
```

It can be done. Here's how, at least for bash.

```
pi@Pi3plus:~$ mkdir directory\ with\ spaces
pi@Pi3plus:~$ ls
Desktop                   Documents   Music     Pictures   python_games   Videos
directory with spaces     Downloads   my_test   Public     Templates
pi@Pi3plus:~$ cd directory_with*
-bash: cd: directory_with*: No such file or directory
pi@Pi3plus:~$ cd directory\ with*
pi@Pi3plus:~/directory with spaces$
```

The backslash character (\) is an escape character. It tells bash "don't treat what follows me as a special character." In this case, instead of interpreting the space as a break between parameters, bash ignores it and puts it in the directory name instead. It's there at the beginning of the second row of files. The only way you can tell is that the words aren't in alphabetical order. You can see it more clearly with ls -l. I've cd'ed into it with a wildcard (cd directory with*). See why it's a problem? Every time you deal with a directory name or filename with spaces in it, you have to escape the spaces, and if you miss one, you'll have the wrong file or directory name. This, combined with rm -r could make a real mess just by being confusing.

GUI designers do a real disservice to everyone by allowing spaces in UNIX-like operating systems, in my opinion. They ignore decades of established practice from the terminal days. Maybe I'm just old and grumpy, but please. For your own sanity, don't put spaces in file or directory names.

Summary

TL;DR? Too long, didn't read? Okay.

- `pwd` tells you what directory you're in. `pwd -P` tells you where you are even if you followed symlinks to get here.

- `ls` tells you what files are there.

- `ls -l` tells you more about the files.

- `ls -lh` tells you the sizes in human readable numbers.

- `ls -R` recursively dives down the directory tree to show you all the directories, from the one you started with on down.

- `du -h` shows you how much space you're using. It's recursive by default.

- `touch` changes the touch date of a file or creates it if it doesn't exist.

- `ln -s` creates a symbolic link to a file's or directory's name.

- `rm` removes files.

- `rm -r` removes files recursively, along with directories, and can make an unholy mess if you're not careful with it.

- Using spaces in Raspbian filenames makes it awkward to handle them from the terminal. Use the escape character (\) before spaces if you have to deal with one.

- `*` is a wildcard character. It tells any command "match any file identical to what came before me". So `cd directory\` with * will match any files that start out that way. This is pretty consistent across most modern operating systems, so I didn't talk about it much.

If you need more help, type man <command name> to get the Linux/ UNIX help pages. They can be a little opaque.

Permissions and Privileges

What if you tried deleting /bin/ls? Could you really break your ability to use the ls command that way? Pop open the terminal window and try it.

```
pi@Pi3plus:~$ rm /bin/ls
rm: remove write-protected regular file '/bin/ls'? y
rm: cannot remove '/bin/ls': Permission denied
pi@Pi3plus:~$
```

Nope. You can't. Let's see why.

```
pi@Pi3plus:~$ ls -l /bin/ls
-rwxr-xr-x 1 root root 108804 Feb 22  2017 /bin/ls
pi@Pi3plus:~$
```

What we're looking at are the permissions field and the owner field, in particular. The file is owned by the root account. (We'll get to accounts right after we're done with permissions and privileges.) The flags mean, if you could read them, that the owning user can read, write/erase, and execute them; group members can read and execute the file; and anyone else (other) can execute it (we'll get to groups when we get to accounts). So we have to ask ourselves, in a steely Clint Eastwood voice, "Are we root? Well, are we?"

Nope.

In a nutshell, that's why we can't delete /bin/ls. It's owned by someone else, and they haven't given us that privilege.

Clear as mud? Read on.

Users and Groups

Raspbian, like most UNIX-like operating systems, supports multiple users. This comes directly from the bad old days when 20 or 30 of us might share, via terminals, one computer with less processing power, and less memory (but much faster disks) than even the Raspberry Pi Zero W. It's persisted because isolating some daemons (like web and email servers) in their own accounts turns out to be a convenient way to keep them secure and out of root's files. (Root, itself, is another user.)

The pi account is a user. The security system only cares about that. Root's a different user, and there are others. How many? Well, let's see. Open the terminal window (you knew that was coming, right?) and type cat/etc/passwd.

cat displays the contents of a text file. Don't worry. Actual passwords haven't been stored in /etc/passwd in years.

```
pi@Pi3plus:~$ cat/etc/passwd
root:x:0:0:root:/root:/bin/bash
```

Lots of accounts cut out.

```
nobody:x:65534:65534:nobody:/nonexistent:/usr/sbin/nologin
pi:x:1000:1000:,,,:/home/pi:/bin/bash
```

Oh hey, there's the pi account. Lots more where that came from has been cut out.

```
lightdm:x:109:113:Light Display Manager:/var/lib/lightdm:/bin/false
```

Look at the information about the pi account.

```
pi:x:1000:1000:,,,:/home/pi:/bin/bash
```

That's the username, pi. The x indicates that there is a password, somewhere. The two numbers are critical. The pi account is user 1000 in group 1000. (Every user has its own group, but there can be other groups as well.) These two values are attached to files we create as the owning user and group values. Our home directory is /home/pi, and we use /bin/bash as our shell.

When you create a file, it's set as owned by the user who created it (1000 in our case), and associated with the group of the user who created it (1000 again). The two values are completely separate, even though the same number has been used for both.

When you try to access the file, you send a request to the kernel. The kernel checks to see if you own the file. If your user number and the file's number match, it's your file. The kernel then checks to see if you've set any permission restrictions on it that would keep you from acting on the file. If you're reading it, the r flag in the (owning) user group better be set. If you're writing (or deleting), the w flag better be set. If you're trying to execute the file as a program, the x flag needs to be set.

If you don't own the file, the kernel checks to see if you're in the same group as the file. Pi's default own group is 1000. If you are, the kernel checks to see if the (owning) user of the file has restricted the file's group access with the second group of three flags. The flags themselves are the same: r for read, w for write/erase, and x for execute.

If you don't own the file and you're not in the group, then you're "other" The kernel checks the third set of flags (from the left) called the "other" flags. Again, the flags do the same things: r for read, w for write/ erase, and x for execute.

There are tools for changing the permissions and groups, but as we're not going to use them, I'm not going to cover them beyond suggesting you look up chmod, chgrp, and chown.

Let's look at /bin/ls again, with our new understanding of what we're reading.

```
pi@Pi3plus:~$ ls -l /bin/ls
-rwxr-xr-x 1 root root 108804 Feb 22  2017 /bin/ls
pi@Pi3plus:~$
```

Now we can see how it is we can execute /bin/ls, but not rm it. The flags, left to right, tell us that /bin/ls is not a directory, and that the owning user (root) can read, write/erase, and execute it. Root's group (also called root) can read but not write/erase and can execute it. And mere riff-raff (other) users like Pi can read the file and execute it. We could make our own copy in our own directory if we wanted to. And we can call (execute it). We can't write/erase it (not to say we didn't try).

File permissions are critical to the Linux security model because, in Linux, *everything is a file*. Devices? Files. Drives? Files. Network connections? Files. And so on. You must understand file permissions, users, and groups if you're going to enjoy working with Raspbian. When you see projects where they tell you "this has to be run as root," what they're often saying is they didn't bother sorting the permissions out correctly.

There are three commands that you can use to change the situation for a given file.

The chown Command

The chown command changes the owning user of a file. Without root privileges, you can't do much with this, so we'll try it with sudo, which I'll explain shortly.

```
pi@Pi3plus ~ $ touch test.txt
pi@Pi3plus ~ $ ls -l test.txt
-rw-rw-r-- 1 pi pi 0 Sep 28 12:27 test.txt
pi@Pi3plus ~ $ sudo chown root test.txt
pi@Pi3plus ~ $ ls -l test.txt
-rw-rw-r-- 1 root pi 0 Sep 28 12:27 test.txt
pi@Pi3plus ~ $
```

You can see that we changed the owning user of the file, but not the group. The chown command takes two parameters. Like this: chown <user you want to own the file> <filename>.

The chgrp Command

Let's change the (owning) user back, so we can get rid of the file from the pi account when we're done with it, and then change its group with the chgrp (change group) command.

```
pi@Pi3plus ~ $ sudo chown pi test.txt
pi@Pi3plus ~ $ sudo chgrp root test.txt
pi@Pi3plus ~ $ ls -l test.txt
-rw-rw-r-- 1 pi root 0 Sep 28 12:27 test.txt
pi@Pi3plus ~ $
```

The chgrp command has the same limitations as chown, so we have to use sudo, and it works the same way: chgrp <the group you want the file to be in> <the filename>.

The chmod Command

It's one of UNIX/Linux's more obnoxious features that the most obvious name for a program was often passed over in favor of a name that's easier to type. In this case, the obvious name for the program that changes the permissions on a file would be chperm. But it's not. It's chmod, for change file mode.

Unlike the other two commands, and because we switched the (owning) user of the file back to pi previously, we can chmod the file without using sudo. The fact that it's still in the root group doesn't matter.

You may have noticed that I've gone to some lengths to call the owner of a file the owning user. This is because chmod does not call the owner of a file the owner. It calls them the user. Another obnoxiously obtuse thing about UNIX/Linux, and one that messes me up to this day.

Anyway, chmod works like this:

```
pi@Pi3plus ~ $ ls -l test.txt
-rw-rw-r-- 1 pi root 0 Apr  4 18:31 test.txt
```

Note that on any file we create we don't actually have execute permission. Let's fix that for this file, despite the fact that it's not a runnable program.

```
pi@Pi3plus ~ $ chmod u+x test.txt
pi@Pi3plus ~ $ ls -l test.txt
-rwxrw-r-- 1 pi root 0  Apr  4 18:31 test.txt
pi@Pi3plus ~ $
```

What I did there was chmod u for user +x to add the execute flag.

Let's give the group execute permissions on this file too.

```
pi@Pi3plus ~ $ chmod g+x test.txt
pi@Pi3plus ~ $ ls -l test.txt
-rwxrwxr-- 1 pi root 0 Apr  4 18:31 test.txt
pi@Pi3plus ~ $
```

See how that went? The g is for group. Because pi is the owning user of the file, we can change the permissions that even the root group can use (in theory).

You can see that other, the unwashed hoards that are neither the owning user nor the group, can only read this file. Let's fix that. We can combine the write/erase and execute permissions into one command.

```
im@Pi3 ~ $ chmod o+wx test.txt
pi@Pi3plus ~ $ ls -l test.txt
-rwxrwxrwx 1 pi root 0 Apr  4 18:31 test.txt
```

Now let's take all the permissions away from the group and other.

```
pi@Pi3plus ~ $ chmod go-rwx test.txt
pi@Pi3plus ~ $ ls -l test.txt
-rwx------ 1 pi root 0 Apr  4 18:31 test.txt
pi@Pi3plus ~ $
```

That's chmod go (group and other) – (take the permissions away) rwx (read, write/erase, execute).

> **Caution**   If you just type chmod +rwx <filename> it does the
> same thing as if you'd typed chmod ugo+rwx <filename>. It
> changes *all three* sets of permissions at once. Be careful waving this
> around, especially if you're doing it with root/sudo.

If you know binary numbers, you can throw the actual mode values at
chmod. I'm not going to get into this much, except to say that x is the ones bit,
w is the twos bit, and r is the fours bit, so chmod 777 <filename> sets the file
with read (4) plus write/erase (2) plus execute (1), for user, group, and other.
You'll still see chmod used that way sometimes. That's how I learned it.

Root and Sudo

Finally, root and sudo. I've been promising them for how long? As much
as the concept of file permissions, the concept of root is fundamental to
Raspbian, and indeed all UNIX-like operating systems.

The Root User

Want to see this kernel we talk about so much? Type this:

```
pi@pi3plus:~$ ls -l /boot/kernel.img
-rwxr-xr-x 1 root root 4622320 Mar 29 16:18 /boot/kernel.img
pi@pi3plus:~$
```

Interesting, no? The root user *owns* the kernel. Yow. The root user is
special because of this. When the kernel checks permissions on a file, the
read and write/erase permissions are simply ignored if the requesting user
is root. Not so with the execute flag. No program will run, even for root, if
the execute permission is not set.

The root user also ignores the owner of the file for purposes of chown,
chmod, and chgrp. When you hear about root privileges, that's what we're
talking about. The root user can treat any file in the system as though it owns it.

> **Note**   Some UNIX-like operating systems have been steadily taking power away from the root user "for security." It makes the systems very hard to manage. Fortunately, Linux is not one of these.

Sudo

Once upon a time, the root user was also the account you logged into to do system maintenance. This meant that your entire system's security hinged on the security of one password that multiple people used and therefore knew.

Today, you almost never log in as root, unless you're running Fedora or Red Hat Linux. Most systems ship with the root *account* disabled, so you can't log in as root. There are multiple approaches to getting system maintenance done without using the *root account*, but the one used by Raspbian, and all Debian-derived Linux distributions, is sudo.

The idea behind sudo is that the system owner (the person who owns the machine itself, or at least has physical access to it) can set a list of commands that you the user charged with maintaining the system can execute with root privileges. You're normally required to type *your* password, in case you left a session logged in and someone else is monkeying with your account. Your use of sudo commands is, ideally, logged, as are any commands you're not allowed to use that you try to use anyway.

On Raspbian, sudo has been set up rather liberally. If you call sudo, you can can do anything the root user can, as the root user, and not have to give a password at all. The assumption is that security is different on a Linux machine that fits in your pocket. So sudo gives you the ability to use root permissions, but you have to take the extra step to use it. This protects you from wiping big chunks of the system out by accident because an rm -r got away from you, and catastrophes like that. It's a reminder to pay attention, because you're using root privilege, and not much more.

Accounts, Users, and Passwords

A lot of people—most people who use Linux and other UNIX-like operating systems, in fact—are often confused by the difference between an account and a user. They're not the same thing. We've already seen that the root *account* is disabled. Here's the difference.

Accounts versus Users

Let's look at the pi account in the /etc/passwd file again. You don't have to go find it; I'll just cut and paste it from the discussion in the "Users and Groups" section.

```
pi:x:1000:1000:,,,:/home/pi:/bin/bash
```

It's a list, broken (delimited) with : marks. The chunk with all the commas between the group and the home directory is where the person's name, what office they're in, and in the bad old days, who pays for their computer time would go in there. Here's an example from basementcat, one of my other Linux machines.

```
jim@basementcat ~ $ grep jim /etc/passwd
jim:x:1000:1000:James Strickland,Downstairs,(xxx)-xxx-xxxx,(xxx)-not-work,
:/home/jim:/bin/bash
jim@basementcat ~ $
```

The point is, the user is 1000, also called jim. It's specified *in* the account entry in /etc/passwd, but it is not the account. That's the difference. The user id is created with the account, normally. As I've hinted earlier, this is important to understand when you execute commands as the root *user* even though the *root account* is disabled.

117

Adding Accounts (and Users)

It's unlikely you'll need to add an account and a user on a Pi, but if you do, the command is adduser. I'm not going to cover the command much, but here's what it looks like.

```
pi@Pi3plus:~$ sudo adduser demo
Adding user `demo' ...
Adding new group `demo' (1001) ...
Adding new user `demo' (1001) with group `demo' ...
Creating home directory `/home/demo' ...
Copying files from `/etc/skel' ...
Enter new UNIX password:
Retype new UNIX password:
passwd: password updated successfully
Changing the user information for demo
Enter the new value, or press ENTER for the default
        Full Name []: demo
        Room Number []: nope
        Work Phone []: nope
        Home Phone []: not this either
        Other []:
Is the information correct? [Y/n] y
pi@Pi3plus:~$
```

Passwords

While we're on the subject of accounts, it's a good time to discuss passwords. We already reset the Pi's password from the Configuration menu, but it shouldn't surprise you to know that there are normal Linux utilities for this as well. I'll cover the command-line one, since it's simplest to use. It's called passwd.

For the ordinary user, this changes your own password.

```
pi@Pi3plus:~$ passwd
Changing password for pi.
(current) UNIX password:
Enter new UNIX password:
Retype new UNIX password:
passwd: password updated successfully
pi@Pi3plus:~$
```

If you're using `passwd` on someone else's account, you'll have to do it with root privileges, from `sudo`. I've created an account called `demo` for this demonstration. Your Pi probably doesn't have one.

```
pi@Pi3plus:~$ sudo passwd demo
Enter new UNIX password:
Retype new UNIX password:
passwd: password updated successfully
pi@Pi3plus:~$
```

If you decide you don't want to change the password after all, just press Return until `passwd` exits with an error message, which you can safely ignore.

You might notice the mentions of UNIX passwords here. This is one of those places where Linux shows its heritage as a kernel plus a lot of utilities built by the OSF (Open Source Foundation) to replace standard UNIX utilities.

Drivers and Memory

Later on, we're going to get into a discussion about drivers. I'm going to introduce the concept now, so it has some time to settle into your mind and it's not completely alien when we start talking about it later. To understand drivers, you have to understand the concept of kernel space and user space in memory.

Memory

Memory is, in its broadest sense, a place to put bytes that isn't inside the CPU. Obviously, if we're going to keep files separate from each other, we'd better keep memory separate too, and this is handled exactly the same way, because everything in Linux is a file.

There are more wrinkles though. Linux, like all UNIX-like operating systems, divides memory into user space and kernel space.

Kernel Space

Kernel space is where the kernel does business. It stores its tables of things like, "who gets which CPU core next?" and "how much memory does this user have?" in kernel space. It also stores all the drivers there. When you talk to the graphics system or the microSD card, or literally anything in the system, a message passes from your program to the kernel, and the kernel decides, based on your privileges and the file permissions, whether to do it for you.

User Space

User space is where all programs that are not part of the kernel run, even if they're owned and run by root. Even mighty systemd runs in user space. Programs in user space should only be able to send messages to the kernel and *ask* the kernel to do things. Security vulnerabilities are, in a nutshell, what you get when this isn't true.

Drivers

A driver, then, is a program that runs in kernel space with the kernel. Once upon a time, drivers had to be compiled *into* the kernel. You didn't plug something in and load a driver; you plugged something in, added code to the kernel, rebuilt the entire kernel, and then rebooted to see if the system would even boot and if the driver did what you want.

Modern Linux kernels let you load and unload drivers from kernel space without rebooting. That's all you need to know right now. Let it soak in. We'll go deeper into the concept in later chapters.

Jargon

In your travels with UNIX-style operating systems, in our case Raspbian Linux, you'll see a lot of strange terms go by. You might wonder how these things got named. Without going into the entire storied history of UNIX-style operating systems, let me say that it was developed in the late 1960s at Bell Labs, but much of modern UNIX grew up in places like the University of California at Berkeley in the early 1970s. The choices of language sometimes get a little colorful, and when they don't, they go toward "easier to type."

This is why a process that most other operating systems would call a server, that is, one that sits in the background waiting for messages from some other process to wake it up and give it something to do, is called a daemon. If you type ps -eaf, which lets you see processes (and threads—we'll get to those much later) you don't own, you can see several daemons: avahi-daemon, udevd, sshd, and so on.

References to GNU or OSF are referring to the GNU and/or Open Source Foundation projects. This means they were written from the beginning to be open source, free to modify, free to use, and free to examine. The OSF set out, decades ago, to replace UNIX (which is proprietary software) with free, open source replacements, from the smallest utilities (gawk—and now mawk—instead of awk) to compilers (GCC versus CC). They intended to replace the kernel too, with the GNU Hurd kernel, but a guy named Linus Torvalds wrote the Linux kernel and beat them to the punch by at least 25 years. (Hurd is, arguably, still not done.) The alliance between the two has been somewhat uneasy.

A distribution of Linux is a Linux kernel with all the associated (usually open source) software to make a complete operating system. Raspbian is a distribution of Linux.

Debian is also a distribution of Linux, and it is the parent of Stretch, which Raspbian is based on (as of this writing), and also of Ubuntu, one of the most popular Linux distributions in the world.

A dependency is where one program depends on another that, from its perspective at least, should be part of the operating system.

A deb file is a Debian-style archive containing a piece of software and a list of dependencies for the software. Debs are read by dpkg, aptitude, or (in our case) apt-get to see if all those dependencies are met, that is, all the other software that a given piece of software needs in order to function are in place. If they aren't, dpkg/aptitude/apt-get will go out to the Internet to servers associated with that Linux distribution and see if they can find those additional pieces of software, checks them for dependencies, and so on, until all the dependencies are met and the new piece of software can be installed and reasonably expected to work.

You might wonder why I've put a little slice of UNIX/Linux history at the end of a short (compared to the books on the subject) chapter on survival Linux for the Raspberry Pi. It's here because you can't get away from the history. It's woven into the fabric of the operating system. I believe that knowing the stories makes Linux, and by extension Raspbian, easier to understand.

Conclusion

You'll need to be able to navigate the filesystem, set passwords, and most importantly shut the system down correctly if your installation of Raspbian is going to keep working reliably. You'll need to understand file permissions and how to change them (using chown, chgrp, and chmod) so you can call files from the command line, and you'll need to know how to install and remove packages with the Debian tools (apt-get). This constitutes survival Linux, and is a tiny fraction of the capabilities of the Raspbian Linux OS. In Chapter 4, you'll get to know C++, and realize that for Arduino regulars, it's really an old friend.

CHAPTER 4

Meet C++

Let's face it, the C and C++ languages have a bad reputation. Hard to learn, obtuse syntax, lots of ways to mishandle memory; you've heard it, I'm sure. You might have heard scuttlebutt that the Arduino sketch language is somehow related to C and C++, but that all the "hard stuff" was taken care of for you by the Arduino desktop application.

The truth is this. Arduino sketches are written in C++. They use the same GNU G++ compiler that Linux uses, albeit configured for 8-bit ATmega CPUs. The Arduino application *does* handle some things for us, and as we make the leap to C++, we'll have to learn to do those for ourselves. Don't worry. I'll walk you through it. It's not that complicated.

What the Arduino Package Really Is

So we can understand what we have to do for ourselves now, let's take a quick look at what Arduino's been doing for us all this time. We'll start by looking at what, exactly, the Arduino application is, and what's in it. To do that, in turn, let's go ahead and put one on the Raspberry Pi.

Install Arduino on Raspberry Pi

Open the web browser on your Pi and go to `http://www.arduino.cc/en/Main/Software`. Be patient, especially if you're on a Pi Zero W. This will take a while. Once you're there, scroll down to "Download the Arduino

© James R. Strickland 2018
J. R. Strickland, *Raspberry Pi for Arduino Users*,
https://doi.org/10.1007/978-1-4842-3414-3_4

IDE" and click on Linux Arm. Time for more patience, while your Pi writes that rather large package to your microSD card.

While you're waiting, you might be wondering why on Earth I want you to put the Arduino desktop software on your Pi. Fair question. The answer is that way down in Chapter 12, called "The Best of Both Worlds," we'll need it. You might also wonder why we're getting it through the web browser instead of apt-get. Didn't I just finish saying that apt-get was easier and faster than graphical installers? Well yes, I did say that. There's one major drawback to apt-get, though, and you might as well find out about it now. The software archives it uses are often behind the times. Nowhere is this more true than the Arduino application. It was ported once, shortly after the Pi was introduced, and hasn't been updated since. By contrast, the Arduino project itself ported and maintains the ARM version we're downloading now. All done? Good. You can try just clicking on the downloaded file like you would on a desktop computer, but I don't recommend it, especially on a Pi Zero W. Instead, crank up the terminal application. (Choose Raspberry menu ➤ Accessories ➤ Terminal, or it's probably in the top panel of your screen.) Here's how you do this the old school way. And you'll get another UNIX/linux command too.

First, cd to the Downloads directory. This is where the Chromium browser puts downloaded files, unless you tell it to put them someplace else. If you do an ls for *.tar.*, you'll see any file with .tar.whatever as its extension. These are called tarballs today. Once upon a time, in a data center far far away, that file would instead be on a magtape. Google 9 track tape if you're curious about that.

```
pi@PiOW:~$ cd Downloads
pi@PiOW:~/Downloads$ ls *.tar.*
arduino-1.8.5-linuxarm.tar.xz
pi@PiOW:~/Downloads$
```

Anyway, the program we'll use to expand the archive is called, unsurprisingly, tar, and since you know it had to do with tapes, it's probably not surprising it stands for Tape Archive. Tar takes a ridiculous number of flags, but here are the ones you'll most often need. (You can also go to man tar if you forget them. I usually have to for anything but expanding archives.)

To expand an archive, you use tar -xf <<tarball name>. To create a new archive, use tar -cf <<tarball name>> <files or directories to go in the tarball>>. Tar's one of those strong, silent types. If you want to see what it's actually doing (because waiting five minutes on a screen where nothing's happening is boring, if nothing else), pass tar the v flag too.

But we're looking at a tar.xz file. The xz stands for x-zip. It's a standard UNIX/Linux data compression tool. The tar file's been compressed. We could uncompress the tar file and then extract it in two steps, but modern tar is smart and can handle compression automatically. When it sees the xz, or a file extension indicating some other compression routine appended to the end, it will do the right thing automatically. Like this.

```
pi@PiOW:~$ cd Downloads
pi@PiOW:~/Downloads$ tar -xvf arduino-1.8.5*
```

Here, I've used a wildcard to avoid typing out the whole filename. The wildcard matches any file with arduino-1.8.5 at the beginning, in this case arduino-1.8.5-linuxarm.tar.xz.

```
arduino-1.8.5/
arduino-1.8.5/lib/
arduino-1.8.5/lib/version.txt
arduino-1.8.5/lib/rsyntaxtextarea-2.6.1.jar
arduino-1.8.5/lib/public.gpg.key
arduino-1.8.5/lib/arduino-core.jar
arduino-1.8.5/lib/batik-svg-dom-1.8.jar
arduino-1.8.5/lib/batik-bridge-1.8.jar
arduino-1.8.5/lib/commons-net-3.3.jar
```

Thousands upon thousands of files later...

```
arduino-1.8.5/tools/WiFi101/tool/firmwares/19.5.2/
arduino-1.8.5/tools/WiFi101/tool/firmwares/19.5.2/m2m_aio_3a0.bin
arduino-1.8.5/tools/WiFi101/tool/firmwares/19.4.4/
arduino-1.8.5/tools/WiFi101/tool/firmwares/19.4.4/m2m_aio_2b0.bin
arduino-1.8.5/tools/WiFi101/tool/firmwares/19.4.4/m2m_aio_3a0.bin
arduino-1.8.5/tools/howto.txt
pi@PiOW:~/Downloads$
```

Next, we need to install the Arduino application. This is easiest from the terminal window too. Just cd into the arduino-1.8.5 (or whatever version you downloaded) directory and type sudo ./install.sh.

```
pi@PiOW:~/Downloads/arduino-1.8.5$ sudo ./install.sh
Adding desktop shortcut, menu item and file associations for Arduino IDE...
touch: cannot touch '/root/.local/share/applications/mimeapps.list':
No such file or directory
/usr/bin/xdg-mime: 803: /usr/bin/xdg-mime: cannot create
/root/.local/share/applications/mimeapps.list.new: Directory nonexistent
 done!
pi@PiOW:~/Downloads/arduino-1.8.5$
```

Now, if you choose Raspberry menu ➤ Programming ➤ Arduino, the Arduino application will start. Be patient, especially if you're on a Pi Zero W. It's slow. Eventually, you'll see the main window open, as shown in Figure 4-1.

Figure 4-1. *Arduino IDE*

What you're looking at here is the Arduino IDE. (It stands for Integrated Development Environment, and has nothing to do with the hard disk standard from the early 1990s. That used to mess me up.) In Figure 4-2, I've opened Geany, the IDE we'll be using on the Pi, beside the Arduino IDE.

IDE

We'll get into this more in the compiler section, but there are two major steps to compiling a computer program: compiling and linking. Compiling means the raw source code is fed to whatever precompiler is involved, then the compiler. When your code comes out of the compiler, it's machine code, but it's not connected to any external libraries you've called, nor to any other code you've included in it. Hooking all that together and producing a single program that will actually run is the job of the linker.

In the old days, when I learned programming, you wrote code in a text editor and then compiled and linked it by hand. Seriously. The first minicomputer operating system I ever used (Digital Equipment's Vax VMS) did it that way. If your program consisted of separate parts, you compiled them separately, and it was up to you to make sure all the parts had been compiled before you linked them in. This process was fraught with errors. (Although in school, most of our programs had only one file, so it was less an issue.) If you forgot to compile a module, you could chase your tail for hours trying to fix a bug that you'd already fixed. Allegedly, this, in fact, was how UNIX make came to be. UNIX make was a godsend. Instead of keeping track of what had and had not been compiled, make checked the touch dates (remember touch dates? the date that shows up in `ls -l`?) of the compiled version of the code against the uncompiled version, and if the uncompiled version (the source code) was later, only then would make compile that code. It saved time and sanity for programmers.

IDEs solve the same problem. Like UNIX make, they keep track of when a given piece of code was last compiled, and whether the source code has been altered since then. You've used this, even if you didn't know it, with the Arduino IDE. If you've used a third-party library and dropped it into a separate tab in the IDE, the Arduino IDE is keeping track of whether you've compiled that library since the last time it was modified.

The Arduino IDE also does syntax coloring (so you can tell comments from code, for example), they match parentheses for you (a godsend, in and of itself), they can help you keep your code neat by indenting or commenting whole blocks at once, and a dozen other fiddly little things that make programming easier. Again, you've probably used these in the Arduino IDE a lot. I certainly did in my previous book about Arduinos.

Compiler

In case you haven't heard the formal definition a dozen times already in your life, a compiler is a program that translates a higher level language, such as C or C++, into machine code. Like we talked about in the IDE section, compilers usually work in cooperation with linkers, to combine compiled programs into an executable image. Any time you tell the Arduino application to compile? That's what it's doing.

In the Linux world, g++ is the default C++ compiler. This tells you nothing, because g++ is a wrapper, in this case around gcc, the GNU project Compiler Collection. (Back in the days when I was building it on a MicroVax II, gcc stood for GNU C Compiler. They changed it as they added more languages.) The usual abbreviation for C++ is cpp, however, so if you type which cpp, you'll get this:

```
pi@PiOW:~$ which cpp
/usr/bin/cpp
pi@PiOW:~$
```

If you did an ls -l on that file, you'd discover that it's a pointer to cpp-6. This calls version 6 and above of GNU cpp. Other distributions of Linux may also have g++ version 5, which is referred to as simply cpp. There's a lot of redirection, and that when you unwind it all, you're really calling gcc with some flags. None of which is that important to us. When you call /usr/bin/cpp, it works.

```
pi@PiOW:~$ /usr/bin/cpp -v
Using built-in specs.
COLLECT_GCC=/usr/bin/cpp
Target: arm-linux-gnueabihf
```

```
Configured with: ../src/configure -v --with-pkgversion='Raspbian
6.3.0-18+rpi1' --with-bugurl=file:///usr/share/doc/gcc-6/README.Bugs
--enable-languages=c,ada,c++,java,go,d,fortran,objc,obj-c++ --prefix=/usr
--program-suffix=-6 --program-prefix=arm-linux-gnueabihf- --enable-shared
--enable-linker-build-id --libexecdir=/usr/lib --without-included-gettext
--enable-threads=posix --libdir=/usr/lib --enable-nls --with-sysroot=/
--enable-clocale=gnu --enable-libstdcxx-debug --enable-libstdcxx-time=yes
--with-default-libstdcxx-abi=new --enable-gnu-unique-object --disable-libitm
--disable-libquadmath --enable-plugin --with-system-zlib --disable-browser-
plugin --enable-java-awt=gtk --enable-gtk-cairo --with-java-home=/usr/lib/
jvm/java-1.5.0-gcj-6-armhf/jre --enable-java-home --with-jvm-root-dir=/usr/
lib/jvm/java-1.5.0-gcj-6-armhf --with-jvm-jar-dir=/usr/lib/jvm-exports/java-
1.5.0-gcj-6-armhf --with-arch-directory=arm --with-ecj-jar=/usr/share/java/
eclipse-ecj.jar --with-target-system-zlib --enable-objc-gc=auto --enable-
multiarch --disable-sjlj-exceptions --with-arch=armv6 --with-fpu=vfp --with-
float=hard --enable-checking=release --build=arm-linux-gnueabihf --host=arm-
linux-gnueabihf --target=arm-linux-gnueabihf
Thread model: posix
gcc version 6.3.0 20170516 (Raspbian 6.3.0-18+rpi1)
COLLECT_GCC_OPTIONS='-E' '-v' '-march=armv6' '-mfloat-abi=hard' '-mfpu=vfp'
'-mtls-dialect=gnu'
 /usr/lib/gcc/arm-linux-gnueabihf/6/cc1 -E -quiet -v -imultilib . -imultiarch
arm-linux-gnueabihf - -march=armv6 -mfloat-abi=hard -mfpu=vfp -mtls-
dialect=gnu
ignoring nonexistent directory "/usr/local/include/arm-linux-gnueabihf"
ignoring nonexistent directory "/usr/lib/gcc/arm-linux-
gnueabihf/6/../../../../arm-linux-gnueabihf/include"
#include "..." search starts here:
#include <...> search starts here:
 /usr/lib/gcc/arm-linux-gnueabihf/6/include
 /usr/local/include
 /usr/lib/gcc/arm-linux-gnueabihf/6/include-fixed
 /usr/include/arm-linux-gnueabihf
 /usr/include
End of search list.
```

See what I mean?

Anyway. That's the compiler we'll be using for our programs in the Pi. It might startle you to know it's the same compiler used by the Arduino application. Try this. Type cd /home/pi/Downloads/Arduino-1.8.5/ hardware/tools/avr/bin. We've just jumped into the Arduino application's directories.

Note   If you plan to use the Arduino application on your Pi for more than experiments, it's a good idea to move it outside the `Downloads` directory and re-run `install.sh`.

Hardware is the directory specific to one type of Arduino. The `avr` directory is for ATmega AVR Arduinos—the uno, the mega, and all the classic ones. The `bin` directory is where the binaries are stored for that type of hardware, that is, compiled programs used to produce the compiled program that will run on the ATmega Arduino.

A quick `ls` shows us that there's a `c++` here.

```
pi@PiOW:~/Downloads/arduino-1.8.5/hardware/tools/avr/bin$ ls -l *c++*
-rwxr-xr-x 2 pi pi 637467 Dec  5  2016 avr-c++
-rwxr-xr-x 1 pi pi 586439 Dec  5  2016 avr-c++filt
pi@PiOW:~/Downloads/arduino-1.8.5/hardware/tools/avr/bin$
```

If we call that compiler, we can pass it a `-v` flag to see what version it is. A quick caveat. We have to specify that we want to load avr-gcc *from this directory*. The bash shell doesn't assume that's what you want by default and will search the usual system directories otherwise. This is when the `.` shortcut becomes the most useful. To do that, precede the file you want to execute with a `.` to tell bash to "run a program from this directory." Like this:

```
pi@PiOW:~/Downloads/arduino-1.8.5/hardware/tools/avr/bin$ ./avr-c++ -v
Using built-in specs.
Reading specs from /home/pi/Downloads/arduino-1.8.5/hardware/tools/avr/
bin/../lib/gcc/avr/4.9.2/device-specs/specs-avr2
COLLECT_GCC=./avr-c++
COLLECT_LTO_WRAPPER=/home/pi/Downloads/arduino-1.8.5/hardware/tools/avr/
bin/../libexec/gcc/avr/4.9.2/lto-wrapper
Target: avr
Configured with: ../gcc/configure --enable-fixed-point --enable-
languages=c,c++ --prefix=/mnt/jenkins/workspace/avr-gcc/label/cm-
raspberrypi2/objdir --enable-long-long --disable-nls --disable-checking
--disable-libssp --disable-libada --disable-shared --enable-lto --with-
avrlibc=yes --with-dwarf2 --disable-doc --target=avr
Thread model: single
gcc version 4.9.2 (GCC)
pi@PiOW:~/Downloads/arduino-1.8.5/hardware/tools/avr/bin$
```

Look familiar? It's an old version of gcc—4.92 versus 6.3.0—but it's fundamentally the same compiler. You've been writing C/C++ code all along and possibly never realized it.

Libraries

I mentioned that the Arduino application was handling some libraries in the background for you. While we're poking around in here, let's look at those too. Use cd to navigate to /home/pi/Downloads/arduino-1.8.5/ hardware/arduino/avr/cores/arduino. Once again, we're looking at just the part of Arduino that's for the avr/ATmega-based boards. A quick ls gives you quite a list.

```
pi@PiOW:~/Downloads/arduino-1.8.5/hardware/arduino/avr/cores/arduino$ ls
abi.cpp                HardwareSerial_private.h  Print.h      WInterrupts.c
Arduino.h              hooks.c                   Server.h     wiring_analog.c
binary.h               IPAddress.cpp             Stream.cpp   wiring.c
CDC.cpp                IPAddress.h               Stream.h     wiring_digital.c
Client.h               main.cpp                  Tone.cpp     wiring_private.h
HardwareSerial0.cpp    new.cpp                    Udp.h        wiring_pulse.c
HardwareSerial1.cpp    new.h                      USBAPI.h     wiring_pulse.S
HardwareSerial2.cpp    PluggableUSB.cpp           USBCore.cpp  wiring_shift.c
HardwareSerial3.cpp    PluggableUSB.h             USBCore.h    WMath.cpp
HardwareSerial.cpp     Printable.h                USBDesc.h    WString.cpp
HardwareSerial.h       Print.cpp                  WCharacter.h WString.h
pi@PiOW:~/Downloads/arduino-1.8.5/hardware/arduino/avr/cores/arduino$
```

All that gets linked with every sketch you write, and any routines you actually call from your sketch are part of the sketch binary that ultimately gets sent to the Arduino. The Arduino app is handling all that in the background. But what about the #includes you sometimes have to do? If you've done some spi or i2c programming on the Arduino and had to use an #include statement to add them, like #include <Wire.h>, you might have wondered where that comes from. They're in there too.

```
pi@PiOW:~$ cd /home/pi/Downloads/arduino-1.8.5/hardware/arduino/avr/libraries
pi@PiOW:~/Downloads/arduino-1.8.5/hardware/arduino/avr/libraries$ ls
EEPROM  HID  SoftwareSerial  SPI  Wire
pi@PiOW:~/Downloads/arduino-1.8.5/hardware/arduino/avr/libraries$
```

You get the idea.

Uploader

There's one other piece of the Arduino puzzle that we have to talk about. We won't use it when programming the Raspberry Pi, but we will be tinkering with it at some length for the last project in this book, "The Best of Both Worlds," so this is as good a time to mention it as any. That part is the uploader. For ATmega/AVR-based Arduinos, it's called AVRDUDE, which stands for AVRDownloaderUploaDEr, according to the website. Like the compiler, it's another standalone project that has been rolled into the Arduino application. It's in the same directory as the compiler: /home/pi /Downloads/arduino-1.8.5/hardware/tools/avr/bin.

```
pi@PiOW:~/Downloads/arduino-1.8.5$ cd /home/pi/Downloads/arduino-1.8.5
/hardware/tools/avr/bin
pi@PiOW:~/Downloads/arduino-1.8.5/hardware/tools/avr/bin$ ls -l avrdude
-rwxr-xr-x 1 pi pi 449459 Dec 16  2016 avrdude
pi@PiOW:~/Downloads/arduino-1.8.5/hardware/tools/avr/bin$
```

AVRDUDE resets the Arduino from whatever it was doing to kick off the bootloader. It signals the bootloader to go into programming mode, then transfers the sketch into the Arduino using the Arduino protocol to verify that the compiled sketch got there in one piece. Then it resets again, and lets the bootloader switch over to sketch mode. At least normally. Our "Best of Both Worlds" project will skip a few of these steps. More on that later.

Meet Geany

In our travels in the Raspberry Pi, we're going to use the Geany IDE. There are certainly others, but Geany is lightweight, relatively simple to use, and if you decide you like it, odds are you can get it for your desktop computer too.

Geany versus the Arduino IDE

You already have the Arduino application running, right? Go ahead and crank up Geany, (choose Raspberry menu ➤ Programming ➤ Geany), and cut/paste the setup() and loop() functions from the empty Arduino sketch into the window on Geany. Now, in Geany, choose File ➤ Save As and give it the name arduino_skel.cpp. (Some filesystems are touchy about ++ in filenames, so cpp is usually used for the extension.)

Interesting, no? Once you save the file, Geany suddenly colors the syntax. This is because Geany is designed to work with lots of different programming languages, and until we saved the file as a .cpp file, it didn't know what kind of file we were editing. It does now. Figure 4-2 shows what it looks like. Sadly, it's in black and white if you're reading the printed version of this book.

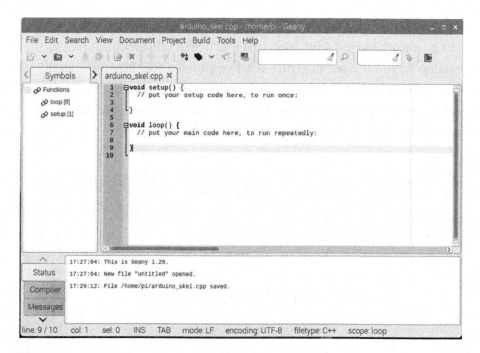

Figure 4-2. *Geany with the Arduino Sketch skeleton*

Note also that Geany has found the two functions we've given it, Loop and Setup, and that they're listed under Symbols in the left-most column. This is a really, really useful thing. If you click on Loop or Setup in the left-most column, Geany takes your cursor there right now. It would do the same if we had multiple files. Now click on one of the braces. See how it highlights the one that matches that one? It highlights in dark blue by default, so you might have to look closely. It does the same thing with (square) brackets, parentheses, and so on. Good modern editors do this. Heck, even nano, my terminal mode editor of choice, can be configured to do syntax coloring. But Geany also manages your files, just like the Arduino IDE does, only easier.

To add a file in Geany, just choose File ➤ New. A new tab will open. Let's go ahead and put a function in it that doesn't do anything, just to practice. As you can see in Figure 4-3, I've added a void function called do_nothing. It returns a void variable type (undefined, or nothing), takes no parameters, and has no code. Go ahead and save it to a file called do_nothing.cpp.

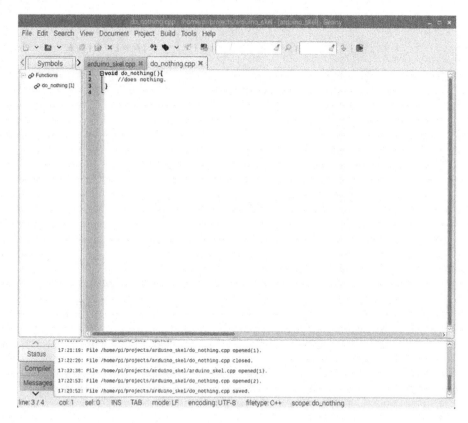

Figure 4-3. *Do nothing function and donothing.cpp*

Here's where Geany really shines. Instead of having a directory of files that might or might not be associated with `arduino_skel.cpp`, we can combine them into a project. Choose Project ➤ New, and when it asks if you want to include all the open files (in our case, `arduino_skel.cpp` and `do_nothing.cpp`) in the project session, choose yes. It may ask to create a `Projects` directory (folder.) Go ahead and let it.

What we've done is to create metadata for the project that lists all the files in the project. However, Geany has not moved our files to the project directory. We can do that with File ➤ Save_As for each open tab. Make sure to save the files into `/home/Pi/projects/arduino_skel` to avoid confusion later. When we go to create new files, however, Geany will use the project's directory as the default.

But wait, as the commercial goes, there's more. Go back to the `arduino_skel.cpp` tab, and at the very top add this: `#include "do_nothing.cpp"`. Because it's included in this project, Geany knows where that file is, so if you press Compile (we'll cover compiling shortly), it will give the compiler the right path to `do_nothing.cpp`. More still. If you click on the right-facing arrow in the Symbols column at the left of the Geany window, shown in Figure 4-4, Geany will tell you exactly where all the files in this project are, and the heading on that column will change to Documents.

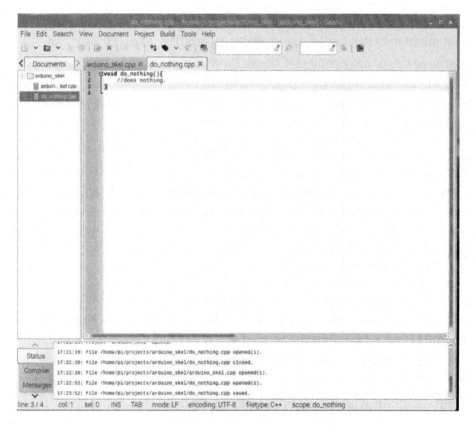

Figure 4-4. *Geany in Documents mode*

I admit. I've been a holdout for the tools of the 80s and 90s—make and text editors—but now that I am used to using the Arduino IDE with Arduino projects and have used Geany (for this book, in fact), I'm sold. Hopefully you are too.

Configuring Geany

Out of the box, as it came with the Raspbian distribution, Geany works pretty well. There are a few issues though. The big one is that while it can compile and build software (they're different, I'll get to that shortly), it can neither run Lint (cppcheck) to check our C++ syntax, nor can it execute (run) whatever we built. Let's fix those problems.

Install Lint (cppcheck)

We won't be using Lint (aka cppcheck) to check our C++ syntax in this book. If you want it, you can fix this problem by typing this:

```
pi@PiOW:~$ sudo apt-get install cppcheck
Reading package lists... Done
Building dependency tree
Reading state information... Done
The following NEW packages will be installed:
  cppcheck
```

Packages get installed...

```
Processing triggers for man-db (2.7.6.1-2) ...
pi@PiOW:~$
```

Basically Geany couldn't make Lint work because the program it was calling, cppcheck, wasn't installed.

Set Up Execute

The execute problem is a bit stranger, and really should be taken care of in the distribution itself. In fact, by the time you read this, it might have been. Feel free to skip ahead to where we actually try to use the Execute button and come back here if it fails.

Hello again. Didn't work? Okay. To make it brief, Geany should be able to run a program we've just built, but as of the August 8th, 2017 version of Raspbian I have, it can't. The terminal window starts, but it hangs. By default, Geany is calling the terminal through the alternatives system. This, in turn, wraps around default applications, like the terminal program, so that if you were to change terminal programs, you don't have to go to Geany and any of dozens of other programs using that terminal and change the terminal call in them. That's great, except that the alternatives wrapper doesn't take the parameters Geany is trying to send it. Bug in the wrapper? Bug in Geany? Bug in LXterminal, the Pi's default terminal program? I don't really know.

We can fix it in Geany's preferences. Choose Edit ➤ Preferences and select the Tools tab in the window that comes up. It should look like Figure 4-5.

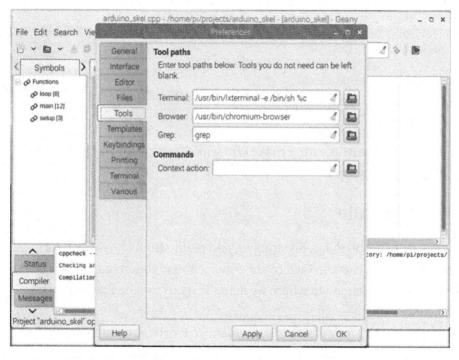

Figure 4-5. *Geany Preferences window*

The Terminal line is what we're after. Yours almost certainly looks different from mine. (Mine's already fixed.) Replace what's in terminal with /usr/bin/lxterminal -e /bin/sh %c and save the configuration file. But let's stop and look at the fix a moment.

That /usr/bin/lxterminal part looks like a call to a program, doesn't it? You're right. That file, lxterminal, is the real name of the Terminal program we've been using right along. If you're reading this more than a few years after 2017, it's possible that's changed. Here's how you tell for sure.

```
pi@PiOW:~$ update-alternatives --list x-terminal-emulator
/usr/bin/lxterminal
pi@PiOW:~$
```

The update-alternatives command works on any Debian-derived system, and it lists what program, of the many options, is being used for a specific function on that Linux installation. In this case, the x-terminal-emulator is the terminal emulator we've selected to run on this Pi.

We're calling lxterminal directly with /usr/bin/lxterminal. Passing lxterminal the -e flag means "execute this program." We then pass it /bin/sh, which is a shell. Once upon a time, sh was a separate, small, lightweight shell called the Bourne shell. If you do an ls -l on /bin/sh, you'll see it's just a symbolic link to our old friend bash, which stands for Bourne Again SHell. It's an improved, open source version of sh. In Linux, they're usually the same thing.

Anyway, the %c is a variable filled in by Geany with the name of the program we'd like to run. So why, you might ask (as I did), not have lxterminal call the file directly? By having lxterminal call /bin/sh first, we get all the environment variables we're used to setting. Environment variables are how bash keeps track of a great many things, most importantly (right now) our current directory. We can then pass just the filename of the compiled program to sh, which runs it in the terminal window. Well. Kind of. Geany wraps our compiled program in a script that gives us more information when it runs.

That's a lot of Linux poking we just did, and a pretty dense explanation of it on my part. We covered all these concepts back in Chapter 3, "Survival Linux," so if you need to look back at them and review, go ahead. That's why that chapter is there.

By the by, if you're wondering, "Does this mean if I do change terminal applications, Geany won't be able to run programs again?" Good catch. Maybe. It depends on whether you uninstall lxterminal. As long as /bin/lxterminal is there, it will work. If it's not there, execute won't work.

Build versus Compile

Okay. Now that we have Geany working right, lets test the building, compiling, and execution functions. We'll use the arduino_skel project for that, but we'll have to add a couple of things to it.

Right now, the arduino_skel.cpp file looks like this:

```
#include "do_nothing.cpp"
void setup() {
  // put your setup code here, to run once:
do_nothing();
}
void loop() {
  // put your main code here, to run repeatedly:
}
```

This isn't a complete program. Just a couple of functions. The truth is, every Arduino sketch you write is that: code in a couple of functions. In the background, the Arduino IDE adds what we're about to add by hand. Add the following function at the bottom of the arduino_skel file.

```
int main(){
    setup();
    while(true){
        loop();
    }
}
```

Your finely tuned Arduino habits should tell you instantly that main is a function, returning an integer. It calls setup, without passing it any parameters, and then it loops forever, calling loop over and over again. This may not be the exact code the Arduino uses, but it does what the Arduino code does. Run setup once, run loop forever.

Go ahead and choose Build ➤ Compile. That compiles the file we've been working on, in this case arduino_skel.cpp. You can run Lint on it too, if you like. But here's the catch. Compile only compiles the one file shown. It only compiles arduino_skel.cpp. It does not compile do_nothing.cpp, and it does not link anything together.

Choosing Build ➤ Build will tell Geany to compile all the files in the project, as needed, and link them together in a finished image, which is an executable program. Go ahead and build the project. I don't recommend executing it. It doesn't do anything, and it loops infinitely at the end, so you'll just have to close the terminal window anyway.

Executing Programs

Let's modify the arduino_skel project to at least produce something we can see, and so it doesn't loop infinitely. Then we can execute it and verify that it, and all our tools, work.

Right now, arduino_skell.cpp looks like this:

```
#include "do_nothing.cpp"
void setup() {
  // put your setup code here, to run once:
do_nothing();
}

void loop() {
  // put your main code here, to run repeatedly:

}
int main(){
    setup();
    while(true){
        loop();
    }
}
```

The first thing we want to do is have it print something in the terminal window. To do this, we need to pull in a library called iostream. You can bet the Arduino IDE does something like it for you, so that `serial.print()` works. We'll do it by hand.

At the top, where we added `#include "do_nothing.cpp"`, we'll include the library. The syntax is a little different. Instead of quote marks, we'll use greater-than/less-than marks. This tells the precompiler that handles the includes to use the system library instead of looking for it in our directory. It looks like this: `#include <iostream.h>`.

Next, we need to fix the infinite loop. Let's change it to a `for` loop. You've probably done these a thousand times in sketches. Edit `main()` so that it looks like this:

```
int main(){
    setup();
    for(int c=0;c<5;c++){
        loop();
    }
}
```

Now let's put some code in the `loop` function, for old time's sake. We'll use a function called `cout`, which we included in iostream. I won't explain what all it does right now, because we'll get into that in the "Write Your First C++ Program" section. It does more or less what `serial.print` does.

```
void loop() {
  // put your main code here, to run repeatedly:
std::cout<<"Sketches are really C++!!!"<<std::endl
}
```

Now choose Build ➤ Build. The compiler will compile both `arduino_skell.cpp` and `do_nothing.cpp`. The linker will go out and find the precompiled library called iostream and link that in, and it will produce the finished image, called `arduino_skell`, and put it in `~/projects/arduino_skell/arduino_skell`. If you do an `ls -l` on that file, you'll see that Geany even set it as executable. So let's execute it.

You should get a new window that looks like Figure 4-6. Normally I won't do screenshots of output windows. Putting the output in as text is much easier to read, but this once it seemed appropriate.

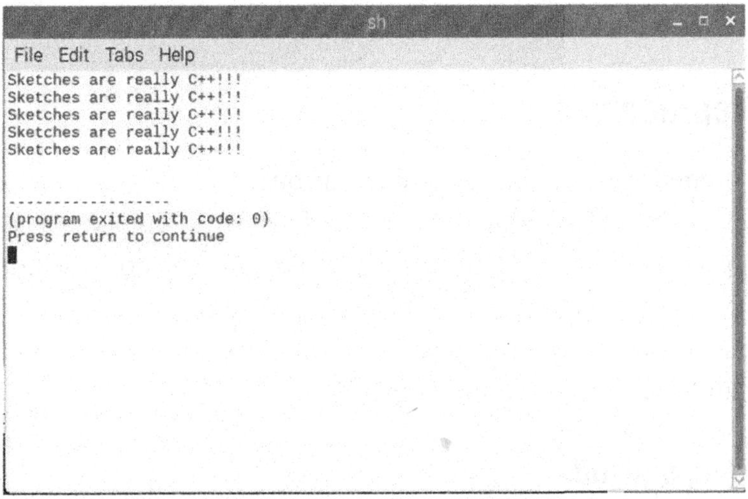

Figure 4-6. *The Output window*

Write Your First C++ Program

So you've already written your very first C++ program, but we left the Arduino training wheels on for that one. To be honest, maintaining them by hand from here on out will be more work than they're worth. So let's go ahead and do a program without them, the C/C++ way.

The C++ Way

Full disclosure. I'm not a C++ expert by any stretch of the imagination. The techniques I'm going to tell you are more "use C++isms, especially objects, when they make sense" rather than pedantically pure C++ structure. Computers don't care about pedantry. If the program works, in many cases, that's all that's required. If you're doing security, aerospace, medical,

145

or other places where any bug might be a major issue, you're probably reading the wrong book, and you might want to read the Raspberry Pi foundation's notice that Pis aren't for that. If you happen to be a C++ expert, all I can say is you know more than I do about it. These programs work (I've tested them). That's all I can promise.

The Preprocessor

I've mentioned the preprocessor in passing, but it's time I give you the heads up on what exactly the preprocessor does. The preprocessor, as the name suggests, is a program that reads your C++ source code (the human readable stuff we're going to write) before compilation takes place. It's best thought of as an interpreted programming language to make C++ programming easier. We've already used it.

Expanding #include

The C/C++ preprocessor interpreted the `#include` directives we put in `arduino_skel.cpp`. It hit that directive, went out and got the `do_nothing.cpp` file, and copied that code into a file along with `arduino_skell.cpp`, before the whole business got sent to the C++ compiler. That's the most common job for the preprocessor.

Macro Expansion

Preprocessor macros are extraordinarily useful. They're also extremely common in the microcontroller world (like Arduino), because they take no memory at runtime. None. A variable can get pretty heavy, memory-wise, when you're dealing with only 4KB of memory, so having constants in that kind of environment is a waste. I used them a ton in my previous book, *Junk Box Arduino*, to substitute for Arduino constants with ambiguous names, to substitute for binary bit patterns, and so forth. Here's an example.

```
#define Control_Port portb
#define Control_DDR ddrb
#define pi 3.14
```

If you've done any Arduino port programming, you know that those port names change depending on what model of Arduino you're on. By abstracting them in a macro, it meant that if you moved my code to say, an Arduino Mega, you just had to change `portb` or `ddrb`, instead of modifying the whole program. That's how macros are expanded. The first term is the macro, the second is its value. So we're defining `Control_Port` and telling the preprocessor to substitute `portb` every time it sees `Control_Port`, `ddrb` for every `Control_DDR`, and `3.14` for every `pi`. Macros can do a lot more than that. They can take parameters and do math and string operations on them. The C/C++ precompiler is, itself, a fairly complete programming language.

In a contest called "Obfuscated C," the story goes, a programmer wrote an entire sieve of Eratosthenes in precompiler macros, and the only C code was the code that printed out the list of prime numbers that was the result. If memory serves, he won the brand new "Best Abuse of the Preprocessor" award. Once compiled, of course, his program would have taken no time to run, since the prime numbers were already generated. It would have taken a long time to compile though. I don't use preprocessor functions in this book. They're tricky and hard to read, and they're well documented online.

Conditional Compilation

C and C++ are funny animals. You can sometimes find yourself in a corner where you have to #include something twice. In `arduino_skel.cpp`, the function `setup()` calls the function `do_nothing()`. Suppose `do_nothing()` calls a third function that is also called by main in `arduino_skel`. Function order can get very fussy, and at times with complex programs, it's possible to get stuck in a situation where there's no right answer when a function can be defined. The C/C++ solution to this conundrum is the function prototype. We'll get to those in later chapters, but the short version is, it provides a placeholder definition for a function to be formally defined later. These, in turn, are often stored in .h files and included at compile time.

Here's where conditional compilation matters. You often break out those function definitions in separate files, but put the skeletons together in the same file. Your compiler will complain if you include the header file twice. Here's how the preprocessor fixes that for you. In your program file and in all the function definition files, you can put this.

```
#ifndef header_included
    #define header_included
    #include "header.h"
#endif
```

What's happening here? Well, #ifndef is "if not defined." If the macro header_included is not defined, it means that the header file has not been included. The next lines are what happen if header_included is not defined. We define it, and then we include the header file.

The last line ends the #ifndef statement. This bit of preprocessor code will #include the header file only if it hasn't already been loaded. When the precompiler goes to roll this particular file into the one big file it will feed to the compiler, if header_included is already defined, it won't run the #include "header.h". I've intended the ifdef code here like we would in C++ and C, but it's often not written that way.

But you can do more with conditional compilation. To get back to the code we talked about in the "Macro Expansion" section, let's say I knew my Arduino sketch was going to be run on more than one type of Arduino. I could put something like this in:

```
#ifdef Cestino        //We're using a Cestino, a type of Arduino-derived board.
#define Control_Port portb
#define Control_DDR ddrb
#elif Mega            //Else if we're using an Arduino Mega 2560
#define Control_Port porte
#define Control_DDR ddre
#endif                //end of the if.
```

You're not limited to putting #ifdefs before the C++ code, either. If you have a function that is specific to one processor but not another, you can #ifdef that function out based on what processor you're using.

We won't use #ifdef much, if at all, but it's a useful thing.

Object-Oriented Programming

You can program a long time in Arduino and not touch object-oriented programming. I've found objects useful from time to time, so I'm going to dive right on in and give you a quick overview of the subject.

There are four major parts to the object-oriented puzzle that you really have to understand, and they're easy to get muddy on. They go by different names and have slightly different rules in different languages, but these are the C++ names.

Objects

An object is a way to put data and code in a single entity. It's like if the toolkit in your car (I'm dating myself again, aren't I?) had literally all the tools you'd ever need to work on the car, and only that car. Every other kind of car has its own tools, and even if my car is the same as your car, each of our cars has its own toolbox, and we can't use each other's.

Attributes

In non-object-oriented programming, attributes are what we'd call variables. They're where the data in an object is stored. Here's one of the big differences. You know how a function can have variables that the rest of the program can't see (local variables)? An object can have private attributes like that. An object can also have public attributes that, if you have an object, you can change with code outside the object.

Methods

Methods are the object-oriented equivalent to functions, except they're contained inside the object. Like attributes, they can be public or private. Because a method is part of the object, whether it's public or private, it can access private attributes and (other) private methods. So to use the car analogy again, if I have a public method called `lug_wrench` and a private attribute called `lugs` (the studs and nuts that hold the wheels on), I can't touch `lugs` because I am not part of the car and its tools, and `lugs` is private. However, I can call `lug_wrench`. It's public. Because `lug_wrench` is part of the car and its tools, it can access `lugs`.

To extend the analogy to its limit without getting silly, if I have a private method called `cheater_bar` (a long piece of heavy pipe you put over the handle of a wrench to increase your leverage), once again, I can't touch either `lugs` or `cheater_bar` because I am not part of the car or its tools. But if `lug_wrench` can call `cheater_bar`, I can call `lug_wrench`, it can call `cheater_bar` and access `lugs`, because it is part of the car and its tools.

The car and its tools are one object. I am code outside the object. `Cheater_bar` is a private method, and `lugs` is a private attribute. `Lug_wrench` is a public method. See?

Classes

So now that you've got a grasp of what an object is, and what it's made of, the next obvious question is, "how do you make them?"

There are two steps. Bear this in mind. It's one of the things that confused me about C++ for a long time. Two steps. The first is to define what we want the object to be. That definition is called a *class*.

A class defines the attributes and methods of the object and gives them their names. For the previous example, it might look like this:

```
class car_and_tools {
    private:
    int lugs=100;          //An integer attribute that stores how tight
                           //the lugs are. Initialized to 100.
    void cheater_bar(){    //A private method to deal with very tight lugs
        //code goes in here
    }   //end of cheater_bar
    public:
    void lug_wrench(){     //A public method for accessing lugs.
        //code goes in here too
    } //end of lug_wrench
}; //End of class.
```

Lugs and the cheater_bar function are private, but lug_wrench is public. It's important, so I'll repeat it. A class is not an object. Nothing is actually created by a class. If I put this code in arduino_skel.cpp, it will compile, but it won't do anything. If I tried to call lug_wrench(), I'd get an error.

Let There Be Objects

When you turn a class into an object, it's exactly the same as creating a variable. Same idea, same syntax.

```
car_and_tools My_VW;
```

This declares an object called My_VW of the type car_and_tools.

Now an object exists. Let's create another one.

```
car_and_tools My_Wifes_Subaru;
```

Done. If I want to use the lug_wrench() method of My_VW, I can call it like this:

```
My_VW.lug_wrench();
```

I can't do anything to `My_Wifes_Subaru` calling methods on `My_VW`. `My_Wifes_Subaru` has its own lug wrench, and I'd call it like this.

```
My_Wifes_Subaru.lug_wrench();
```

I can't touch the `lugs` attribute of either object because they're defined in the class as private. I can't touch the `cheater_bar()` method in either object because they're defined in the class as private. I know, I'm repeating myself, but these are the fundamentals of object-oriented programming. Do they make sense now?

Good. Enough lecture. Let's go write a program.

TicTac

The first program we're going to write in C++ really has nothing to do with Raspberry Pi-specific programming. It runs just as well on my Mac as it did on the Raspberry Pi I wrote it on. (I used `Pi3plus`, if you wondered. It's faster.) We're going to write a tic-tac-toe program. In the interest of keeping it really simple, we're not even going to write an opponent. We'll make it a two player game. (A good opponent would involve some game theory. A quick and easy opponent would always win. Tic-Tac-Toe is not a very good game.)

Planning

Maybe it's my age, that I grew up in the days of pencil and paper, and that I was about 10 when I first got my hands on a computer, but I've found that when I plan a program on paper, it works better. Laziness forces me to keep things simple. You don't have to use pencil and paper, but it's a good idea to plan the program, especially when it comes to the objects and data structures in it. Prior preparation prevents poor performance, or so they say.

Rules

The rules of tic-tac-toe are pretty simple. You and your opponent take turns placing Xs and Os on the board until one or the other (or more often neither) of you gets three in a row horizontally, vertically, or diagonally. (Yeah, the Elle King song is running through my head now too. Sorry.) So the program needs to represent the board in data. It needs to be able to tell if someone won. And it needs a way for players to put their data in. If that sounds like there's an object involved, you've got a good ear.

Objects

There's only one object we need in this program. It's called the_board, of the class board. Go ahead and write that down. We need a class called board.

```
class board{
};
```

Attributes

The board class needs to store all the moves in the game. To make it easy to picture how all this code works, we'll represent those moves as a two-dimensional array of chars. (Single characters.) Yes, a boolean would use less memory. Don't worry about it. You're programming a Raspberry Pi now. Your Pi has at least 256MB of RAM. The fact that we're using nine bytes of RAM to store data we could fit in nine bits doesn't matter. We'll call it board_data.

No code outside the board object needs to talk to board_data, so we'll make it private. So write that down in the board class.

```
class board{
    private:
        char board_data[3][3];
};
```

Methods

The board class needs to be able to see if anyone has won. While that method needs to be accessed from the outside, it's going to be a huge monster of a method. Let's break it down further.

If you think about it, you can check all the possible victory conditions with three types of checks. A check across, a check vertically, and a check diagonally. So let's create methods to do those things. No code outside the board object needs to access these smaller methods, so we'll make them private. We'll fill the actual code in later.

```
class board{
    private:

    char board_data[3][3];

    bool check_across(){
    }
    bool check_vert(){
    }
    bool check_diag(){
    }
};
```

We'll need a public method so that code outside an object of the board class can see if the board is in a winning state. But by now, there's something that should have you screaming at me. The board_data array is not initialized. Anywhere. That is a great way to get pseudo-random results, and that's not what we're looking for, so we need to create two public methods: one to initialize the array, and one to check to see if a player has won.

Actually we need more methods than that. We need a method to display the board on the terminal window. We also need a way for players to make their moves. Okay. Let's write all those down too.

Actually wait.

The only time we're going to call the method that initializes the board_data array is when the object is first instantiated. It'd be nice if C++ could just call that for us, wouldn't it? It can. If you name a public method the same thing as the class name, it's called the constructor, and C++ will call it when the object is created. As the name might suggest, there is also a destructor, if you need one. It's also a public method and it's the class name again, only with a tilde (~) in front of it. Like this:

```
class board{
    public:
    board(){

    //code goes here

    }
    ~board(){
    //code would go here too.
    }
}; //end of the board class
```

C++ actually has a default constructor and destructor, so if you don't have to do anything special for one or the other, you don't need to include one. We need a constructor to initialize board_data, but the default destructor is just fine. So let's write that down too.

```
class board{

    private:
    char board_data[3][3];

    bool check_across(){

    }

    bool check_vert(int col, char player){

    }

    bool check_diag(){

    }
```

```
    public:

    board(){

    }

    void display(){

    }

    bool win_check(){

    }

    void player_move(){

    }
}; //end of board class.
```

It's more complicated than a sketch, but not much more complicated. You may have written sketches with objects already. If so, you're ahead of the game. If not, and you're looking at the class and wondering how much worse this is going to get, the answer is not much. Most of the complexity is right here in the skeleton. Each of those methods is straightforward code. You've done functions harder than these if you've done much Arduino programming. And with all the heavy lifting done in objects of the board class, main() is pretty simple too, as you'll see.

So let's get coding.

Coding

I'm not going to walk you through writing each of these functions. As I said, they're not complicated at all. I'm going to throw the code at you, annotate it in spots above and beyond my already lengthy comments, and figure you've done this enough to follow along.

Note   Do comment your code, even if you're the only person who will ever see it. You might have to try to understand it again a few years down the road, and future you will thank present you for it.

The Class

Here's the actual board class, in all its glory, comments intact.

```
class board{
    private:

        /* Private variable: board_data
         * ------------------------------------------------
         * What it is:
         * -------------
         * a two dimensional array of characters.
         *
         * What it's for:
         * -------------
         * stores all the X or O values. Represents the board.
         * ------------------------------------------------
         */
        char board_data[3][3];

        /* Private method: check_across
         * ---------------------------
         * Parameters: int row, char player
         * Returns: a boolean value (true or false)
         *
         * How it works:
         * -------------
         * given a row and a player, start at the Oth
         * column in that row and traverse that row of the array
         * to the 2nd position. If any of those chars are NOT
         * equal to player, return false, otherwise return true.
         * ------------------------------------------------
         */
        bool check_across(int row, char player){
            for (int c=0;c<=2;c++){
                if (board_data[row][c]!=player) return (false);
            }
            return(true);
        }

        /* Private method: check_vert
         * ---------------------------
         * Parameters: int col, char player
         * Returns: a boolean value (true or false)
         *
```

```
* How it works:
*  ------------
* Given a column and a player, start at the 0th
* row in that column and traverse that column vertically
* to the 2nd position. If any of those chars are NOT
* equal to player, return false, otherwise return true.
*  ------------------------------------------------
*/
bool check_vert(int col, char player){
    for (int c=0;c<=2;c++){
        if (board_data[c][col]!=player) return(false);
    }
    return(true);
}

/* Private method: check_diag
*  ---------------------------
* Parameters: bool up, char player
* Returns: a boolean value (true or false)
*
* How it works:
*  ------------
* If up is false
*     Loop on c.
*         Using the value of c as both row and column,
*         check each value in the board_data array at
*         that position (c,c). If it's not equal to player,
*         return false. If c goes past 2, return true.
*
* Otherwise (up is true) -
*     Initialize d as an int with the value 2
*         Loop on c from 0 to 2
*         if the char in board data at row d, column c is
*         not equal to player, return false. otherwise
*         decrement d and repeat. The c variable will be
*         incremented automatically by the for loop.
*     If c goes past 2, return true.
*  ------------------------------------------------
*/
bool check_diag(bool up,char player){
    if (!up){
        for (int c=0;c<=2;c++){
            if (board_data[c][c]!=player) return(false);
        }
```

```
    }else{
        int d=2;
        for (int c=0;c<=2;c++){
            if (board_data[d][c]!=player) return(false);
            d--;
        }
    }
    return(true);
};

public:
/* Public method: board
 * ---------------------------
 * Parameters: none.
 * Returns: nothing.
 *
 * How it works:
 * -------------
 * This method is the class constructor. It's called when
 * an instance of the "board" class is created.
 * The functionality is classic stuff: a pair of nested loops.
 * The outer for loop loops on c. This will be the row.
 *     The inner for loop loops on d.
 *         Set board_data at the addresses c and d to the empty character.
 *     increment d
 *     When d gets bigger than 2 increment c.
 * When c gets bigger than 2, exit.
 * --------------------------------------------------
 */
board(){
    for (int c=0;c<=2;c++){ //outer loop
        for (int d=0;d<=2;d++){//inner loop
            board_data[c][d]=(char)0; //set the element of the array
        }//end of inner loop
    }//end of outer loop
}
```

We just declared the constructor. You noticed, right?

```
/* Public method: display
 * ---------------------------
 * Parameters: none.
 * Returns: nothing.
 *
```

```
 * How it works:
 * -------------
 * This method is all about pretty-printing the board_data
 * array. First, we print the column number line.
 * After that, it's a classic nested for loop to traverse
 * the board_data array by rows.
 *
 * Of note: while this method is public (can be called by
 * private entities), because it is part of the board class,
 * it can access board's private variables. It could call
 * board's private methods too, but does not.
 *
 * Loop on c
 *     Every time the c loop increments, we're at a new
 *     row, so  print the row's coordinate value
 *     Loop on d.
 *     If board_data at row c, column d is empty
 *     (which will make the value logically false),
 *     print three blank spaces. Otherwise print
 *     board_data at row c column d, with a blank
 *     space on each side. If d (the column) is less
 *     than 2, print a pipe character(|). This forms the
 *     vertical lines in the tic-tac-toe board. Increment
 *     d. When the d loop gets past 2 and exits, print
 *     an endl. This ends the line so we start at the
 *     left margin for the next line. If c is less than 2,
 *     print the horizontal line for the crosshatch.
 *     Increment c. When the c loop exits, we've gone
 *     through all the elements in the board_data
 *     array. Print an endl to give some whitespace.
 * -------------------------------------------------
 */
void display(){
    std::cout<<"  (0) (1) (2)"<<std::endl; //column numbers
    for(int c=0;c<=2;c++){
        std::cout<<"("<<c<<")"; //row number
        for (int d=0;d<=2;d++){
            if (!board_data[c][d]){
                std::cout<<"   ";
            }else{
                std::cout<<" "<<board_data[c][d]<<" ";
            }
            if (d<2) std::cout<<"|";
        }//end of d loop (columns)
```

```
        std::cout<<std::endl;
        if (c<2) std::cout<<"   --- --- ---"<<std::endl;
    }//end of c loop (rows)
    std::cout<<std::endl;
}//end of method.

/* Public method: win_check
 * ---------------------------
 * Parameters: player, a char.
 * Returns: a boolean (true or false).
 * What it does:
 * -------------
 * Tic-Tac-Toe is a simple game. There are only 8 win
 * conditions, so we'll just check them all. I'm playing
 * more boolean games here. In boolean, only false plus
 * false is false, so any true returned by any of the checks
 * will be preserved.
 * Of note: While this method is public (can be called by
 * outside entities), because it is part of the board class,
 * it can call board's private methods. It could access
 * private variables too, but it doesn't.
 *
 * How it works:
 * -------------
 * Set the boolean "won" to false.
 * Loop on c.
 *     Add whatever check_across on row c returns.
 *     Add whatever check_vert on column c returns.
 * Increment c.
 * When loop c exits, check both diagonals (top left to
 * bottom right and bottom left to top right) and add their
 * results to won. Return won. If any of the win conditions
 * has occurred, it will be true.
 * ------------------------------------------------
 */
bool win_check(char player){
    bool won=false;
    for (int c=0;c<=2;c++){
        won+=check_across(c,player);
        won+=check_vert(c,player);
    }//end of the c loop
    won+=check_diag(false,player);
    won+=check_diag(true,player);
```

```
    if (won) std::cout<<"Player "<<player<<" Won."<<std::endl;
    return(won);
}//end of the win_check method

/* Public method: player_move
 * --------------------------
 * Parameters: player (a char)
 * Returns: a boolean (true or false).
 *
 * What it does:
 * -------------
 * The player_move method does two things. Given a
 * player name, it asks the player for a row and a column
 * for that player's move. It then checks the move to
 * make sure it's not out of range (no values greater than
 * 2) and that the box the player chose is not already taken.
 * Of note: while this method is public (can be called by
 * private entities), because it is part of the board class,
 * it can access board's private variables. It could call
 * board's private methods too, but does not.
 *
 * How it works:
 * -------------
 * Set a boolean called "Valid" to false.
 * Set integers "row" and "column" to zero
 * Loop on valid not being true,
 *      Ask the player to enter coordinates.
 *      Input (cin) the row and the column
 *      If the element of board_data at row and col is empty
 *      //and//
 *  if row is less than 3 //and// if column is less than 3:
 *          thank the user, set the value in board_data,
 *          and set valid to true.
 *      Otherwise tell the user that the coordinates they
 *      gave were  invalid.
 * Go back to the beginning of the valid loop.
 * If valid is true, exit from the method.
 * ------------------------------------------------
 */
void player_move(char player){
    bool valid=false;
    int row=0,col=0;
    std::cout<<"Player "<<player<<", it's your move."<<std::endl;
    std::cout<<"Enter Coordinates"<<std::endl;
```

```
while (!valid){
    std::cout<<"Row: ";
    std::cin>>row;
    std::cout<<"Column: ";
    std::cin>>col;
```

I use boolean logic a lot. It's very important to differentiate between a binary and (&) and a logical and (&&). A binary and (&) takes two binary values and returns a third. If you pass it a char, that's eight bits. Say, 0b00000001 and 0b00000011. If you *and* those two values together, you get 0b00000001. Only the leading 1 is true in both values. The point is, binary ands don't work at all when you pass them a boolean variable (true or false). For that you need a boolean, or logical, and (&&). If it sounds like I chased my tail for some time writing this program because I forgot that, I did.

By the by: 0bxxxx is notation for a binary literal, just as 0x precedes hexadecimal literals. It's part of the C++ standard as of 2014, and was part of GNU C++ long before that. If you're also coding for the Arduino, I strongly recommend against using their B prefix for binary values. It only works with values up to eight bits. 0b always works.

```
if ((board_data[row][col]==(char)0) && (row<3) && (col<3)){
            std::cout<<"Thank You."<<std::endl;
            board_data[row][col]=player;
            valid=true;
        }else{
            std::cout<<"Invalid Coordinates. Please try
            again."<<std::endl;
        } //end of if

    } //end of while valid is not true loop

} //end of method

}; //end of the board class
```

Just in case you didn't already know, // is an alternative notation for comments. Multiline comments are surrounded with /* and */.

Main

So with most of the game taken care of in the board object class, what's left for main to do? Not a whole lot, and that's fine. The ideal main() doesn't do a lot of heavy lifting. The idea is that somehow objects in code might be reusable without a lot of custom code to make them go in main(). How realistic that is, I don't honestly know, but that's the ideal.

Our main needs to do three things, really. It needs to instantiate a board class object, display the board, then loop back and forth between players, display the board and getting moves until someone wins.

And that's exactly what it does.

Note that main *must* return an integer variable. This tells Linux whether or not there were errors during the program's run.

```
int main(){
    bool we_have_a_winner=false; //has anyone won?
    char player='X'; //what player is playing?
    board the_board; //instantiate the object the_board

    while(!we_have_a_winner){ //loop on we_have_a_winner being false
        the_board.display(); //display the board
        the_board.player_move(player); //have the player move
        we_have_a_winner=the_board.win_check(player); //see if they won

        if (player=='X'){ //if player X was playing
            player='O'; //set player to O
        }else{
            player='X'; //otherwise set player to X
        }//end of the if
    }//end of the loop

    the_board.display(); //display the final board
    return 0; //return zero, telling Linux that there were no errors
}
```

Cout Is Not Serial.print

It's tempting to use std::cout just the same as we used serial.print in Arduino. They are *not* the same thing. Because this is C++, cout and cin are objects. The commands we're actually issuing are << (the stream insertion operator) and >> (the stream extraction operator). They are formatted input and output operators, and they're smart enough (barely) to recognize what type of variable or attribute they're being asked to put data into or get data out of. The problem is, the stream may have other stuff in it. For cout, this is seldom a problem. For cin, it can make quite a mess, because anything left in the stream will be read the next time cin is accessed. In later programs we'll get into more serious input protection, when we need it. For tictac.cpp, just bear in mind that if you feed it bad input values, it will go into an infinite loop and give you an error message. By default, C++ and its ancestor C are horrible at handling user input in general, but especially character strings. I guarantee you that you'll miss the Arduino string class long before we're done. We'll use a better mechanism as we get into later chapters.

Compiling

Go ahead and build the tictac.cpp file, whether you type it in by hand or load it from the example code available for this book. Remember, build, not just compile. We want iostream linked in.

Running

When you click Execute, a new terminal window should pop up, and this is what should be in it.

```
    (0) (1) (2)
(0)   |   |
    --- --- ---
(1)   |   |
    --- --- ---
(2)   |   |

Player X, it's your move.
Enter Coordinates
Row:
```

Remember when we told Geany what to do explicitly to execute a program? This is the result. Go ahead and play the game through.

```
    (0) (1) (2)
(0)  |   |
    --- --- ---
(1)  |   |
    --- --- ---
(2)  |   |

Player X, it's your move.
Enter Coordinates
Row: 1
Column: 1
Thank You.
    (0) (1) (2)
(0)  |   |
    --- --- ---
(1)  | X |
    --- --- ---
(2)  |   |

Player O, it's your move.
Enter Coordinates
Row: 0
Column: 0
Thank You.
    (0) (1) (2)
(0) O |   |
    --- --- ---
(1)  | X |
    --- --- ---
(2)  |   |

Player X, it's your move.
Enter Coordinates
Row: 2
Column: 1
Thank You.
    (0) (1) (2)
(0) O |   |
    --- --- ---
(1)  | X |
    --- --- ---
(2)  | X |
```

```
Player O, it's your move.
Enter Coordinates
Row: 1
Column: 0
Thank You.
   (0) (1) (2)
(0) O |   |
   --- --- ---
(1) O | X |
   --- --- ---
(2)   | X |

Player X, it's your move.
Enter Coordinates
Row: 0
Column: 1
Thank You.
Player X Won.
   (0) (1) (2)
(0) O | X |
   --- --- ---
(1) O | X |
   --- --- ---
(2)   | X |

------------------
(program exited with code: 0)
Press return to continue
```

See the line that says (program executed with code: 0)? That's the script Geany generates to run our program talking. That 0 is what main returns. If you run tictac.cpp from a terminal window directly, like this—~/projects/tictac/tictac—you won't get that. If you run it in its own terminal, like this—lxterminal -e ~/projects/tictac/tictac or lxterminal -e ./tictac if you're in the project directory already—you'll notice that when the game ends, the terminal window closes immediately.

Congratulations. You've written a C++ program, with nothing Arduino-related involved.

The Code

Here's the complete source code for `tictac.cpp`, including all my
comments and the usual GNU copyleft boilerplate. Geany will insert that
for you, if you choose File ➤ New ➤ New (with template) ➤ main.cxx
when you create the file, instead of the usual File ➤ New.

```
/*
 * tictac.cxx
 *
 * Copyright 2017 Jim Strickland
 *
 * Standard GNU boilerplate:
 * This program is free software; you can redistribute it
 * and/or modify it under the terms of the GNU General Public
 * License as published by the Free Software Foundation;
 * either version 2 of the License, or (at your option) any later version.
 * This program is distributed in the hope that it will be
 * useful, but WITHOUT ANY WARRANTY; without even the
 * implied warranty of MERCHANTABILITY or FITNESS FOR A
 * PARTICULAR PURPOSE. See the GNU General Public
 * License for more details.
 * You should have received a copy of the GNU General Public
 * License along with this program; if not, write to the Free
 * Software Foundation, Inc., 51 Franklin Street, Fifth Floor,
 * Boston, MA 02110-1301, USA.
 *
 */

/* tictac
 * version 1.0
 * language: c++
 * This program exists solely to demonstrate basic C++ programming concepts,
 * like objects, classes, and methods. It is two player, so there is no
 * programmed opponent (game theory would be too much).
 */

/* Iostream gives us cin and cout, among other things we
 * won't be using. These functions let us talk to the terminal.
 * It also defines the std:: namespace. Note that every time
 * we call cin or cout we have to tell C++ what namespace
 * those functions are in. There are ways around that, but for
 * this first program we'll go ahead and do it explicitly.
 * Also, I forgot about the workaround.
 */
```

```
#include <iostream>

/* Class Declaration
 * -------------------------------------------------
 *
 * Private methods:
 * -------------------------------------------------
 * check_across - checks a horizontal line for wins.
 * check_vert - checks a vertical line for wins.
 * check_diag - checks a diagonal line for wins.
 * -------------------------------------------------
 *
 * Public Methods:
 * -------------------------------------------------
 * board - constructor. Sets all chars in board_data to empty.
 * win_check - checks to see if the player given has won.
 * player_move - interacts with the player to get coordinates and call wincheck
 * -------------------------------------------------
 * There's no custom destructor. When we'd destruct the
 * object, the program is terminating anyway.
 * -------------------------------------------------*/
class board{
    private:

    /* Private variable: board_data
     * -------------------------------------------------
     * What it is:
     * -------------
     * a two dimensional array of characters.
     *
     * What it's for:
     * -------------
     * stores all the X or O values. Represents the board.
     * -------------------------------------------------
     */
    char board_data[3][3];

    /* Private method: check_across
     * ---------------------------
     * Parameters: int row, char player
     * Returns: a boolean value (true or false)
     *
```

```
* How it works:
* ------------
* given a row and a player, start at the 0th
* column in that row and traverse that row of the array
* to the 2nd position. If any of those chars are NOT
* equal to player, return false, otherwise return true.
* ----------------------------------------------
*/
bool check_across(int row, char player){
    for (int c=0;c<=2;c++){
        if (board_data[row][c]!=player) return (false);
    }
    return(true);
}

/* Private method: check_vert
* --------------------------
* Parameters: int col, char player
* Returns: a boolean value (true or false)
*
* How it works:
* ------------
* Given a column and a player, start at the 0th
* row in that column and traverse that column vertically
* to the 2nd position. If any of those chars are NOT
* equal to player, return false, otherwise return true.
* ----------------------------------------------
*/
bool check_vert(int col, char player){
    for (int c=0;c<=2;c++){
        if (board_data[c][col]!=player) return(false);
    }
    return(true);
}

/* Private method: check_diag
* --------------------------
* Parameters: bool up, char player
* Returns: a boolean value (true or false)
*
```

```
* How it works:
* -------------
* If up is false
*     Loop on c.
*         Using the value of c as both row and column,
*         check each value in the board_data array at
*         that position (c,c). If it's not equal to player,
*     return false. If c goes past 2, return true.
*
* Otherwise (up is true) -
*     Initialize d as an int with the value 2
*     Loop on c from 0 to 2
*         if the char in board data at row d, column c is
*         not equal to player, return false. otherwise
*         decrement d and repeat. The c variable will be
*         incremented automatically by the for loop.
*     If c goes past 2, return true.
* ------------------------------------------------
*/
bool check_diag(bool up,char player){
    if (!up){
        for (int c=0;c<=2;c++){
            if (board_data[c][c]!=player) return(false);
        }
    }else{
        int d=2;
        for (int c=0;c<=2;c++){
            if (board_data[d][c]!=player) return(false);
            d--;
        }
    }
    return(true);
};

public:
/* Public method: board
 * ---------------------------
 * Parameters: none.
 * Returns: nothing.
 *
 * How it works:
 * -------------
 * This method is the class constructor. It's called when
 * an instance of the "board" class is created.
 * The functionality is classic stuff: a pair of nested loops.
 * The outer for loop loops on c. This will be the row.
```

```
*       The inner for loop loops on d.
*           Set board_data at the addresses c and d to
*           the empty character.
*       increment d
*       When d gets bigger than 2 increment c.
* When c gets bigger than 2, exit.
* ------------------------------------------------
*/
board(){
    for (int c=0;c<=2;c++){ //outer loop
        for (int d=0;d<=2;d++){//inner loop
            board_data[c][d]=(char)0; //set the element of the array
        }//end of inner loop
    }//end of outer loop
}

/* Public method: display
* ---------------------------
* Parameters: none.
* Returns: nothing.
*
* How it works:
* -------------
* This method is all about pretty-printing the board_data
* array. First, we print the column number line.
* After that, it's a classic nested for loop to traverse the
* board_data array by rows.
*
* Of note: while this method is public (can be called by
* private entities), because it is part of the board class,
* it can access board's private variables. It could call
* board's private methods too, but does not.
*
* Loop on c
*       Every time the c loop increments, we're at a new
*       row, so print the row's coordinate value
*       Loop on d.
*           If board_data at row c, column d is empty
*           (which will make the value logically false),
*           print three blank spaces. Otherwise print
*           board_data at row c column d, with a blank
*           space on each side.
*           if d (the column) is less than 2, print a pipe
*           character(|). This forms the vertical lines in the
*           tic-tac-toe board. Increment d.
```

```
*      When the d loop gets past 2 and exits, print an
*      endl. This ends the line so we start at the left
*      margin for the next line. if c is less than 2, print
*      the horizontal line for the crosshatch. Increment c.
* When the c loop exits, we've gone through all the
* elements in the board_data array. Print an endl to give
* some whitespace.
* -------------------------------------------------
*/
void display(){
    std::cout<<"    (0) (1) (2)"<<std::endl; //column numbers
    for(int c=0;c<=2;c++){
        std::cout<<"("<<c<<")"; //row number
        for (int d=0;d<=2;d++){
            if (!board_data[c][d]){
                std::cout<<"   ";
            }else{
                std::cout<<" "<<board_data[c][d]<<" ";
            }
            if (d<2) std::cout<<"|";
        }//end of d loop (columns)
        std::cout<<std::endl;
        if (c<2) std::cout<<"   --- --- ---"<<std::endl;
    }//end of c loop (rows)
    std::cout<<std::endl;
}//end of method.

/* Public method: win_check
* ---------------------------
* Parameters: player, a char.
* Returns: a boolean (true or false).
* What it does:
* -------------
* Tic-Tac-Toe is a simple game. There are only 8 win
* conditions, so we'll just check them all. I'm playing
* more boolean games here. In boolean, only false plus
* false is false, so any true returned by any of the checks
* will be preserved.
* Of note: While this method is public (can be called by
* outside (entities), because it is part of the board class,
* it can call board's private methods. It could access
* private variables too, but it doesn't.
*
```

```
 * How it works:
 * -------------
 * Set the boolean "won" to false.
 * Loop on c.
 *      Add whatever check_across on row c returns.
 *      Add whatever check_vert on column c returns.
 * Increment c.
 * When loop c exits, check both diagonals (top left to
 * bottom right and bottom left to top right) and add their
 * results to won. Return won. If any of the win conditions
 * has occurred, it will be true.
 * ------------------------------------------------
 */
bool win_check(char player){
    bool won=false;
    for (int c=0;c<=2;c++){
        won+=check_across(c,player);
        won+=check_vert(c,player);
    }//end of the c loop
    won+=check_diag(false,player);
    won+=check_diag(true,player);
    if (won) std::cout<<"Player "<<player<<" Won."<<std::endl;
    return(won);
}//end of the win_check method

/* Public method: player_move
 * --------------------------
 * Parameters: player (a char)
 * Returns: a boolean (true or false).
 *
 * What it does:
 * -------------
 * The player_move method does two things. Given a
 * player name, it asks the player for a row and a column
 * for that player's move. It then checks the move to make
 * sure it's not out of range (no values greater than 2) and
 * that the box the player chose is not already taken.
 *
 * Of note: while this method is public (can be called by
 * private entities), because it is part of the board class,
 * it can access board's private variables. It could call
 * board's private methods too, but does not.
 *
```

```
* How it works:
* -------------
* Set a boolean called "Valid" to false.
* Set integers "row" and "column" to zero
* Loop on valid not being true,
*     Ask the player to enter coordinates.
*     Input (cin) the row and the column
*     If the element of board_data at row and col is
* empty //and//. If row is less than 3 //and// if column is
*         less than 3: thank the user, set the value in
*         board_data, and set valid to true.
*     Otherwise tell the user that the coordinates they
*     gave were invalid.
* Go back to the beginning of the valid loop.
* If valid is true, exit from the method.
* ------------------------------------------------
*/
void player_move(char player){
    bool valid=false;
    int row=0,col=0;
    std::cout<<"Player "<<player<<", it's your move."<<std::endl;
    std::cout<<"Enter Coordinates"<<std::endl;

    while (!valid){
        std::cout<<"Row: ";
        std::cin>>row;
        std::cout<<"Column: ";
        std::cin>>col; // &&
        if ((board_data[row][col]==(char)0) && (row<3) && (col<3)){
            std::cout<<"Thank You."<<std::endl;
            board_data[row][col]=player;
            valid=true;
        }else{
            std::cout<<"Invalid Coordinates. Please try again."<<std::endl;
        } //end of if

    } //end of while valid is not true loop

} //end of method
}; //end of the board class
```

```
/* main function
 * ---------------------------
 * Parameters: nothing
 * Returns: an integer (C++ requires this)
 *
 * How it works:
 * -------------
 * Create the boolean "we_have_a_winner" and set it false
 * Create the char "player" and set it to X. (X always starts)
 * Instantiate an object of the board class (above) called
 * the_board
 * Loop on we_have_a_winner being false
 *     Call the "display" method on the_board.
 *     Call the "player_move" method on the_board, and tell it which player.
 *     Call the "win_check" method on the_board for the player.
 *     If we've been dealing with the X player, set the
 *     variable player to O. Otherwise it must be O, so set it to X.
 * End of the while we_have_a_winner is false loop, which means someone won.
 * Display the final board.
 * Exit, returning zero to tell Linux there were no errors.
 * ------------------------------------------------
 */
int main(){
    bool we_have_a_winner=false; //has anyone won?
    char player='X'; //what player is playing?
    board the_board; //instantiate the object the_board

    while(!we_have_a_winner){ //loop on we_have_a_winner being false
        the_board.display(); //display the board
        the_board.player_move(player); //have the player move
        we_have_a_winner=the_board.win_check(player); //see if they won

        if (player=='X'){ //if player X was playing
            player='O';   //set player to O
        }else{
            player='X'; //otherwise set player to X
        }//end of the if
    }//end of the loop

    the_board.display(); //display the final board
    return 0; //return zero, telling Linux that there were no errors
}//end of the program.
```

Conclusion

The Arduino software is made up of the Arduino IDE, the GNU C++ compiler for AVR, Wiring, the standard interface for the various AVR flavors' built-in hardware, and the AVRDUDE uploader for transferring compiled code to the Arduino. For the Pi, we'll use the Geany IDE, which is quite similar to Arduino's, and GNU C++ for ARM Linux (it comes with Raspbian). We can run the code directly on the Pi where we wrote it. We'll use WiringPi in place of Wiring, and we'll cover that in depth in Chapter 5.

CHAPTER 5

Meet WiringPi

So we have programs running on the Pi, and that's a good thing. It's really the key to the whole process, even if TicTac didn't do more than play a simple screen game. For the Pi to do what Arduinos do, though, we need to be able to control their GPIO ports. For that, we'll use the WiringPi library. It's included in modern versions of Raspbian by default.

What Is WiringPi?

On the Arduino, you undoubtedly used the pin family of functions, like `pinMode(pin)`, `digitalRead(pin)`, and `digitalWrite(pin,HIGH/LOW)`. Those come from a project called Wiring, originally written by Hernando Barragán, and is about half of everything we know and love about Arduino. (The other half is Processing, in which the IDE is written, and which gave us the notion of sketchbooks and sketches. The version used for Arduino is typically years out of date.) WiringPi is a library of C/C++ functions that works the same way for the Raspberry Pi, written by Gordon Henderson. Essentially, it provides a familiar interface for those of us who came from the Arduino world to the GPIO pins.

As with the Arduino, you can *do* all this without going through WiringPi (or Wiring, in the case of Arduino), but you're starting to deal with registers and addresses that are not very well documented, and that are subject to change with different versions of the Pi. There's a good

© James R. Strickland 2018
J. R. Strickland, *Raspberry Pi for Arduino Users*,
https://doi.org/10.1007/978-1-4842-3414-3_5

tutorial on Pieter-Jan Van de Maele's blog here: `http://www.pieter-jan.com/node/15`, but I confess I have not tried it. Normally this goes against my grain, hiding complexity with an abstract library, but in this case I think it's worth it.

Raspbian has a built-in GPIO interface library, but it's for Python. For those of us coding in C and C++, it's not very useful.

WiringPi Functions

WiringPi is a set of C functions—an API (Application Programming Interface). These functions break down into five general types: setup functions, wiring functions, thread functions, time functions, and other functions, mostly information. I'm going to skip over the PWM functions, because they're complicated to explain and we don't use them in this book.

Setup

There are three separate functions to initialize WiringPi. You only need to call one, and we only use one of them in this book. Nevertheless, for completeness, here they are.

wiringPiSetup

The `wiringPiSetup()` function sets up the WiringPi library to use the WiringPi pin numbers. I don't recommend this. While yes, it does theoretically mean that you'd have to change your code when the Raspberry Pi foundation changes which Broadcom GPIO line does what, my opinion is that it's worth it. I feel the same way about Arduino, to the point that the only Arduino-compatible I've ever designed from scratch reorganized the pin numbers to reflect the pin numbers on the IC package.

This meant that there were holes in the pin map—when a given pin was power, ground, clock, or whatever—but that you could always refer to the IC and know what pin was what when you tried to program it.

wiringPiSetupGpio

`wiringPiSetupGpio()` does the same thing as `wiringPiSetup`, except that it uses the Broadcom GPIO pin numbers. These are not in any particular order around the GPIO header, but they are defined for sure by Broadcom, which makes the system chip in your Pi. That's as close to canonical as I can think of. This is the setup used by all the code in this book and referred to in the text as well.

wiringPiSetupSys

`wiringPiSetupSys()` sets WiringPi up to use the `/sys/class/gpio` interface, which is the standard interface as provided by Raspbian. Normally, according to the website, WiringPi accesses the hardware directly. It's useful when you don't want your program to have access to all the GPIO pins via the GPIO group (we'll cover that later) or running as root (don't do this).

Wiring

The wiring functions are the ones you're most familiar with, coming from the Arduino world. Most of them have counterparts in Arduino/Wiring, although some require additional hardware to use with the Pi. (The Pi has no analog pins, for example, but this functionality can be added with external hardware.)

pinMode

```
void pinMode(int pin_number,int mode)
```

The pinmode() function, like its Arduino counterpart, is used to tell WiringPi what you want that pin to do. There are four modes defined: INPUT, OUTPUT, PWM_OUTPUT, and GPIO_CLOCK. Returns nothing.

INPUT

The INPUT mode sets the pin up to listen for an input. Instead of having a high and low state (when unconnected to anything else), the pin goes "high impedance." This means that the pin can be swung high or low with very little current. INPUT mode is also subject to the effects of pullup/pulldown resistors. Unlike the Arduino, these are set with a separate command that we'll get to later.

OUTPUT

OUTPUT mode sets the GPIO pin up to source or sink current. If it's then set high, it will source up to 3.3v, at up to 16mA per pin, not to exceed 51mA total. This isn't a lot of current. There's a hard limit of 51mA total due to the voltage regulator on the Pi, rather than the system chip itself.

An ATmega328P-PU based Arduino can source 40mA at 5v per pin, and a maximum of 200mA for the whole Arduino, unless it's a surface mount ATmega, in which case it can source 400mA, thanks to dual VCC lines. The dual ground lines of an ATmega328P-PU based Arduino mean it can *sink* up to 400mA.

Note   I've said this before, and I'll say it again. The Raspberry Pi cannot source or sink more than 3.3v through any GPIO pin. Be careful when you wire things to the GPIO port. There are 5v pins there just waiting to fry a GPIO line.

GPIO_CLOCK

Sets the pin up for outputting a user-selectable clock. This is roughly similar to setting up one of the Arduino's timers to generate a steady clock signal. A pin set up this way can be connected to one of a number of clock sources with a specific divisor to get a wide variety of frequencies.

digitalWrite

```
void digitalWrite(int pin,int value)
```

Sets the pin HIGH or LOW. The values HIGH and LOW are defined by the library, but you can also use 1 and 0 for them. According to the WiringPi website, any value above 0 will work for HIGH, but only 0 will work for LOW.

This function requires a pinMode of OUTPUT on that pin prior to writing. Returns nothing.

digitalWriteByte

```
void digitalWriteByte(int value)
```

Writes an 8-bit value to the first eight GPIO pins. It does this in two write operations instead of eight, so it's considerably faster than turning pins on by hand.

Very important: digitalWriteByte writes to the first eight WiringPi GPIO pins. The Broadcom pin number equivalents, in order, are: BCM17, BCM18, BCM27, BCM22, BCM23, BCM24, BCM25, and BCM4.

Sadly, there is no corresponding digitalReadByte, so those of us hoping to do the kinds of operations we're used to with Arduino port(x) commands are pretty much out of luck. Returns nothing.

Requires a pinMode of OUTPUT on that pin prior to writing. Returns nothing.

digitalRead

`int digitalRead(int pin)`

Reads the pin's value and returns HIGH or LOW (1 or 0, respectively), depending on the pin's state.

Requires a `pinMode` of INPUT on that pin prior to reading.

pullUpDnControl

`void pullUpDnControl(int pin, int pud)`

This function sets or clears the pullup/pulldown resistor in a given pin.

Sometimes, leaving a pin's value floating can cause trouble. The input is *so* sensitive that any random electrical noise can push it over its trigger threshold. This is especially problematic when dealing with interrupts. It's a good idea to set input pins to a default state. You can do it externally with pullup or pulldown resistors (pull the pin high to +3.3v (usually) or down to ground, respectively), or if the noise isn't too great, you can use the internal resistors in the Pi's system chip.

The values pud can be set to are PUD_OFF and PUD_DOWN for a pulldown resistor and PUD_UP for a pullup resistor.

This is the same concept as using the input pullup resistors in an Arduino by either sending a `digitalWrite(HIGH)` to an input pin or setting the `pinMode` to INPUT_PULLUP in more recent versions of Arduino. The Arduino does not have internal pulldown resistors.

Requires a `pinMode` of INPUT. Returns nothing.

Threads

We'll get to threads in greater depth a couple of chapters from now. For right now, threads are a way to break code into parts that can run simultaneously and let them do just that. If you have multiple cores, multiple threads really can run simultaneously. There are three thread functions.

PI_THREAD

PI_THREAD() is a function wrapper that allows the code you put in it to run as a separate thread from the main program. It's activated by piThreadCreate().

piThreadCreate

```
int piThreadCreate(name)
```

If you pass this function the name of one of your functions declared with the PI_THREAD declaration, the function runs in its own thread. This means that it's still part of the parent process, but that it's scheduled and will execute on its own. Requires the PI_THREAD declared function.

Returns 0 on a successful thread start, or something else if the thread did not start.

piLock

```
void piLock(int keyNum)
```

Threads share variables. If one thread is modifying a variable and another thread wakes up and reads the variable, it's impossible to predict what was really in the variable at the moment it was read. To prevent this, you'd surround the update of the variable with a piLock and a piUnlock. PiLock takes a single integer variable from 0 to 3 and returns nothing.

piUnlock

```
void piUnlock(int keyNum)
```

The inverse of piLock(), this function unlocks the lock and allows threads to wake up normally as the Linux scheduler sees fit.

Interrupts

As with threads, we're going to get into interrupts at considerable depth in upcoming chapters, so I'm going to gloss over what they are here. An interrupt is a hardware circuit in a microcontroller or microprocessor that forces the CPU to jump to an "interrupt vector" and execute the instructions there until the code sends the CPU back to what it was doing. It's a very powerful technique to let a CPU seem to do two things at once. WiringPi's interrupt system is very similar to the one in Arduino, although the declaration of the interrupt service routine (ISR) is somewhat more relaxed, and the setup is slightly different.

There's only one function involved.

wiringPiISR

```
int wiringPiISR(int pin, int edgeType, void (*function)(void))
```

This gets a little complicated. `Pin` and `edgeType` are pretty straightforward. As usual, they're integers. `Pin` is the pin number, which thankfully respects whichever pin numbering scheme you've selected. In our case, it will happily digest the Broadcom GPIO numbers we've been using. The `edgeType` parameter is another integer, with values undoubtedly #defined in the headers for WiringPi. These can be `INT_EDGE_FALLING`, `INT_EDGE_RISING`, or `INT_EDGE_SETUP`. A falling edge means the interrupt will fire as the pin goes from high to low. A rising edge means the interrupt will fire as the pin goes from low to high. Setting the interrupt `INT_EDGE_SETUP` means you configured the falling or rising setting somewhere else, and it should not be changed.

So what is `void (*function) (void))`? It's a pointer that points to the void function. Clear as mud? Probably. Let's talk about pointers a little.

Pointers

Pointers are one of the more complicated aspects of C and C++. Here's what's going on. Everything in memory has an address. If you declare an integer variable, call it my_int, the Pi allocates four bytes of RAM and puts the address of the first byte in a table of variables. So when you access my_int to set it to something, the program has to go to the variable table and find my_int, look up that address, then go to that address in memory and write your data. The address doesn't change, only what's in RAM at that address.

With me so far? Good.

When you create a pointer, you are asking for a variable that holds an address.

So if you declare a pointer to an integer int *my_pointer, you can't store an integer in it. That pointer is a place where the address of your data can be stored. It can't store an integer directly, because by itself, it has no memory allocated to it. If you declare another integer—int my_int;—the memory is allocated, and your variable gets declared as normal. If you want my_pointer to point at my_int's memory, you need to ask C/C++ for the address of my_int. You do that with the & symbol. So my_pointer=&my_int sets my_pointer to the address of my_int. This is useful when you want one piece of code that can access variable names you don't know yet. There are also ways to allocate memory and get an address without declaring a variable, but that's getting beyond the scope of this book. There are good tutorials on C and C++ pointers elsewhere on the net.

Here's the thing about memory. On a von Neumann architecture like the Pi's system chip, it's literally true that everything is in the same bucket we call RAM. Variables and code. So a function name is just like a variable. It's a name in a table associated with an address in memory where the code is. You can, in fact, have a pointer to a function.

Pointers to functions are exactly what's going on with `wiringPiISR`. The `wiringPiISR` function takes a void pointer (a pointer set to nothing when the program starts) as its parameter. Since the pointer is set up to point to functions, we also have to deal with any parameters the function can take. ISRs can take no parameters, so the declaration explicitly sets the parameter field to void.

It's easier than that to use. We'll be doing that later in this chapter.

Note   On Harvard Architecture devices like the ATmega microcontrollers that Arduinos use, instructions and data are actually separated, and it's nearly impossible to get bytes from one side to the other. That's a job for the compiler to sort out.

Speaking of the compiler, the variable table I've mentioned is not likely to be how the compiler really goes about it. From our perspective as programmers, however, it's functionally what happens.

Time

Like the Arduino core, Linux provides a number of clocks for measuring various orders of magnitude of time. Sadly, none of them are as simple as the `millis()` and `micros()` functions in Arduino, and the `delay()` and `delayMicroseconds()` functions are not standard C/C++ functions. Not to worry, WiringPi has us covered. There are four timing-related functions. (If you're interested in doing it the Linux way, you're looking for the `clock_gettime()` function. I found those functions poorly documented and very difficult to use.)

Caution   The timing functions rely on a system clock that may not get updated in a timely fashion if interrupts occur.

---

millis

```
unsigned int millis (void)
```

This function returns an unsigned integer of the number of milliseconds since one of the wiringPiSetup functions was called. It works exactly the same way millis() in Arduino does.

Caution   Very important: The 32-bit unsigned integer (uint32_t) millis returns will roll over in about 49 days. Calling a wiringPiSetup function again does not reset it, and more than one call to one setup function either does nothing (at best) or causes a fatal error.

This function takes no parameters.

micros

```
unsigned int micros(void)
```

Works exactly the same way millis does, except that the value this function returns is microseconds.

Note   The 32-bit unsigned integer (uint32_t) that micros() returns will roll over in just over an hour.

This function takes no parameters.

delay

```
void delay(unsigned int howLong)
```

As with the Arduino, there's also a delay function, which causes the program to sit and wait for a certain number of milliseconds. It takes an unsigned integer (uint32_t) of seconds, meaning the delay can be no longer than 49 or so days.

This function returns nothing.

delayMicroseconds

```
void delayMicroseconds(unsigned int howLong)
```

This function does exactly the same thing delay() does, except with microseconds (1/1000th of a millisecond). Since it depends on the same timer as the millis and micros clock, and that clock may be delayed in updating by interrupts, you should be aware that delayMicroseconds is not always accurate. This function takes an unsigned integer (uint32_t) of how many microseconds to delay, and the program sits and does nothing for that period of time. This function returns nothing (void).

Thoughts

This is by no means comprehensive documentation of the WiringPi library. The library is big and gets bigger all the time as new modules and GPIO peripherals are supported. I've covered the parts we're actually going to use in this book, and to make the point that a lot of the functionality you're used to from Wiring in Arduino sketches is available with WiringPi.

There is reasonably comprehensive documentation on the WiringPi library at the author's website at http://www.wiringpi.com/reference.

GPIO Command

WiringPi also includes a command-line utility called GPIO, which has special privileges set so that you can call it, but it runs with the privileges of its owner, root. For some manipulations of the GPIO system, you need this. I'm only going to cover one GPIO command, in no small part because it's all I've used. Full documentation is available at `http://wiringpi.com/the-gpio-utility/`.

Pinouts

I've found only one use for the GPIO utility thus far, and that's getting the canonical list of what pins do what on *this* Pi, with *this* version of WiringPi. That command is `gpio readall`. Its output is shown in Figure 5-1.

```
pi@PiOW:~$ gpio readall
+-----+-----+---------+------+---+-Pi ZeroW-+---+------+---------+-----+-----+
| BCM | wPi |   Name  | Mode | V | Physical | V | Mode |  Name   | wPi | BCM |
+-----+-----+---------+------+---+----++----+---+------+---------+-----+-----+
|     |     |    3.3v |      |   |  1 || 2  |   |      | 5v      |     |     |
|   2 |   8 |   SDA.1 |   IN | 1 |  3 || 4  |   |      | 5v      |     |     |
|   3 |   9 |   SCL.1 |   IN | 1 |  5 || 6  |   |      | 0v      |     |     |
|   4 |   7 | GPIO. 7 |   IN | 1 |  7 || 8  | 1 | IN   | TxD     | 15  | 14  |
|     |     |      0v |      |   |  9 || 10 | 1 | IN   | RxD     | 16  | 15  |
|  17 |   0 | GPIO. 0 |   IN | 1 | 11 || 12 | 1 | IN   | GPIO. 1 | 1   | 18  |
|  27 |   2 | GPIO. 2 |   IN | 1 | 13 || 14 |   |      | 0v      |     |     |
|  22 |   3 | GPIO. 3 |   IN | 0 | 15 || 16 | 1 | IN   | GPIO. 4 | 4   | 23  |
|     |     |    3.3v |      |   | 17 || 18 | 1 | IN   | GPIO. 5 | 5   | 24  |
|  10 |  12 |    MOSI |   IN | 1 | 19 || 20 |   |      | 0v      |     |     |
|   9 |  13 |    MISO |   IN | 1 | 21 || 22 | 1 | IN   | GPIO. 6 | 6   | 25  |
|  11 |  14 |    SCLK |   IN | 1 | 23 || 24 | 1 | IN   | CE0     | 10  | 8   |
|     |     |      0v |      |   | 25 || 26 | 1 | IN   | CE1     | 11  | 7   |
|   0 |  30 |   SDA.0 |   IN | 1 | 27 || 28 | 1 | IN   | SCL.0   | 31  | 1   |
|   5 |  21 | GPIO.21 |   IN | 1 | 29 || 30 |   |      | 0v      |     |     |
|   6 |  22 | GPIO.22 |   IN | 1 | 31 || 32 | 0 | IN   | GPIO.26 | 26  | 12  |
|  13 |  23 | GPIO.23 |   IN | 0 | 33 || 34 |   |      | 0v      |     |     |
|  19 |  24 | GPIO.24 |   IN | 0 | 35 || 36 | 0 | IN   | GPIO.27 | 27  | 16  |
|  26 |  25 | GPIO.25 |   IN | 0 | 37 || 38 | 0 | IN   | GPIO.28 | 28  | 20  |
|     |     |      0v |      |   | 39 || 40 | 0 | IN   | GPIO.29 | 29  | 21  |
+-----+-----+---------+------+---+----++----+---+------+---------+-----+-----+
| BCM | wPi |   Name  | Mode | V | Physical | V | Mode |  Name   | wPi | BCM |
+-----+-----+---------+------+---+-Pi ZeroW-+---+------+---------+-----+-----+
```

Figure 5-1. *GPIO readall output*

The table you get is organized like this. The inner two columns under "Physical" are the physical pins of the GPIO port of the Raspberry Pi you're using, 1-40, alternating sides. This is so you can find the pin you're looking for on the WiringPi breakout board you're using, or on the Pi itself.

The V columns are the voltage levels currently on the pins, where 0 is LOW and 1 is HIGH. These are logical values. The exact voltages on those pins may be somewhat different, though not much. Whether that is set by the Pi or by external circuitry is subject to the next columns.

The mode columns tell you whether your pin is set as an input or an output. All the pins shown on this `gpio readall` call are set as inputs. Once you run the program we're about to write in this chapter, some of them will be outputs. You should always explicitly set the pin's input/output state regardless. Some pins have no mode. That's because they're not GPIOs. They're power rails or grounds. The mode column will also tell you if a pin is in an alternate mode. To be brief, most of the GPIO pins have other functionality connected to them. You can switch which function the pin has in software. If it's not the norm, `gpio readall` will tell you in the mode column, by listing the mode as ALT<some number>. There are lists of the alternate functions for each pin, or you can wade through the Broadcom documentation for the system chip you're using and get the full skinny on it.

The name columns are the names. If you're looking for the MOSI, MISO, and SCLK pins to hook up something with SPI, this is a useful column. The GPIO numbers listed are the *WiringPi* GPIO numbers. This gets confusing because different breakout boards number things differently. The Adafruit board I use, for example, lists the Broadcom GPIO numbers (BCMs) that we use in this book, and as the Pi foundation lists them, but only for pins that don't have a function other than GPIOs. That's unfortunate, in my opinion, since each pin can have multiple functions, and there isn't room to list them all. It's here that the WiringPi numbering scheme irritates me most, because it's unique to WiringPi.

The last four columns (two on each side) are the wPi numbers and the BCMs. My advice is to pick a numbering scheme, most likely BCM, look your pin numbers up on that, then go inward on this table to the physical pin.

GPIO Group and Privileges

Remember in Chapter 3, "Survival Linux," when I mentioned privileges? Remember how I also said *everything* in Linux is a file? Well, the access system by which WiringPi controls your GPIO pins is, at some level, a file, and you need permission to use it. Unsurprisingly, it's owned by root.

Fortunately, the group set on the GPIO interface system is not root, but GPIO.

It's worth checking to make sure your pi account is a member of the GPIO group, so it can access the GPIO pins. To do this takes a little more Linux.

```
pi@PiOW:~$ groups
pi adm dialout cdrom sudo audio video plugdev games users input netdev gpio
i2c spi
pi@PiOW:~$
```

The groups command will list which groups your pi account is a member of. If gpio and i2c are not in this list, you'll have problems running the programs we're going to create in this book. To do that, we'll use the usermod command. As with all Linux commands, usermod has dozens of options, of which we'll be using two: -a and -G. The -a tells usermod to *append* the group to your list of groups, rather than set your list of groups to this group alone. The -G flag (must be capitalized) tells usermod you want to modify the user's list of supplementary groups. Full documentation on usermod can be had by typing man usermod. Some web searching to find out how to use it might be in order too.

Hooking Up WiringPi in Geany

There's one last little gotcha that we need to deal with when we're writing programs that use WiringPi. We have to tell Geany to look for the WiringPi library. Most importantly, we have to tell WiringPi to add it every time we start a new project. Programs that use WiringPi won't *build* without it, although they'll *compile* just fine. Here's what that looks like on a piece of test code I wrote to check how digitalWritebyte works.

```
g++ -Wall -o "writebyte" "writebyte.cpp" (in directory: /home/pi)
/tmp/cc5JYx08.o: In function `main':
writebyte.cpp:(.text+0xc): undefined reference to `wiringPiSetup'
writebyte.cpp:(.text+0x14): undefined reference to `delay'
```

Lots more errors...

```
collect2: error: ld returned 1 exit status
Compilation failed.
```

To fix this problem, create your project, then create at least one C++ file to go in it. Otherwise, Geany won't know what language you're using and won't give you the right options, or it won't have the right project open.

Choose Build ➤ Set Build Commands. Look on the list of C++ commands. The second one (unless Geany's changed a lot between my "now" and your "now") is build. Edit the command field for build to add -l wiringPi, as shown in Figure 5-2. (That's a lowercase L, by the way, not an i or a 1.) Note also that the command window scrolls. Make sure you don't break up an existing flag.

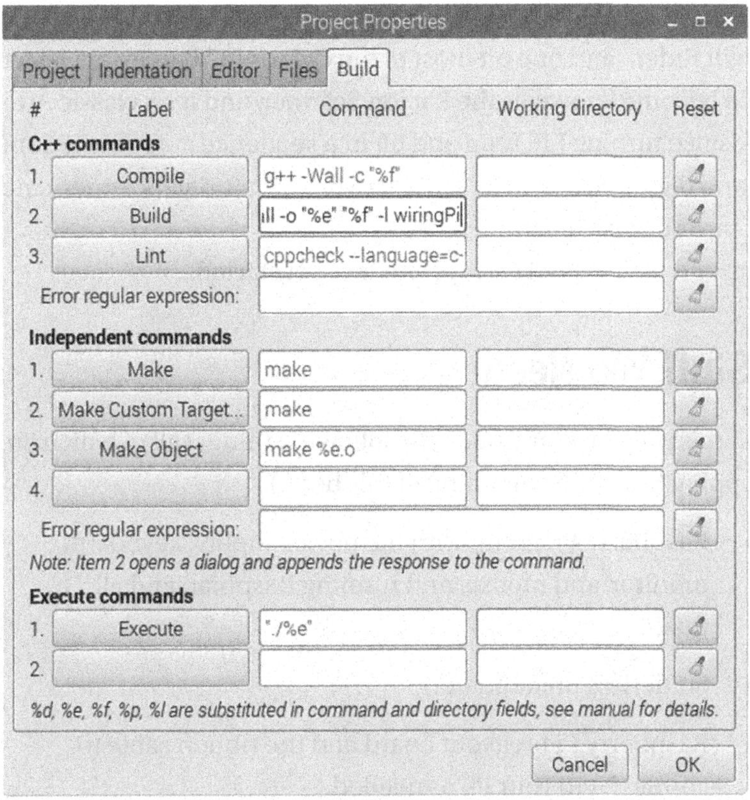

Figure 5-2. *Editing the project properties*

Click OK when you're done. Remember. Every new project must have this treatment.

Build the Larson (Memorial) Scanner

Here's where we (finally) get to a hardware project. If you've been around the block in the Arduino world, you've done at least one Larson Scanner, and you know the story behind them. If not, read on.

The late Glenn A. Larson was the producer of (among many, many other TV series) the original "Battlestar Galactica" and "Knight Rider." Both those series featured visual scanners that were shown to the viewing audience as a sequence of lights scanning back and forth. One on the car in "Knight Rider," and one on most of the Cylons in "Battlestar Galactica." It's since become known as the Larson Scanner, and it's a classic Arduino project, since turning LEDs on and off in a sequence amounts to some delays and digitalWrites. I call it the Larson (Memorial) Scanner, since Larson passed away in 2014.

So round up your LED arrays and let's get started.

The Stuff You Need

To build this project, you'll need the following things (all of which are on the shopping list at the beginning of this book):

- Raspberry Pi, set up with the power supply, keyboard, monitor, and mouse, and running Raspbian and all that.

- Solderless breadboard.

- Raspberry Pi breakout board and the ribbon cable to connect it to your Pi, as needed.

- Hookup wire or jumpers.

- LED arrays and the datasheet for them. Note: If you're not using the Kingbright DC10GWA or one of the other colored variants of it, you'll need to work out how to hook your LED arrays up and what dropping resistor is required on your own. These particular arrays have 10 independent LEDs each, with no common cathodes or anodes. If you must go with a common cathode or anode type, go with a common anode. That way, the wiring will be different (easier), but the software can be the same.

- You can use just about any 10-segment LED bar graphs, so long as their current demands aren't more than what the Pi can deliver (we'll get to that later), but watch out. Some larger bar graphs are wired with the expectation that you'll multiplex your pins rather than use one pin per LED, as we're going to do here for clarity. Multiplexing is interesting and fun, but I'm not covering it in this book. The Kingbrights also have an adequate, easy-to-read datasheet, which can't be said for may other types.

- The 220Ω resistor.

Survival Ohm's Law

It's possible to go through a great many tutorials in the Arduino world without learning Ohm's law. It's important right now for sizing our dropping resistor, and to keep the load on each pin of the Pi below 15mA. It's important to know Ohm's law, but with LED dropping resistors, as long as you err on the side of too much resistance, all it does is make the LED a little dimmer. Still, let's cover Ohm's law for those who don't already know it.

Ohm's law states that between any two points on a circuit, there is a directly proportional relationship between current and voltage. That relationship is called the resistance. This relationship can be described mathematically by I=V/R. I is the current in Amperes, V is the voltage, and R is the resistance. This function can be algebraically transformed to solve for current (I) or voltage (V) or resistance (R). So to apply that to our LED dropping resistor needs, we do the following.

We know from the datasheet that the Kingbright DC10GWA's LEDs have a typical voltage drop of 2.2v. We know that our positive rail coming out of the Raspberry Pi's GPIO breakout is 3.3v. That means our resistor needs to dissipate 1.1v at no more than 15mA. We know volts and amps (Milliamps are thousandths of amps—make sure to keep track of the units), so we'll solve for resistance.

First, let's reshuffle the Ohm's law equation a bit. We know I, we know V, we need R.

If we multiply both sides of the equation by R, we get IR=V. It gets us volts, which isn't what we want, but it also gets R out of the fraction so we can mess with it. If we then divide both sides of the equation by I (current), we get R=V/I. That version of the equation gives us what we need.

So. V is 1.1 and current is .015. Divide 1.1 by .015 and we get about 73 Ohms (Ω). That's the minimum size our resistor must be to protect the LED and the output of the Raspberry Pi.

There's a catch. We have a lot more than one LED. With the Larson Scanner, only one should be on at any given time, but just in case something weird happens with the code, let's go with about three times the minimum resistor. You'll recall I chose a 220Ω resistor in the shopping list. This is it. But let's verify how much current the resistor will be dealing with with nearly three times the resistance.

I=V/R. Volts is 1.5, resistance is 220Ω. 1.1/220 is 0.005 or so Amps (5mA).

So we know the resistance we need. We also need to determine the watts the resistor will be dissipating. In case it wasn't clear, resistors dissipate energy as heat, so the wattage limit of a resistor is how much heat it can dissipate without going up in smoke.

Watts is equal to VI—volts times amps. We're dropping 1.1v with 5mA of current. 1.1*.005 is 0.0055 watts. Five and a half milliwatts. A 1/8-watt resistor should handle this with ease, considering they can dissipate 125mW. So a 1/4-watt, 220Ω resistor will be fine, right? Well, let's see. If we have all the LEDs on, we're dealing with 20 times the current. 20*5mA is 100mA, or 0.1 amps. 0.1*1.1v is about .11 watts.

Considering a 1/8-watt resistor is only rated for 0.125 watts, that's a little high. You never really want to run a resistor more than half its rated wattage. They get hot. A 1/4-watt resistor has more than twice the current. The Pi's only rated to deliver half that current to all the pins combined, so with a 1/4-f resistor, we've ensured that the Pi will go up in smoke before our resistor will. That's a good thing.

So in the end, was my one-watt resistor necessary? Not in the slightest. I have those resistors on hand from working with vacuum tube electronics where whole watts and hundreds of volts are the norm. They also look better under the camera.

Schematic

Having gathered the parts and revisited Ohm's law, let's get started building the project. Figure 5-3 shows the schematic.

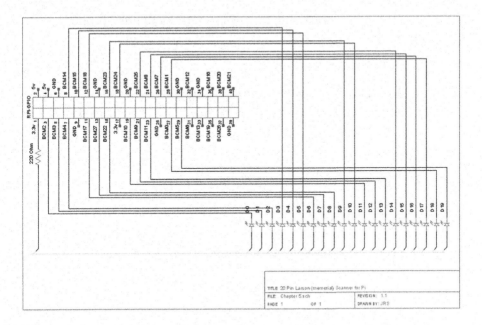

Figure 5-3. *Larson Memorial Scanner schematic*

Construction

If your breakout board or your Pi needs pins soldered in, now's the time.

Soldering

If you don't know how to solder, I recommend the tutorials on EEVblog, starting with EEVblog #180. You can find it here: https://www.youtube.com/watch?v=J5Sb21qbpEQ. Don't like video? There's another good tutorial on Adafruit's website here: https://learn.adafruit.com/adafruit-guide-excellent-soldering. I learned from both these sources, and my printed circuit board electronics began working after that. It's easier to learn from videos.

Caution   You only get two eyes in this life. Be careful with them. Always wear eye protection when you solder. Every time. Flux fumes aren't good for your lungs, either, so make sure you have proper ventilation.

If you don't already have one, I strongly suggest getting a *temperature* controlled soldering station. I'm on my second—an old industrial unit from the late 1980s with interchangeable tips that determine the temperature.

All soldered up? Good. Soldering is fun.

Wiring Up

Figure 5-4 shows what my setup looks like.

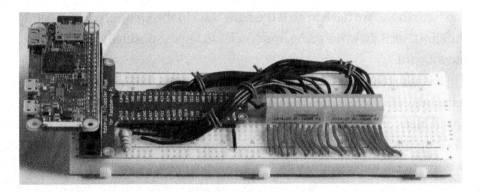

Figure 5-4. *Larson (Memorial) Scanner*

That's my Pi Zero W sitting on the edge of the breakout board. I mentioned it looked good in photos. Go ahead and put your breakout board at one end of your breadboard. The closer to the edge of the breadboard it is, the better. All the projects we're going to do have to fit in the remaining space.

Dropping Resistor

Next, take the 220Ω (Ohm) resistor and connect it from physical pin 1, the 3.3v line, to the positive rail on that side of your breadboard. Don't have a rail like that? You can do it with wire, too, but it will be messier.

This is going to be our dropping resistor for all the LEDs, in case that wasn't clear earlier.

Anode Lines

As you can see in the schematic, we're going to wire the anodes of our LEDs together on one bus. The positive rail of the breadboard being driven by the dropping resistor is that bus. If your LED array already has common anodes, so much the better. You'll only have to wire two of them. The Kingbrights I'm using have no interconnections between LEDs, so if

201

you have those, we have to do it the hard way. In the picture, you can see the short, straight wires going from each LED to the positive rail of the breadboard.

If you're reading the ebook version, you can see that those wires are red, and on the schematic, the positive rail/bus is green. If not, the figures are all black and white, so just follow where the connections go. Wire all 20 LEDs up this way. Make sure your arrays have the anode side toward the positive rail of the breadboard.

Style

In Figure 5-4, you'll see I've hanked some of the lines together in groups and let them rise up over the breadboard in what's called flying leads. You don't have to do it this way, but with complex wiring like this, it swiftly gets messy if you don't. I didn't invent this technique. I saw it done here: `http://forum.6502.org/viewtopic.php?f=4&t=3329` and thought it looked nice in photos. It worked well in my previous book, too.

Switched Cathode Lines

You can (hopefully) see in the schematic that the Raspberry Pi will be switching the cathode lines from `HIGH` (off) to `LOW` (on). You may also note that the cathode lines are in groups of two to four. This was to make a complex (and rather messy) schematic somewhat easier to read. You could hank the lines together that way if you wanted, to make it easier to debug.

Following the schematic, wire BCM2 (physical pin 3), BCM3 (physical pin 5), and BCM4 (physical pin 7), to diodes 0, 1, and 2, respectively, counting left to right. Congratulations, the first three LEDs are hooked up.

Whether you wire one side of the breakout board at a time or try to go in order of the physical pins doesn't really matter, so long as the BCM numbers and the LED numbers line up. If they don't, or you're using LEDs with a common cathode and you have to wire the anodes, you'll have to modify the code a bit on your own.

Continue wiring each group of BCM lines to their corresponding LEDs until you have all 20 wired up (0-19). It's tedious, but not that complicated. I really suggest hanking the wires though. Even more than I did.

The Project

Open Geany, choose Project ➤ New, close whatever project is open, and name your new project Larson. Now choose Document ➤ Set Filetype ➤ Programming Languages ➤ C++ source file to tell Geany what kind of file we're dealing with, even though we haven't written anything yet. It's easier this way. Next, choose Build ➤ Build Commands and, in the build line (line 2), add -l wiringPi. Choose File ➤ Save As, call it Larson.cpp, and make sure to save it in the project directory. You're ready. Let's write some code.

The Program

If you've skipped ahead and looked at the section called "The Code," that's the full code as I wrote it, compiled it, and above all tested it, just like it was in the last chapters. I've mentioned this before, but it's worth repeating. Comments are your friends. If you have to revise this code later, having the guts laid out in text explanation where you can see them will save you far, far more time than it takes to write them now.

Preprocessor Definitions and Inclusions

We know we need wiringPi.h, because we're talking to the GPIO pins. We'll also be using delay, which is a WiringPi call. We'll need iostream if we want to echo anything to the terminal for debugging, which we probably will, so let's include that too.

Let's also define a couple of macros: LEDs for the number of LEDs we're addressing, and `delaymils` for the number of milliseconds between LEDs switching on and off. These are both handy for debugging, since you can light smaller groups of the LEDs at a time by changing LEDs, and you can lengthen the time between them to make sure they're coming on in the right order, which is important. These will be filled in by the preprocessor at compile time.

```
#include <iostream>
#include <wiringPi.h>
#define LEDs 20
#define delaymils 40
```

Namespace

There's a certain amount of disagreement in my (online) sources as to whether hardcoding the namespace is a good idea. If we ever somehow hooked up a library that defined custom versions of cout and endl, this would be a bad idea. It's a safe bet for this program that we won't. We only need iostream for debugging. So we'll go ahead and set it here.

```
using namespace std;
```

The pins Array

Remember how I said it was really important to make sure you connected the GPIOs to the LEDs in the same order that I did? This is where that matters. This is an array of integers, the size defined in LEDs and initialized to the GPIO lines, in order by the LED they're connected to. So LED 0 is connected to BCM2, LED1 is connected to BCM3, and so on. If your arrays are different or you wired them differently, this is one of the places you'll have to change things. It should really be in one line, but there's only so much room on a page of this book.

```
int pins[LEDs] = {2,3,4,14,15,18,17,27,22,23,24,10,9,11,25,8,7,1,0,5};
```

The main() Function

We're not writing Arduino code anymore. And in this program, there aren't any objects needed, there aren't any external functions needed, and we can roll all the stuff that setup() and loop() would do into main. The Larson (Memorial) Scanner is a pretty simple beast. We'll complicate it more later.

We start out by declaring main() as an int that takes no parameters, to make C++ happy. Then we declare an integer, c, and initialize it to 0.

```
int main(void){
    int c=0;
```

Initialize WiringPi

Set WiringPi up to use the Broadcom GPIO numbers. We'll always use this version.

```
    wiringPiSetupGpio();
```

Initialize the Pins

Go through the array of BCM numbers in order of the LEDs and set them all as outputs, then set them HIGH (off) as well. The cout is here for debugging. I have commented it out. You can uncomment it as needed.

Note that flush (or std::flush if we didn't have that namespace set) makes cout print *right now* as opposed to waiting until the loop ends.

```
    for (c=0;c<LEDs;c++){
        //cout<<"Setting pin "<<pins[c]<<"to output\n"<<flush;
        pinMode (pins[c],OUTPUT);
        digitalWrite(pins[c],HIGH);
    }
```

Loop Forever

Does this feel like we've just finished the setup() function and we're going to the loop() function? We have. We just haven't broken them out into functions. There was no need.

Loop while true is true. Which is always the case, except in politics.

```
while(true){
```

Loop Through the LEDs from Low to High

Loop on c from 0 to the last time c is less than LEDs. Turn diode c on by setting that pin LOW. Wait delaymils milliseconds, then if c is not 0, meaning there was no previous LED, switch the previous LED (one left of the current position) off by setting the pin HIGH. There's a cout for debugging here too. It gets very spammy when switched on.

```
for (c=0;c<LEDs;c++){
    //cout << "switching" << pins[c] <<"\n"<< flush;
    digitalWrite(pins[c],LOW);
    delay(delaymils);
    if (c>0) digitalWrite(pins[c-1],HIGH);
}
```

Loop Through the LEDs from High to Low

We've scanned from left to right, and the last LED is lit on the right side. Now we need to go the other way. The last LED will be switched on (HIGH) even though it was left that way by the previous loop. That's fine. The scan needs to pause slightly at each end.

Loop on c from LEDs -1 (because the array goes 0 to 19) to 0 and decrement c at the end of each loop. You knew you could do that, right? The c variable is once again the index of the diodes, going from 19 to 0. Go to the pins array, look up that BCM GPIO number, and switch that pin on (LOW). Then wait delaymils milliseconds, and if c is less than LEDs (we're not on the rightmost LED), turn the next LED to the right off by setting the pin HIGH.

```
for (c=LEDs-1;c>=0;c--){
    //cout << "switching" << pins[c] <<"\n"<< flush;
    digitalWrite(pins[c],LOW);
    delay(delaymils);
    if (c<LEDs)digitalWrite(pins[c+1],HIGH);
}
```

End the Loop Forever

We never actually stop looping forever, at least from the perspective of this program, but we have to close the loop.

```
}
```

End the Main() Function

We'll never get here either, but once again, to keep C++ happy, we'll tell it that if we ever *do* get here, we should return a 0, telling the operating system that nothing went wrong.

```
    return 0;
}
```

First Run

Unless you've uncommented the cout lines, the window that pops up when you run this program from Geany will be remarkably...empty. To end the program, click on that window and press Ctrl+C (Control and lowercase c). This is how you stop programs, if they'll stop at all. You can also just close the window. Since the Larson process is a child of the sh window called by Geany, the process will end when the window closes. You'll probably wind up with a couple of LEDs left on. It's not a problem.

The Code

As always, here's the code, exactly as you'll be able to download it from the official archive for this book.

```
/*
 * larson.cpp
 *
 * Copyright 2017 Jim Strickland <jrs@jamesrstrickland.com>
 *
 * Standard GNU boilerplate:
 * This program is free software; you can redistribute it and/
 * or modify it under the terms of the GNU General Public
 * License as published by the Free Software Foundation;
 * either version 2 of the License, or (at your option) any
 * later version.
 *
 * This program is distributed in the hope that it will be
 * useful, but WITHOUT ANY WARRANTY; without even the implied
 * warranty of MERCHANTABILITY or FITNESS FOR A PARTICULAR
 * PURPOSE.  See the GNU General Public License for more details.
 *
 * You should have received a copy of the GNU General Public
 * License along with this program; if not, write to the
 * Free Software Foundation, Inc., 51 Franklin Street,
 * Fifth Floor, Boston, MA 02110-1301, USA.
 *
 */

/*
 * larson
 * This program implements the classic "Larson (Memorial)
 * Scanner",albeit a 20-pin Raspberry Pi version. It //requires//
 * a Pi with a 40-pin GPIO bus, or it won't call the right pins
 * in wiringPi.
 * It exists to demonstrate the use of wiringPi in its most
 * basic mode, digitalWrite.
 */

/* Iostream gives us cin and cout, which we might need for
 * debugging. wiringPi is the star of this show, the software
 * interface to the GPIO pins.
 * We define LEDs as 20, both to set the index of the pins array,
 * and as the maximum index value of the loop that reads it.
 * Likewise delaymils is a constant value of how many
 * milliseconds to wait between changing LEDs.
 */
```

```
#include <iostream>
#include <wiringPi.h>
#define LEDs 20
#define delaymils 40

/*
 * We're only using one namespace in this program, so it's safe
 * to set this program's default namespace to std.
 */
using namespace std;

/*
 * There's no good reason to use an object here, so we'll use a
 * global variable instead. This is the array that maps the pin
 * numbers in the order they're plugged into the LED arrays to
 * its own index value (from 0 to LEDs).
 */
int pins[LEDs]={2,3,4,14,15,18,17,27,22,23,24,10,9,11,25,8,7,1,0,5};

/*
 * Main()
 * Parameters: none
 * Returns: an integer to tell the system its exit status.
 *
 * How it works:
 * -------------
 * Initialize the integer c at zero. C will be a counter. This
 * isn't really necessary, since it's initialized in the for
 * loop below, but it's good practice.
 *
 * Initialize wiringPi
 * Call the wiringPiSetupGpio() function. This function
 * configures the program's interface with the wiringPi/GPIO
 * system. Critically, it sets it up to use the Broadcom GPIO
 * numbers instead of earlier wiringPi specific pin numbers,
 * physical pin numbers, or anything else.
 *
 * Initialize pins
 * In a for loop, we set all the pins to output mode and high.
 * We're using them for output.
 * Note Bene: We are switching the //low// or cathode side of
 * each LED. When the GPIO is //HIGH//, the LED is //off// Only
 * when the GPIO is //LOW// does current flow. So we set them
 * all high at initialization to turn all the LEDs off.
```

```
 *
 * Loop Forever scanning from low to high and high to low.
 *          Scan Low to High LED #. Starting with LED 0,
 *                  turn the LED on,
 *                  wait delaymils,
 *                  then turn the previous LED off.

 *          Scan High to Low by LED number.
 *                  Switch the current LED on,
 *                  Wait delaymils,
 *                  then switch the previous LED off.
 *
 * We'll never reach the return(0).
 */

int main(void){
    int c=0;
    //Initialize WiringPi.
    wiringPiSetupGpio();

    //Initialize Pins.
    for (c=0;c<LEDs;c++){
        //cout<<"Setting pin "<<pins[c]<<"to output\n"<<flush;
        pinMode (pins[c],OUTPUT);
        digitalWrite(pins[c],HIGH);
    }

    //Loop forever switching the LEDs on and off in sequence.
    while(true){

        //Loop from 0 to LEDs - "scan" from low LED # to high.
        for (c=0;c<LEDs;c++){
            //cout << "switching" << pins[c] <<"\n"<< flush;
            digitalWrite(pins[c],LOW);
            delay(delaymils);
            if (c>0) digitalWrite(pins[c-1],HIGH);
        }

        //Loop from LEDs to 0 - scan from high LED # to low.
        for (c=LEDs-1;c>=0;c--){
            //cout << "switching" << pins[c] <<"\n"<< flush;
            digitalWrite(pins[c],LOW);
            delay(delaymils);
            if (c<LEDs)digitalWrite(pins[c+1],HIGH);
        }
    }
    return 0;
}
```

Conclusion

The WiringPi library provides an easy interface to the Pi's various hardware capabilities, including GPIO pins. It's very similar (deliberately) to Arduino's Wiring library, and we'll be using it extensively in the projects to come. It's pre-installed in Raspbian. To get to know WiringPi, we built the Larson (Memorial) Scanner project, which lights 20 LEDs in a sequence from left to right, then right to left. In Chapter 6, we'll dig into input and output with GPIO in more detail.

CHAPTER 6

Input and Output

As pretty as the Larson (Memorial) Scanner is, it's also a good demonstration of the Raspberry Pi's GPIO controls using WiringPi. In this chapter, we'll modify the circuit (slightly) and the program (a bit more) so that we can read data in as well. We'll do it two ways, since it's not a very big topic by itself: polled and interrupt driven. Once again, WiringPi makes this easy.

Let's go ahead and modify the circuit first.

The Stuff You Need

We're adding exactly one part and some wire for this project. It's a short list.

- Raspberry Pi and Larson (Memorial) Scanner build from Chapter 5.

- One normally open PCB pushbutton switch. SPST (Single Pole Single Throw) is fine. I got mine in a bag of 20 from Adafruit on special some years ago. We'll go into switches a little more later in this chapter.

- More hookup wire.

© James R. Strickland 2018
J. R. Strickland, *Raspberry Pi for Arduino Users*,
https://doi.org/10.1007/978-1-4842-3414-3_6

The Revised Circuit

The schematic in Figure 6-1 should look pretty familiar. It'd be easy to miss the one change, that switch, SW1, that's connected from the positive rail for diode power to BCM12, physical pin 32. There's nothing special about that pin. It was just handy—the next one in line.

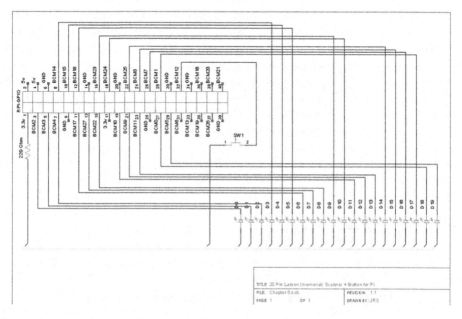

Figure 6-1. *Larson (Memorial) Scanner schematic with a pushbutton input*

Some Words About Pushbutton Tactile Switches

Ah, the lowly PC board pushbutton switch. Simple, mechanical, nearly as cheap as dirt, and filled with interesting gotchas for those who've never played with them. Most of you probably have, already, so I'll keep this as brief as I can.

The pushbutton switch I'm using, despite having four external pins that connect to my breadboard, is an SPST (single pole single throw), normally open type. Single pole means there's only one path through the

214

switch. Single throw means you can throw the switch into only one *on* position. Normally open means the switch is off by default. Like a lot of terms in electronics and other industries, these terms come from much earlier times, and they're easier to understand if you've seen the original. Figure 6-2 is a patent drawing from 1895, showing a simple knife switch. I've annotated it to show throws and poles.

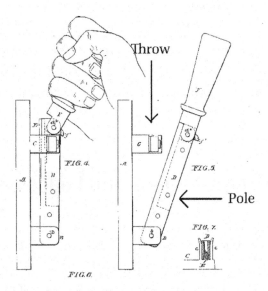

Figure 6-2. *Pole and throw on an 1890s knife switch*

If you took a pushbutton switch apart, and got a magnifying glass, what you'd probably find is that the button is a plastic dot, with a part that sticks out in the middle that pushes on a small, round, slightly domed, springy piece of metal. At the perimeter of that piece of metal is one cylindrical contact. The metal dome rests on it. Inside that cylindrical contact, separated by empty air from both the dome and the outer contact, is a second cylindrical contact. When you press the button, it forces the middle of the dome downward so that the metal touches the inner contact as well as the outer contact. It's all enclosed, and much, much smaller, but it does the same thing.

One set of gotchas involves the external pins of the switch. So far as I can tell, there's no systematic method to predict which pins are connected when the button is pushed. If your switch has a datasheet, it will tell you. If, like mine, your switches came in a bag on clearance from somewhere, finding that datasheet may be a problem.

My suggestion? Use your multimeter set for Ohms to find out which set of pins is connected together when the switch is closed. Modern ones will beep. If not, the meter will still show (nearly) zero resistance. The resistance will be infinite or thereabouts when the switch is open.

There's another gotcha that we'll talk about a little later, but keep it in the back of your mind for now. Switches bounce. Your finger pressure isn't as steady in computer time (milliseconds to nanoseconds) as it is in human time. Physical switch contacts vibrate. And so on.

Some Words About Pullup and Pulldown Resistors

For those who've not used them, inputs can be a little fussy. They expect a logical high (voltage above about 2.2v) or logical low (voltage below about 0.8v). But what if, as we have, you've put a switch to one of those voltages? What happens to the voltage when the switch is open and the line isn't connected to anything?

The answer, quite often, is that because the input is quite sensitive (high impedance), your wire plus the input circuitry becomes a radio and random level changes are sent into the input. If they happen to cross the high or low thresholds, that value gets sent.

To avoid this, pullup and pulldown resistors are used. Just as the name suggests, a pullup resistor pulls the input to whatever logical high voltage you've connected it to. A pulldown resistor pulls the input down to whatever logical low voltage you've connected it to. In digital logic, it's very important that your inputs are all at a known state. Like the Arduino, the

Pi has internal pullup resistors. It also has pulldown resistors. These were covered already in Chapter 5, "Meet WiringPi." As a reminder, the pullups are between 50kΩ and 65kΩ and the pulldowns are between 50kΩ and 60kΩ. We'll deal with them in the code.

Note   The logic voltages are approximations based on similar Broadcom products, as reported by this website: `http://www.mosaic-industries.com/embedded-systems/microcontroller-projects/raspberry-pi/gpio-pin-electrical-specifications`.

The Pi foundation has not officially documented these values. One of the great frustrations with the Raspberry Pi is a lack of formal technical documentation.

Button_Polled

We're ultimately going to write two versions of this program, and both of them are new versions of Larson. We'll start by copying the code over and building a project around it.

The Project

One of the things Geany doesn't do well is move files between projects. We'll just do it with the terminal window. Make sure Geany is closed, then start the terminal. Type `cd ~/projects` and press Return. Then type `mkdir button_polled` and press Return. This will be our new project's directory.

Now type this:

```
cp ./Larson/Larson.cpp ./button_polled/button_polled.cpp.
```

A quick `ls` of the `button_polled` directory should look like this:

```
pi@PiOW:~$ cd projects
pi@PiOW:~/projects$ cp ./Larson/Larson.cpp ./button_polled/button_polled.cpp
pi@PiOW:~/projects$ ls button_polled
button_polled.cpp
pi@PiOW:~/projects$
```

Now we have to create a project in Geany and add `button_polled.cpp` to that project. So choose Project ➤ New and create a project called `button_polled`. Geany will set up the correct directory, not because it's smart about these things, but because we named the project the same thing as the directory. Project created, but it's empty. Next, choose File ➤ Open and select `button_polled.cpp`. It will open in Geany as normal. Now when you save the project, the project will contain `button_polled.cpp`.

One more thing. Like we did in the last chapter, you'll need to set the build flags to include `-l wiringPi` or the project won't build.

Note   As you may have guessed, a .geany file is just a text file that tells Geany what files are in the project and where they're located, along with our build instructions, and a lot of other information. Feel free to look inside, but I don't recommend altering it by hand.

Code Modification

Okay. Project created. Scroll down to the `#includes` and `#defines` section, and add this: `#define button_pin 12`. From now on, we'll use the macro `button_pin` to refer to the pin the button is wired to. This way if you ever want to move the button to a different pin, you can update the software easily. It should look like this:

```
#include <iostream>
#include <wiringPi.h>
#define LEDs 20
#define delaymils 40
#define button_pin 12
```

As always, note the lack of a semicolon in preprocessor macro definitions.

Next, scroll down to main, just after the loop where we initialize the pins, and set the pin as an input, and turn on its pulldown resistor. Like this:

```
pinMode(button_pin,INPUT);
pullUpDnControl(button_pin,PUD_DOWN);
```

The pin initialization section should look like this when you're done:

```
//Initialize Pins.
for (c=0;c<LEDs;c++){
    //cout<<"Setting pin "<<pins[c]<<"to output\n"<<flush;
    pinMode (pins[c],OUTPUT);
    digitalWrite(pins[c],HIGH);
}
pinMode(button_pin,INPUT); //set button_pin's pinmode to input.
pullUpDnControl(button_pin,PUD_DOWN);
```

One more bit of code to change. We need to actually poll the pin. In case this is new to you, polling means reading the pin inside a loop, over and over again. We have a number of loops here, so we can just put it at the top of the main loop for the scanner. You may have already seen the disadvantage of putting it there, but I'm making a point that will become obvious when we run the program.

Scroll down to the loop forever that begins while (true) and add the following lines:

```
if((bool)digitalRead(button_pin)){
cout<< "Button is Pressed" << endl;
}
```

If the button is pressed when we reach this part of the loop, we'll print a message to the terminal window. The beginning of the main loop should look like this:

```
while(true){
        if((bool)digitalRead(button_pin)){
            cout<< "Button is Pressed" << endl;
        }
```

That's it. Those are all the mods we have to do. Go ahead and build the project and execute it. The Larson Scanner should work as it did before, and if you press the button, you should the message on the screen that it's been pressed. Rocket science this is not. Hint. Hold the button down for about a second and a half. Here's where I make that point I was talking about earlier.

If you hadn't seen the glaring defect in using the main loop for polling, you've certainly seen it now. The outermost loop in main() only cycles every 1.6 seconds, assuming a delaymils of 40. After all, 40ms times 40 (one full cycle of the scanner) is 1600ms, or 1.6 seconds. Polling *always* has this problem. If the system gets up to something else, if your code gets delayed by something else, the polling won't happen until it's done. There are times when this is the right thing to do, when you're dealing with a system that runs in real-time, like Arduino, or even more so: assembly language programs on Arduino or similar platforms. In Linux, there's no way to know when the program will poll next. There's a better way, and I'll show it to you right after the full source code for button_poll, which follows.

The Code

```
/*
 * button_polled
 *
 * Copyright 2017 Jim Strickland <jrs@jamesrstrickland.com>
 *
 * Standard GNU boilerplate:
 * This program is free software; you can redistribute it
 * and/or modify it under the terms of the GNU General Public
 * License as published by the Free Software Foundation;
 * either version 2 of the License, or (at your option) any
 * later version.
 *
 * This program is distributed in the hope that it will be
 * useful, but WITHOUT ANY WARRANTY; without even the implied
 * warranty of MERCHANTABILITY or FITNESS FOR A PARTICULAR PURPOSE.
```

```
 * See the GNU General Public License for moredetails.
 *
 * You should have received a copy of the GNU General Public
 * License along with this program; if not, write to the Free Software
 * Foundation, Inc., 51 Franklin Street, Fifth Floor, Boston,
 * MA 02110-1301, USA.
 *
 */

/*
 * button_polled
 * This project is, in most respects, a duplicate of  Larson(memorial)
 * scanner project, save that it connects a
 * momentary switch between BCM12 and the LED drive positive
 * rail. I'll call the changes out where they appear.
 */

/* Iostream gives us cin and cout, which we might need for * debugging.
 * WiringPi is the star of this show, the software interface to the GPIO pins.
 * We define LEDs as 20, both to set the index of the pins
 * array, and as the maximum index value of the loop that reads it.
 * Likewise delaymils is a constant value of how many
 * milliseconds to wait between changing LEDs.
 */
#include <iostream>
#include <wiringPi.h>
#define LEDs 20
#define delaymils 40

/* New for button_polled: button_pin is the BCM pin number that
 * our button is connected to. This way it can be changed easily.
 */
 #define button_pin 12

/*
 * We're only using one namespace in this program, so it's safe
 * to set this program's default namespace to std.
 */
using namespace std;

/*
 * There's no good reason to use an object here, so we'll use a
 * global variable instead. This is the array that maps the pin
 * numbers in the order they're plugged into the LED arrays to
 * its own index value (from 0 to LEDs.)
 */
```

```
int pins[LEDs]={2,3,4,14,15,18,17,27,22,23,24,10,9,11,25,8,7,1,0,5};

/*
 * Main()
 * Parameters: none
 * Returns: an integer to tell the system its exit status.
 *
 * How it works:
 * -------------
 * Initialize the integer c at zero. C will be a counter. This
 * isn't really necessary, since it's initialized in the for
 * loop below, but it's good practice.
 *
 * Initialize WiringPi
 * Call the wiringPiSetupGpio() function. This function
 * configures the program's interface with the WiringPi/GPIO
 * system. Critically, itsets it up to use the Broadcom GPIO
 * numbers instead of earlier WiringPi specific pin numbers,
 * physical pin numbers, or anything else.
 * New for button_polled: initialize button_pin as an input,
 * and turn onthe pin's pulldown resistor.
 *
 * Initialize pins
 * In a for loop, we set all the pins to output mode and high.
 * We're using them for output.
 * Note Bene: We are switching the //low// or cathode side of each LED.
 * When the GPIO is //HIGH//, the LED is //off// Only when the GPIO is
 * //LOW// does current flow. So we set them all high at
 * initialization to turn all the LEDs off.
 *
 * Loop Forever scanning from low to high and high to low.
 *         Scan Low to High LED #. Starting with LED 0,
 *             turn the LED on,
 *             wait delaymils,
 *             then turn the previous LED off.
 *
 *         Scan High to Low by LED number.
 *             Switch the current LED on,
 *             Wait delaymils,
 *             then switch the previous LED off.
 *
 * We'll never reach the return(0).
 */
```

```
int main(void){
    int c=0;
    //Initialize WiringPi.
    wiringPiSetupGpio();

    //Initialize Pins.
    for (c=0;c<LEDs;c++){
        //cout<<"Setting pin "<<pins[c]<<"to output\n"<<flush;
        pinMode (pins[c],OUTPUT);
        digitalWrite(pins[c],HIGH);
    }
    pinMode(button_pin,INPUT); //set button_pin's pinmode to input.
    pullUpDnControl(button_pin,PUD_DOWN);

    //Loop forever, switching the LEDs on and off in sequence.
    while(true){
        if((bool)digitalRead(button_pin)){
            cout<< "Button is Pressed" << endl;
        }
        //loop from 0 to LEDs - "scan" from low LED # to high.
        for (c=0;c<LEDs;c++){
            //cout << "switching" << pins[c] <<"\n"<< flush;
            digitalWrite(pins[c],LOW);
            delay(delaymils);
            if (c>0) digitalWrite(pins[c-1],HIGH);
        }

        //loop from LEDs to 0 - scan from high LED # to low.
        for (c=LEDs-1;c>=0;c--){
            //cout << "switching" << pins[c] <<"\n"<< flush;
            digitalWrite(pins[c],LOW);
            delay(delaymils);
            if (c<LEDs)digitalWrite(pins[c+1],HIGH);
        }
    }
    return 0;
}
```

Button_Interrupt

Interrupts, as I mentioned in Chapter 5, "Meet WiringPi," are different. In a traditional computing environment like Arduino, where your program has full control over the processor while it's running, an interrupt is a hardware

223

signal that causes the processor to stop running the code it's running and jump to a specific address called an interrupt vector. It runs that code, then jumps back, usually within a few milliseconds.

It's more complicated in Linux (everything's more complicated in a multiuser, multitasking operating system), but WiringPi gives us interrupts that look, on the face of them, like the real thing. They'll solve our problems with button_polled nicely.

The Project

You can probably guess how we'll create the project for button_interrupt. Pretty much the same way as we created button_polled, except we'll combine the "create a directory" and "copy the file over" steps into one. Close Geany.

Go ahead and open a terminal window. Make sure you're in the projects directory with cd ~/projects . Now we'll use cp, the copy command, and a flag I've not shown you before, -r, to duplicate the whole directory. The -r flag does for cp what it does for rm: tells the command to recurse, that is, to go into any subdirectories and process them the same way. So cp -r says "copy this directory and everything in it." So if we type cp -r button_polled button_interrupt, we'll have everything copied over. We will want to go in and rename the new copy of button_polled to button_interrupt, so we don't confuse the heck out of ourselves later. Here's what all that looks like.

```
pi@PiOW:~$ cd ~/projects
pi@PiOW:~/projects$ cp -r button_polled button_interrupt
pi@PiOW:~/projects$ cd button_interrupt
pi@PiOW:~/projects/button_interrupt$ ls button_polled  button_polled.cpp
pi@PiOW:~/projects/button_interrupt$ rm button_polled
pi@PiOW:~/projects/button_interrupt$ mv button_polled.cpp button_interrupt.cpp
pi@PiOW:~/projects/button_interrupt$ ls button_interrupt.cpp
pi@PiOW:~/projects/button_interrupt$
```

Once that's done, go ahead and create a project called `button_interrupt` and add `button_interrupt.cpp` to it the same way you did last time.

Modifying the Code

We need to add a #define the debounce time in milliseconds. It looks like this: #define `button_debounce_delay` 100. Here is the code.

```
#include <iostream>
#include <wiringPi.h>

#define LEDs 20
#define delaymils 40

/* Set the button pin to 12. Also define the debounce delay. */

#define button_pin 12
#define button_debounce_delay 100 //milliseconds
```

Remember how I said the physical switch could bounce, and that your finger can chatter? The interrupts in WiringPi are fast enough to pick that up. (Polling is too, but only with a very short, tight loop, unlike the one we used in `button_polled`.) We could easily wind up with far more presses than we want, and if they did something important, that'd be a problem. There's an added wrinkle. If another interrupt comes in while your interrupt service routine (ISR) is running, your ISR may be called from the beginning again.

Debouncing

The solution is called *debouncing*. It's a really simple concept. If you know that meaningful button presses have to be a certain amount of time apart, make sure that presses closer together aren't read. There are two ways to do this. The traditional electronics way is with a capacitor and (often) a resistor. The resistor limits the current available to charge the capacitor, and the capacitor only conducts the voltage it's charged to. Essentially, a resistor-capacitor pair is an electronic time delay.

225

With microcontrollers and microprocessors, it's even easier. Just put a delay in the code and ignore the interrupt if it happens faster than that. Traditionally in Arduino code, you can also call `nointerrupts()` to disable (or mask) interrupts while your ISR is running. There's no provision for this in WiringPi directly. WiringPi remembers one additional interrupt and handles it when the ISR completes. Interrupts after the first one are ignored.

In order to debounce the circuit, we'll need to keep track of the time between button presses. Since the ISR is not running between presses, this needs to be a global variable. We know `millis()` returns an unsigned 32-bit integer (`uint32_t`), so that's what our global needs to be too. While we're at it, let's go ahead and declare an integer for how many times the button's been pressed. But there's a catch.

The compiler does a lot of stuff behind the scenes, including caching of variables. Since we're calling the ISR externally, the caching may not be up to date when the ISR runs, which means our variable may not have been updated the next time we read it. It's true that it may work. In fact, in the prototype for this code, it did work. Still, having variables that may not be up to date is no way to run a program.

To solve this, we need to tell the compiler that this variable may be updated any time, by means it may not know about, and that it shouldn't optimize the variable. To do this, We declare it `volatile`. Like this.

```
volatile int button_presses=0;
volatile uint32_t last_time_interrupt_fired=0;
```

Now the compiler knows how we're going to use these variables and will set them up accordingly. There will be some code in the ISR that uses these variables to actually do the debouncing, although you can probably see how it's going to work. We've also set `last_time_interrupt_fired` to a known value. Zero. Always important.

You probably noticed I define `button_debounce_delay` as 100ms in the macro. Why 100ms? Because in my tests, I was not able to press the button faster than that, even tightening my forearm until it shook and pressing the button on each shake. Your hands may be faster. Feel free to set the `debounce_delay` shorter if you find you can push the button fast enough that it misses interrupts.

A Quick Aside About Variable Types

You may have noticed that I tend to assert explicit types (`uint32_t`) rather than using the normal declarations (unsigned int, unsigned long int, etc.). This habit comes from Arduino, where the length of an `int` in bits is different between platforms. By declaring "I want a 32-bit, unsigned integer, dang it," I get the number of bits I expect every time.

The Interrupt Service Routine

As long as we're talking about the Interrupt Service Routine (ISR), let's go ahead and write it. Like they've undoubtedly told you in the Arduino world, an ISR needs to be short and sweet—interrupt, do some small amount of work, and then return. If we dilly dally too long in the ISR, we may miss additional interrupts when they happen. How does five lines strike you?

```
void button_ISR(void){
    uint32_t time_since_last_interrupt=millis()-last_time_interrupt_fired;
    last_time_interrupt_fired=millis();

    if (time_since_last_interrupt >button_debounce_delay){
        cout<<"Time Since Last Interrupt:"<<time_since_last_interrupt<<endl;
        cout<<"Button Pressed "<<++button_presses<<" Times."<<endl;
    }
}
```

An ISR takes no arguments and returns nothing. Anything else won't compile, so we pass it a void as its arguments and declare it as a void type for its return variable.

Next, we declare another uint32_t to hold a time value and set it to the difference between last_time_interrupt_fired and millis(), which is the total time since the program started.

If time_since_last_interrupt is greater than button_debounce_ delay, we print the value of time_since_last_interrupt. We also print the value of button_presses, but the sneaky ++ preceding that variable name means "increment this variable by 1 beforehand."

Main()

The first new thing Main needs to do is initialize last_time_interrupt_ fired to something sensible. Like the current value of millis(). Go ahead and add this line to main, right underneath wiringPiSetupGpio().

```
last_time_interrupt_fired=millis();
```

Pin initialization is exactly the same, so we don't have to touch it. We do need to hook the ISR up, however, and we should do that *after* the pins are initialized, so the interrupt doesn't fire immediately because the pin happened to be set high from whatever happened before button_ interrupt ran. You always want your pins in a known state before you hook an interrupt to one of them. It can be hard to see and harder to track down why an interrupt is firing spuriously if you don't. Here's the ISR hookup line.

```
wiringPiISR(button_pin,INT_EDGE_FALLING,&button_ISR);
```

What does it all mean? Well, we're calling the wiringPiISR function, which will do the hooking up for us. We pass it the pin the button is connected to, tell it we want it to activate when the pin falls from logical high to logical low, and that button_ISR is the interrupt service routine.

Why INT_EDGE_FALLING? When you press the button and *let go of it*, two events happen. There's a rising edge, and a falling edge. In this case, it's a matter of personal preference which one to choose, and I chose the falling edge. If it's important to catch the rising edge (say, you want to know when the button is first touched and it doesn't matter if it's held down), then you'd hook it to INT_EDGE_RISING. If you want two interrupts per button press, you can hook it to INT_EDGE_BOTH, and the interrupt will fire on the rising and the falling edge both, in case you wanted to time the length of the button press or something.

Next, scroll down to the while(true) loop and cut these lines out.

```
if((bool)digitalRead(button_pin)){
    cout<< "Button is Pressed" << endl;
}
```

And we're done. When you run the program, you should get the usual Larson Scanner. Pressing the button, no matter how fast you move your finger, should get you output for each press. The output should look something like this. Feel free to try and press the button and let up on it in less than 104ms.

```
Time Since Last Interrupt:5310
Button Pressed 1 Times.
Time Since Last Interrupt:999
Button Pressed 2 Times.
Time Since Last Interrupt:2135
Button Pressed 3 Times.
Time Since Last Interrupt:5476
Button Pressed 4 Times.
Time Since Last Interrupt:247
Button Pressed 5 Times.
Time Since Last Interrupt:104
Button Pressed 6 Times.
Time Since Last Interrupt:113
Button Pressed 7 Times.
Time Since Last Interrupt:118
Button Pressed 8 Times.
Time Since Last Interrupt:122
Button Pressed 9 Times.
Time Since Last Interrupt:127
Button Pressed 10 Times.
```

The Code

As always, here's the complete code, in case some of the modifications weren't clear.

```
/*
 * button_interrupt.cpp
 *
 * Copyright 2017 Jim Strickland <jrs@jamesrstrickland.com>
 *
 * Standard GNU boilerplate:
 * This program is free software; you can redistribute it and/
 * or modify it under the terms of the GNU General Public
 * License as published by the Free Software Foundation;
 * either version 2 of the License, or (at your option)
 * any later version.
 *
 * This program is distributed in the hope that it will be
 * useful, but WITHOUT ANY WARRANTY; without even the implied
 * warranty of MERCHANTABILITY or FITNESS FOR A PARTICULAR
 * PURPOSE. See the GNU General Public License for more details.
 *
 * You should have received a copy of the GNU General Public
 * License along with this program; if not, write to the Free
 * Software Foundation, Inc., 51 Franklin Street, Fifth Floor, Boston,
 * MA 02110-1301, USA.
 *
 */

/*
 * button_interrupt
 * This program is derived from button_polled and Larson.cpp,
 * and is used to demonstrate WiringPi's interrupt functionality.
 * Most of the button_polled code has been replaced.
 */

/* Iostream gives us cin and cout, which we might need for debugging.
 * WiringPi is the star of this show, the software interface to the GPIO pins.
 * We define LEDs as 20, both to set the index of the pins array,
 * and as the maximum index value of the loop that reads it.
 * Likewise delaymils is a constant value of how many
 * milliseconds to wait between changing LEDs.
 */
```

```
#include <iostream>
#include <wiringPi.h>

#define LEDs 20
#define delaymils 40

/* Set the button pin to 12. Also define the debounce delay. */

#define button_pin 12
#define button_debounce_delay 100 //milliseconds

/* Define a static int to hold the number of button presses,
 * and a 32-bit unsigned integer to hold the time value of the
 * last time the interrupt fired. This is for debouncing.
 */
volatile int button_presses=0;
volatile uint32_t last_time_interrupt_fired=0;

/*
 * We're only using one namespace in this program, so it's safe
 * to set this program's default namespace to std.
 */
using namespace std;

/*This is the Interrupt Service Routine that will be called
 * when we press the button. It takes no parameters and returns
 * nothing, as must all ISRs.
 *
 * How it works:
 * ------------
 * First, we declare another 32-bit unsigned integer to hold
 * of millis(), since we'll use the value twice and we'd prefer
 * it didn'tchange. We store the value of millis() minus the
 * value of the last_time_interrupt_fired static unsigned 32- bit integer in it.
 * Next, we update last_time_interrupt_fired with the current value of millis().
 * If time_since_last_interrupt is greater than the button_
 * debounce_delay,which is a preprocessor macro of some number
 * of milliseconds, then print a message on the screen and exit.
 * If not, just exit.
 */
void button_ISR(void){
    uint32_t time_since_last_interrupt=millis()-last_time_interrupt_fired;
    last_time_interrupt_fired=millis();

    if (time_since_last_interrupt >button_debounce_delay){
        cout<<"Time Since Last Interrupt:"<<time_since_last_interrupt<<endl;
        cout<<"Button Pressed "<<++button_presses<<" Times."<<endl;
    }
}
```

```
/*
 * There's no good reason to use an object here, so we'll use a
 * global variable instead. This is the array that maps the pin
 * numbers in the order they're plugged into the LED arrays to
 * its own index value (from 0 to LEDs.)
 */
int pins[LEDs]={2,3,4,14,15,18,17,27,22,23,24,10,9,11,25,8,7,1,0,5};

/*
 * Main()
 * Parameters: none
 * Returns: an integer to tell the system its exit status.
 *
 * How it works:
 * -------------
 * Initialize the integer c at zero. C will be a counter. This
 * isn't really necessary, since it's initialized in the for
 * loop below, but it's good practice.
 *
 * Initialize WiringPi
 * Call the wiringPiSetupGpio() function. This function
 * configures the program's interface with the WiringPi/GPIO
 * system. Critically, it sets it up to use the Broadcom GPIO
 * numbers instead of earlier WiringPi specific pin numbers,
 * physical pin numbers, or anything else.
 *
 * Initialize pins
 * In a for loop, we set all the pins to output mode and high.
 * We're using them for output.
 * Note Bene: We are switching the //low// or cathode side of each LED.
 * When the GPIO is //HIGH//, the LED is //off// Only when the
 * GPIO is //LOW// does current flow. So we set them all high
 * at initialization to turn all the LEDs off.
 *
 * Loop Forever scanning from low to high and high to low.
 *         Scan Low to High LED #. Starting with LED 0,
 *             turn the LED on,
 *             wait delaymils,
 *             then turn the previous LED off.
 *
 *         Scan High to Low by LED number.
 *             Switch the current LED on,
 *             Wait delaymils,
 *             then switch the previous LED off.
 *
 * We'll never reach the return(0).
 */
```

```
int main(void){
    int c=0;
    //Initialize WiringPi.
    wiringPiSetupGpio();

    //Initialize interrupt timer variable.
    last_time_interrupt_fired=millis();

    //Initialize Pins.
    for (c=0;c<LEDs;c++){
        //cout<<"Setting pin "<<pins[c]<<"to output\n"<<flush;
        pinMode (pins[c],OUTPUT);
        digitalWrite(pins[c],HIGH);
    }
    pinMode(button_pin,INPUT); //set button_pin's pinmode to input.
    pullUpDnControl(button_pin,PUD_DOWN); //turn the pin's pullup/pulldown off

    //Hook up button_ISR as an interrupt service routine on button_pin.
    wiringPiISR(button_pin,INT_EDGE_FALLING,&button_ISR);

    //Loop forever switching the LEDs on and off in sequence.
    while(true){

        //loop from 0 to LEDs - "scan" from low LED # to high.
        for (c=0;c<LEDs;c++){
            //cout << "switching" << pins[c] <<"\n"<< flush;
            digitalWrite(pins[c],LOW);
            delay(delaymils);
            if (c>0) digitalWrite(pins[c-1],HIGH);
        }

        //loop from LEDs to 0 - scan from high LED # to low.
        for (c=LEDs-1;c>=0;c--){
            //cout << "switching" << pins[c] <<"\n"<< flush;
            digitalWrite(pins[c],LOW);
            delay(delaymils);
            if (c<LEDs)digitalWrite(pins[c+1],HIGH);
        }
    }
    return 0;
}
```

Conclusion

In this chapter, we explored reading input both by polling and by using WiringPi's interrupt service. We used this knowledge to add a button to the Larson (Memorial) Scanner project and wrote two programs, one that polls the button, and one that reads it via the WiringPi interrupt. We learned two more ways to treat the Raspberry Pi like an Arduino. But the Pi is not an Arduino. It has a complex, multiprocessing operating system (Raspbian) between our code and the "bare metal" of the system chip. So in the next chapter, we'll dig into running multiple processes and how to code them.

CHAPTER 7

One Pi, Multiple Processes

Up until now, we've been focusing on getting you up to speed in Linux enough to be comfortable using Raspbian, and getting you up to speed in WiringPi enough to do things you already knew how to do with Arduino. Here's where those two paths merge. From here on, we'll be doing things with the Raspberry Pi that you can't easily do with Arduino without adding a lot of (expensive) shields or buying a (somewhat expensive) Arduino Yun. The first of those things is multitasking.

Up until now, we've been treating the Pi like we treat an Arduino Uno. Run this program. Pick up interrupts. Run as fast as you can. Run forever until you're powered off. We can do that. It's perfectly reasonable, but in the background the Pi has had a lot more going on. It's been keeping track of what WiFi networks are available. It's been our development environment. And so on. The Pi, like all modern desktop computers, is a multitasking machine, and Linux is a multitasking operating system.

I'm not going to go into a lot of depth as to how that works, but a quick overview might be helpful. To start with, we need to understand processes, and what happens to them, a little better.

© James R. Strickland 2018
J. R. Strickland, *Raspberry Pi for Arduino Users*,
https://doi.org/10.1007/978-1-4842-3414-3_7

Processes

A process is, essentially, a program being run and the resources that are allocated to it. You can think of any Arduino sketch, running on an Arduino Uno, as a process, the one and only process on the Arduino. Interrupts interrupt the existing code stream (you could think of it as a thread and not be far wrong) and activate a different one temporarily, then return back to the original code stream. If loop() ever ended, the process would terminate, and the Arduino would sit there doing nothing at all.

Linux processes are the same, more or less, but how they get those resources is radically different. Linux processes get all their resources from the Linux kernel. The kernel gives the process its memory on request and handles all requests for memory access. The kernel controls access to all the peripherals—the keyboard, the mouse, the screen, etc.—and allows (or doesn't allow) access to any given program, based on its security profile (file permissions and whether it's running as root). Most interesting to us at this point, the kernel also determines *when* and *how long* any given process gets to use the CPU core, or cores, if you have a multi-core Pi. This is called the scheduler.

Scheduling

If we were writing an operating system with a scheduler on the Arduino, we might put the scheduler in an ISR (ISR1) and hook the interrupt line to a clock so it fires perhaps every ten milliseconds. We then load two other sketches into memory (sketch A and sketch B) and start the first one.

After a hundredth of a second, the clock fires the interrupt. ISR1 wakes up, tells the CPU to push all its internal registers being used by sketch A out into memory, then jumps to sketch B. A hundredth of a second later, the clock fires the interrupt again, and we switch back to sketch A the same way. Congratulations, we've invented preemptive multitasking. (Cooperative multitasking, now mostly extinct, let individual programs tell the system when it could switch tasks/processes. Which was fine until one of those programs hung, when it hung the whole system. Classic MacOS did this.)

Cooperative multitasking is great. Splitting the processor between the two processes evenly is great (and the basis, roughly, of real-time operating systems), except that sketch A is reading a water level indicator, and we're polling that indicator far faster than it's capable of changing. Half our cycles are being wasted. So we hook the water level indicator up to another interrupt and hook *that* interrupt to an ISR (ISR2) that sets a flag on process A when it fires. The next time ISR1 fires, it reads that flag. If it's false, ISR1 doesn't wake sketch A up. If ISR2 has fired and the flag is true, the next time ISR1 fires, it will wake sketch A up, read the data from the sensor, and everything proceeds as normal. That's great, because it frees compute resources for sketch B, except when sketch A wakes up. Above all, we keep the CPU busy, and we switch contexts (sketches) fast enough that the user isn't really aware of it.

Now we have a preemptive multitasking scheduler. We could come up with ways to enforce whose memory is whose, so sketches don't interfere with each other. Ideally the CPU would have a protected area of memory to put the scheduler in and we could keep the memory table in there too. While we're at it, we could (if the CPU supported it) come up with ways to swap memory in and out of the memory map from another device (probably a drive of some kind, or an SD card). If we added graphics control, network protocols, and a lot of other things…well, we'd pretty much have a kernel that does what the Linux kernel does.

So okay. Linux runs multiple processes at the same time. If you have a multicore Pi, it can *literally* run multiple processes at the same time, one on each core. Otherwise you're switching between at least two (dozens, really) of processes including the kernel itself. Switching is very fast. What does that buy us for designing projects on the Raspberry Pi?

How about two Larson Scanners at the same time? Interesting, yes? Let's make that happen.

Designing Larson_Multiprocess

What we want is for each array of ten LEDs to scan independently. We could split the program in half, effectively, and run it twice. In fact, when I first developed this project, I did exactly that. But there's an easier way. We'll use the Linux fork() command.

Fork

According to the man page (man fork), the fork function is a member of the unistd.h, the POSIX standard library. POSIX, in case you wondered, is an IEEE standard defining how UNIX and UNIX-like operating systems' resources are called by programs. It makes porting programs from one UNIX-like platform to another much, much easier if the program was written to go through POSIX for its interaction with the operating system.

Note   Don't let the TLAs (three letter acronyms) intimidate you. An API (Application Programming Interface) is just a series of functions that let you use the resources the operating system in your programs. The wiringPi library provides the WiringPi API. The Arduino core provides the Arduino API. We've been using APIs right along.

What fork() does is simple. Make a nearly exact copy of *this* process. Copy this process's memory and whatnot to the new one, then start the new process at the same point in the program. Both processes are running at the same time (again, literally if you have multiple cores, whereas they only appear to with a single core).

The differences are that the new process is a child of the first one, and that it has its own process ID. There are other, more subtle differences that you can read about in man fork. These are the ones that are important to us right now. Remember how systemd started all those other processes, or how the bash shell starts a process for at least some of its more complicated commands? Fork, frequently with additional stuff, is how it's done. We know how to start the new process. What else do we need?

Well, if we're going to have two scans running at the same time in two separate processes, and if they all start out with the same program, we'll have to have two versions of the scan code, so each one can scan with only half the LEDs. But let's face it, it's much easier to cut that code out of main() and make it into a function, and then just call it twice with different settings.

The original Larson.cpp scan code made a few assumptions that aren't true anymore: that we always start with the 0th LED and end with the one at LEDs -1. For two scanners, we'll need to change those. Also, the dual Larson Scanner looks better if the two "eyes" aren't both scanning left to right at the same time. For aesthetic purposes, we'll have them start at opposite ends of the LED arrays.

Right. Make scan into a function, use fork(), for which we'll need uinstd.h. Anything else? Well...there is one thing. One of Larson.cpp's deficiencies is that if you quit Larson by pressing Ctrl+C on the Geany running window, it leaves the LEDs on. What's actually happening there?

Signals

Pressing Ctrl+C tells the Geany window to interrupt, which causes it to close. When it closes, it takes its child, our program, with it. Specifically, Ctrl+C causes bash to send a SIGINT signal to the Geany window's process, and the Geany window process forwards that signal to its children. When our process, running Larson.cpp, gets that signal, it terminates right away, and whatever LEDs were switched on, stay on.

It'd be nice if we could have Larson_multiprocess clean up after itself before it terminates by turning all the LEDs off, but we have no way of knowing what Larson will be doing when that SIGINT is coming. There's no way to poll for it. If that sounds like a job for an interrupt service routine, you're *exactly* right. Signals are the UNIX/Linux equivalent to interrupts, and signal handlers are the equivalent of ISRs. (WiringPi is actually doing some fakery in its interrupts. I'll cover that in the next chapter.) By default, SIGINT tells the process to exit, and (if it's not hung), it will. We can trap that signal with a signal handler. We can have our program turn off all the LEDs and exit gracefully. We could even have the program trap and ignore the signal completely, but let's not. If we're going to mess with signals, there's another library we'll need. Unsurprisingly, it's called csignal.

Note   Libraries that are part of the C/C++ standard don't have .h at the end. Libraries that aren't (such as wiringPi.h, unistd.h, and any libraries you create) must. An .h file defines prototypes for all the functions in the library, and will have the needed #include for the library itself built in.

Okay. Move scan to a function so we can operate both LED arrays separately. Fork to start a process for the second array of LEDs. Add a signal handler so we turn off the LEDs and exit gracefully. Add csignals.h and unstd.h. That sounds like a plan to me. Let's get started.

Code Changes

Make a copy of Larson.cpp and create a new project with it called Larson_multiprocess.

New #includes

First, let's get the #includes taken care of. Just add #include <csignal> and #include <unistd.h> somewhere in the includes. I grouped my standard libraries and nonstandard libraries together. You don't have to.

You don't even have to put them all at the top, but it's easier to find them up there.

```
#include <iostream>
#include <csignal>
#include <wiringPi.h>
#include <unistd.h>
#define LEDs 20
#define delaymils 40
```

New Global Variables

The namespace and pins[] array are unchanged, but we do need to declare another global variable. As with #includes, I like to keep global variable declarations together. We need a boolean. This will be the variable that our signal handler switches to false when we get a SIGINT. It needs to be volatile for exactly the same reasons the ISR's globals did. So here are the globals as they are now. We need to initialize it as true. The reason for this will become clear shortly.

```
int pins[LEDs]={2,3,4,14,15,18,17,27,22,23,24,10,9,11,25,8,7,1,0,5};
volatile bool running=true;
```

Scan Function

Next, we need to split the scan code out of main() and make it more flexible. Just cut everything from while(true){ to the end of that loop } out of main and paste it under the global variable declarations.

It will need a function declaration. We'll call it scan(). It returns nothing, so we'll make it a void function. It needs to be able to work between arbitrary start and end points, and it needs to be able to start at either end of the LED array. We could pass scan() the start and end points explicitly, but let's just pass it a boolean that tells it whether it's running

241

the low-order LEDs (0-10) or the high-order LEDs (11-20). Let's pass it a second so it knows whether to start at the low end or the high end of its LED array too. That looks like this:

```
void scan(bool low_order_LEDs,bool start_low){
```

Variables and Setup

We need a few more variables. Three integers and a boolean, to be exact. We're using c the same way we did in main. We'll add localLEDs, which will be the highest LED we can use (plus one), and localzero, which will be the lowest LED we can use. We'll add a boolean called localstart_low, which we'll initialize to the parameter start_low, but clear later once the scan is running. We'll also add some code to set localzero and localLEDs up correctly.

```
int c=0;
int localLEDs;
int localzero;
bool localstart_low=start_low;

if (low_order_LEDs){
    localzero=0;
    localLEDs=(LEDs/2);
}else{
    localzero=(LEDs/2);
    localLEDs=LEDs;
}
```

Logic Changes

Remember how we were looping on while(true) which meant loop forever? Remember how that's the loop we want to stop if we get a SIGINT? Remember I said I'd explain what the running volatile boolean was for? Replace true with running. Now our scan loop will scan forever until our signal handler switches running to false.

```
while(running){
```

Next, we need to handle localstart_low. If it's true, we want to start at localzero and scan up to localLEDs. If it's false, we want to go the other way. If you think about it, our scanning function is really *two* scans: one going from localzero to localLEDs, and one going back. If localstart_ low is false, all we really need to do is skip the first scan (the low to high scan) and start with the second one. So let's wrap the low to high scan in an if-then, switching on localstart_low. But wait. We only want this to happen once, otherwise we'll never scan from low to high. So our if-then becomes an if-then-else. If localstart_low is true, we scan as normal. If it's false, we skip the low-to-high scan, set localstart_low to true, and then do the high-to-low scan. Next time we get to our conditional, localstart_low will be true, and we'll go on scanning as usual. Could this have been done more efficiently? Probably. We could have made the scan function only do one scan per call, but that'd be a lot of recoding and reconceptualizing the program. It's only a demo. This will work.

Finally, make sure you also switch all references to LEDs to localLEDs, and 0 to localzero.

Here's what that looks like.

```
if (localstart_low){
    for (c=localzero;c<localLEDs;c++){
        //cout << "switching" << pins[c] <<"\n"<< flush;
        digitalWrite(pins[c],LOW);
        delay(delaymils);
        if (c>localzero) digitalWrite(pins[c-1],HIGH);
    }
}else{
    localstart_low=TRUE;
}

for (c=localLEDs-1;c>=localzero;c--){
    //cout << "switching" << pins[c] <<"\n"<< flush;
    digitalWrite(pins[c],LOW);
    delay(delaymils);
    if (c<localLEDs)digitalWrite(pins[c+1],HIGH);
}
    }
}
```

SIGINT Handler Function

We also need to add a function to handle the SIGINT signal. Like ISRs, a signal handler is in two parts: the function and the hookup down in the main() function. We're writing the function first. It's a void function, and the csignal library requires that it take an integer parameter for the signal number. If we wanted to, we could make this handler handle many other signals by decoding the signal number and determining what to do from there. SIGINT is a signal 2, in case you wondered.

```
void SIGINT_handler(int signal_number){
    running=false;
}
```

Short, sweet, and to the point. Since we're only hooking it to the SIGINT signal, we don't have to decode signal_number. Just set running to false and exit.

Changes in Main()

Here's where all the groundwork we've laid comes together, which is exactly what's supposed to be in main(). First, we'll hook up the signal handler. That's done with the signal() function, and we pass it the signal number and the signal handler function name. If you suspected that SIGINT is defined in unistd.h, you suspected right. You could use 2 there, but on some systems the signals are numbered differently. Probably not a good habit to get into.

```
int main(void){
    signal(SIGINT,SIGINT_handler);
```

While we're handling system stuff, let's handle the fork here too.

```
    pid_t process_id=fork();
```

There's quite a bit going on in that call. A `pid_t` data type is "system defined data type for process IDs." Defined in `unistd.h`? Yep. It's usually an unsigned integer, but how wide, exactly, can vary a lot. This way is safer. We declare the variable `process_id` and put the `process_id` returned by the `fork()` call in it.

Initialize WiringPi

WiringPi has to be initialized exactly once per process. Since we now have two processes, both of them need to initialize WiringPi, so we let both processes do exactly that.

```
//Initialize WiringPi
wiringPiSetupGpio();
```

Set Up the GPIO Pins

Up until now, both the parent process and the child process have been doing the same things (theoretically) simultaneously. But we only need to initialize the GPIO hardware once. Since fork returns a process ID of 0 to the child process, and the process ID of the child process to the parent process, we can switch on whether the process ID is greater than 0 to know whether this code is running in the parent or the child process.

Let's initialize the GPIO pins from the parent process only, and while we're at it, start the parent process's scan, with the parameters `low_order_` LEDs as true (use the LEDs from 0 to 10) and `start_low` false (start from the highest LED in this group). This will make this process scan from LED 10 to LED 0 the first time, then scan normally after that.

```
if (process_id>0){//parent process If we're in the parent process...

for (int c=0;c<LEDs;c++){
    pinMode (pins[c],OUTPUT);
    digitalWrite(pins[c],HIGH);
}
```

Loop through all the pins from 0 to LEDs-1 and set the pinModes to output. Then set them high (off).

```
scan(true,false);
```

Scan the low-order LEDs (0-10) and do not start low (i.e., start on the highest LED, most likely 10, then scan down to 0).

```
}else{ //child process
    scan(false,true);
}
```

Otherwise (process_id is 0, meaning the code is running on the child process), scan the high-order LEDs (11-20) and start low (LED 11). No matter which process we are, we'll stay in one of these two calls to scan forever unless we catch a SIGINT. If/when that happens, we'll fall out of whichever loop we're in and move to the following code.

Exit Gracefully

If we get here, no matter which process we're running in, we've fallen out of one of the two scan() loops. That should only happen if we've caught a SIGINT, and the signal handler is set to false.

```
for (int c=0;c<LEDs;c++){
    digitalWrite(pins[c],HIGH);
}
```

Turn all the pins off by setting them to HIGH.

```
return 0;
}
```

Return 0 to Linux and exit the program.

Note   As an aside, the only signal we can't trap is a signal 9, SIGKILL. That tells the kernel to "terminate this process no matter what it's doing and no matter what it wants." Ever send a `kill -9 <process id>` to a Linux program from the terminal window? If I told you that kill is a program for sending signals to processes, would it make it clear what that does? We'll mess with that a little once we have `Larson_multiprocess` running.

The Code

As always, here's the full code for this project, replete with my comments.

```
/* Larson_multiprocess.cpp
 *
 * Copyright 2017 Jim Strickland <jrs@jamesrstrickland.com>
 *
 * Standard GNU boilerplate:
 * This program is free software; you can redistribute it and/
 * or modify it under the terms of the GNU General Public
 * License as published by the Free Software Foundation;
 * either version 2 of the License, or (at your option) any
 * later version.
 *
 * This program is distributed in the hope that it will be
 * useful, but WITHOUT ANY WARRANTY; without even the implied
 * warranty of MERCHANTABILITY or FITNESS FOR A PARTICULAR
 * PURPOSE.  See the GNU General Public License for more details.
 *
 * You should have received a copy of the GNU General Public
 * License along with this program; if not, write to the Free
 * Software Foundation, Inc., 51 Franklin Street, Fifth Floor,
 * Boston, MA 02110-1301, USA.
 *
 */
```

```
/*
 * Larson_multiprocess
 * This program implements the classic "Larson (memorial)
 * scanner", albeit a 20 pin Raspberry Pi version, with two
 * "eyes," each running in its own pthread It //requires// a Pi
 * with a 40 pin GPIO bus, or it won't call the right pins in wiringPi.
 * Several modifications from Larson.cpp. First, we install a
 * signal handler to turn all the LEDs off when we get an interrupt signal.
 * Next, we split the actual scanning out of main and into a function.
 * It is no longer hardcoded to run forever, only as long as
 * running is true, which it is until a SIGINT is caught. Then
 * we clean up the LEDs and exit.
 */

/* Iostream gives us cin and cout, which we might need for debugging.
 * wiringPi is the star of this show, the software interface to
 * the GPIO pins. pthread.h gives us the Linux thread library.
 * It's included in wiringPi too, so we don't //technically//
 * have to include it here, but it's bad business to depend on
 * declarations in other libraries.
 *
 * We define LEDs as 20, both to set the index of the pins array,
 * and as the maximum index value of the loop that reads it.
 * Likewise delaymils is a constant value of how many milliseconds
 * to wait between changing LEDs.
 */

#include <iostream>
#include <csignal>
#include <wiringPi.h>
#include <unistd.h>
#define LEDs 20
#define delaymils 40

/*
 * We're only using one namespace in this program, so it's safe
 * to set this program's default namespace to std.
 */
using namespace std;
```

```
/*
 * There's no good reason to use an object here, so we'll use a
 * global variable instead. This is the array that maps the pin
 * numbers in the order they're plugged into the LED arrays to
 * its own index value (from 0 to LEDs.)
 */
int pins[LEDs]={2,3,4,14,15,18,17,27,22,23,24,10,9,11,25,8,7,1,0,5};
volatile bool running=true;

/* void scan(bool low_order_LEDs, bool start_low)
 * Parameters:
 *     low_order_LEDs is a boolean that tells scan whether it's
 *         scanning from the 0th LED to 10. If this parameter
 *         is false, we're scanning from LED 10 to LED 20.
 *     start_low is a boolean that tells scan whether to start
 *     at the lowest led and scan up, or the highest led and
 *     scan down.
 *         This only effects the //first// scan.
 * Returns nothing.
 *
 * How it Works:
 * -------------
 * Basically the guts of main() in Larson.cpp, but we have to
 * do some processing of local variables first.
 * Initialize c at 0 for safety.
 *
 * Declare localLEDs and localzero. These are the maximum and
 * minimum LEDs this particular instantiation of scan should
 * scan between.
 *
 * Initialize localstart_low to start_low. If it's false, we
 * start high on the first scan.
 *
 * Set up localzero and localLEDs.
 * If we were passed low_order_LEDs as true,
 *         set localzero to 0 and localLEDs to LEDs divided
 *         by 2. (This value is probably 10, but who knows how
 *         many LEDs those wily users have hooked up?)
 * Otherwise (low_order_LEDs is false),
 *         set localzero to LEDs divided by 2 and localLEDs
 *         to LEDs.
 *
```

```
* Loop as long as running is true. It's set false by the signal handler.
* (This means we may get as much as one full scan between the
* signal being caught and scan exiting. That's ok.)
*           If localstart_low is TRUE
*               Scan Low to High LED #. Starting with localzero,
*                   turn the LED on,
*                   wait delaymils,
*                   then turn the previous LED off.
*           else set localstart_low TRUE.
*               (start_low and localstart_low only effect the
*               first scan.)
*               Scan from high to low
*                   Switch the current LED on,
*                   Wait delaymils,
*                   then switch the previous LED off.
*/
void scan(bool low_order_LEDs,bool start_low){
    int c=0;
    int localLEDs;
    int localzero;
    bool localstart_low=start_low;

    //set up localzero and localLEDs
    if (low_order_LEDs){
        localzero=0;
        localLEDs=(LEDs/2);
    }else{
        localzero=(LEDs/2);
        localLEDs=LEDs;
    }
    while(running){ //loop forever as long as running is true.
        if (localstart_low){
            //if localstart_low is true, loop from localzero to
            // localLEDs - "scan" from low LED # to high.
            for (c=localzero;c<localLEDs;c++){
                //cout << "switching" << pins[c] <<"\n"<< flush;
                digitalWrite(pins[c],LOW);
                delay(delaymils);
                if (c>localzero) digitalWrite(pins[c-1],HIGH);
            }
```

```
        }else{
            //if localstart_low was false, we skipped the low-
            //to-high part of the scan and came here. We only
            //want this to happen on the first scan, so when we
            //GET here, set localstart_low true. Then do the
            //high-to-low part of the scan as usual.
            localstart_low=TRUE;
        }

        //loop from localLEDs to localzero - scan from high LED # to low.
        for (c=localLEDs-1;c>=localzero;c--){
            //cout << "switching" << pins[c] <<"\n"<< flush;
            digitalWrite(pins[c],LOW);
            delay(delaymils);
            if (c<localLEDs)digitalWrite(pins[c+1],HIGH);
        }
    }
}

/* SIGINT_handler
 * Parameters:
 * signal_number, an integer
 * Returns: nothing.
 *
 * How it works
 * -----------
 * Very much like a wiringpiISR interrupt handler, signal_
 * handler iscalled by a system event, namely a signal being
 * raised. In this case we're looking for SIGINT, a macro for
 * the signal we get when ctrl-c is pressed in the geany run window.
 * This handler only fires if SIGINT is raised, so no decoding logic is needed.
 */
void SIGINT_handler(int signal_number){
    running=false;
}

/*
 * Main()
 * Parameters: none
 * Returns: an integer to tell the system its exit status.
 *
```

```
 * How it works:
 * --------------
 * Declare the variable process_id as type pid_t. This is an
 * integer of some kind, but what kind exactly is platform
 * specific. We initialize that variable with a call to fork(),
 * which starts a child process identical to the parent we're
 * in, with all the same variables except process_id. The
 * child's process id is stored in the parent's process_id
 * variable. The child's own process_id variable will be set
 * to 0. Forked processes start at the next
 *
 * Initialize wiringPi. Both the parent and child processes must do this.
 * If process_id is greater than 0, we're the parent process.
 *          Initialize the pins. Only needs to happen once -
 *          there's only one set.
 *          scan the low order LEDs, starting with the highest
 *          one (LED 10, most likely. (low_order_leds true,
 *          start_low false)
 * else
 *          We don't need to initialize the pins again, and we
 *          already initialized wiringPi, so just scan the high
 *          order LEDs starting with the lowest one. (low_order_
 *          leds false, start_low true)
 *
 * Scan only returns if the signal handler sets running to
 * false, so if scan returns, turn all the LEDs off and exit.
 */

int main(void){
    //connect up the signal handler to fire on SIGINT.
    signal(SIGINT,SIGINT_handler);

    //fork the child process and store its PID in process_id on
    //the parent process. The fork() call returns 0 to the
    //child process.
    pid_t process_id=fork();

    //Initialize wiringPi
    wiringPiSetupGpio();

    if (process_id>0){//parent process
            //Initialize Pins.
    for (int c=0;c<LEDs;c++){
```

```
    //cout<<"Setting pin "<<pins[c]<<"to output\n"<<flush;
    pinMode (pins[c],OUTPUT);
    digitalWrite(pins[c],HIGH);
  }
    scan(true,false);
  }else{ //child process
    scan(false,true);
  }
  //If we get here, scan has exited, most likely because the
  //signal handler has set running to false. So turn all the
  //LEDs off and exit.
  for (int c=0;c<LEDs;c++){
    digitalWrite(pins[c],HIGH);
  }
  return 0;
}
```

Running the Program

Click the paper-airplane icon on Geany to run `Larson_multiprocess`. You should get two separate scans starting at the center and moving outward. Got two scans that cross over each other and run through all 20 LEDs? It's not a bug. It's an optical illusion. Put your finger on the line where the two LED arrays meet in the center, and you'll see the true movement of both scans. They should stay more or less in sync, but there aren't any guarantees that they will, since we haven't provided any code for that. What happens on your screen should look like Figure 7-1.

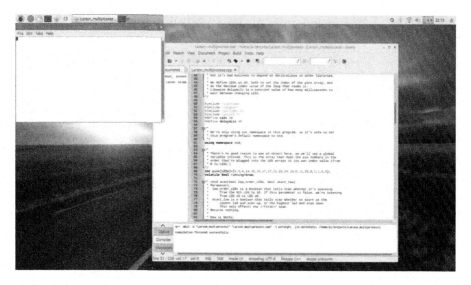

Figure 7-1. *Geany running Larson_multiprocess*

If you move your mouse to the window marked sh (at the top left of the screen in Figure 7-1—yours may be somewhere else), you're talking to the terminal session actually running `Larson_multiprocess`. Click on that window and press Ctrl+C.

The window will go away, and the LED arrays should clear. They may not clear at exactly the same time (they don't on my Pi Zero W, at least) because the two processes receive signals from sh at different times, and just like with the button, each process has to wait for the end of a scan cycle before it checks the running boolean. Is it working? Excellent. Let's break it.

Processes in Linux

Remember how I mentioned the `kill` command for sending signals to processes, and I said I'd get to that later? Now is that time. In the Arduino world we'd just reboot the microcontroller, but that's a little more painful on Raspberry Pi. Plus we might want to keep some of these processes around. Go ahead and restart `Larson_multiprocess` from the Geany Run button. You may have to press it twice.

Listing Running Processes

The first thing we need is to see what we're doing. Let's have a look at our processes, shall we? To do that, we'll need some more UNIX/Linux terminal-window skills.

We'll use a command called ps (process status). Kick off another terminal window and type ps. You should get something like this.

```
pi@PiOW:~$ ps
  PID TTY          TIME CMD
 1380 pts/2    00:00:00 bash
 1522 pts/2    00:00:00 ps
pi@PiOW:~$
```

By default, ps looks at its own bellybutton. So there's ps, on process 1522, and there's the bash shell I called it from, on 1380. Your process IDs will almost certainly be different. Interesting, but not very useful. If you go through the ps man pages (practically a novel from the length), you'll find that to get all the processes owned by this user, you use the -a flag. So ps -a gets you this:

```
pi@PiOW:~$ ps -a
  PID TTY          TIME CMD
  585 tty1     00:00:00 bash
 2217 pts/1    00:00:00 Larson_multipro
 2218 pts/1    00:00:00 Larson_multipro
 2220 pts/2    00:00:00 ps
pi@PiOW:~$
```

Now we're getting somewhere. Those two processes marked Larson_multipro are the ones we created. That's great. Let's kill one. Hint. The child will have a higher number than the parent. In my list of processes, 2218 is the highest process in the list of Larson_multipro. So what signal do we want to send it? Well, SIGINT, obviously, but here's a list of all the signals kill can send. You get it by typing kill -L (capital L).

```
pi@PiOW:~$ kill -L
 1) SIGHUP      2) SIGINT      3) SIGQUIT     4) SIGILL      5) SIGTRAP
 6) SIGABRT     7) SIGBUS      8) SIGFPE      9) SIGKILL    10) SIGUSR1
11) SIGSEGV    12) SIGUSR2    13) SIGPIPE    14) SIGALRM    15) SIGTERM
16) SIGSTKFLT  17) SIGCHLD    18) SIGCONT    19) SIGSTOP    20) SIGTSTP
21) SIGTTIN    22) SIGTTOU    23) SIGURG     24) SIGXCPU    25) SIGXFSZ
26) SIGVTALRM  27) SIGPROF    28) SIGWINCH   29) SIGIO      30) SIGPWR
31) SIGSYS     34) SIGRTMIN   35) SIGRTMIN+1 36) SIGRTMIN+2 37) SIGRTMIN+3
38) SIGRTMIN+4 39) SIGRTMIN+5 40) SIGRTMIN+6 41) SIGRTMIN+7 42) SIGRTMIN+8
43) SIGRTMIN+9 44) SIGRTMIN+10 45) SIGRTMIN+11 46) SIGRTMIN+12 47) SIGRTMIN+13
48) SIGRTMIN+14 49) SIGRTMIN+15 50) SIGRTMAX-14 51) SIGRTMAX-13 52) SIGRTMAX-12
53) SIGRTMAX-11 54) SIGRTMAX-10 55) SIGRTMAX-9  56) SIGRTMAX-8  57) SIGRTMAX-7
58) SIGRTMAX-6 59) SIGRTMAX-5  60) SIGRTMAX-4  61) SIGRTMAX-3  62) SIGRTMAX-2
63) SIGRTMAX-1 64) SIGRTMAX
pi@PiOW:~$
```

There's signal 2, SIGINT, the only one we're trapping in Larson_
multiprocess. So if we type kill -2 2218 or kill -SIGINT 2218 (either
one will work), the child process should exit. It will actually try to turn out
all the LEDs, but since the parent process is still running, the scan will keep
going on the low LEDs.

```
pi@PiOW:~$ kill -SIGINT 2218
pi@PiOW:~$ ps -a
  PID TTY          TIME CMD
  585 tty1     00:00:00 bash
 2217 pts/1    00:00:00 Larson_multipro
 2218 pts/1    00:00:00 Larson_multipro <defunct>
 2254 pts/2    00:00:00 ps
pi@PiOW:~$
```

The ps command now shows that the process is defunct, and you
should have only one "eye" working in the scanner. Go ahead and kill the
other one the same way.

```
pi@PiOW:~$ kill -2 2217
pi@PiOW:~$ ps -a
  PID TTY          TIME CMD
  585 tty1     00:00:00 bash
 2255 pts/2    00:00:00 ps
pi@PiOW:~$
```

Note that with the parent process gone, the defunct child is no longer shown either. If we go the other way and send a SIGINT to the parent, this happens:

```
pi@PiOW:~$ ps -a
  PID TTY          TIME CMD
  585 tty1     00:00:00 bash
 2307 pts/1    00:00:00 Larson_multipro
 2308 pts/1    00:00:00 Larson_multipro
 2322 pts/2    00:00:00 ps
pi@PiOW:~$ kill -2 2307
pi@PiOW:~$ ps -a
  PID TTY          TIME CMD
  585 tty1     00:00:00 bash
 2308 pts/1    00:00:00 Larson_multipro
 2323 pts/2    00:00:00 ps
pi@PiOW:~$
```

The child, with its parent gone, becomes the parent process.

Let's send it a different signal. How about a -9? Go ahead and restart Larson_multiprocess once more.

```
pi@PiOW:~$ ps -a
  PID TTY          TIME CMD
  585 tty1     00:00:00 bash
 2329 pts/1    00:00:00 Larson_multipro
 2330 pts/1    00:00:00 Larson_multipro
 2333 pts/2    00:00:00 ps
pi@PiOW:~$ kill -9 2329
pi@PiOW:~$ ps -a
  PID TTY          TIME CMD
  585 tty1     00:00:00 bash
 2330 pts/1    00:00:00 Larson_multipro
 2334 pts/2    00:00:00 ps
pi@PiOW:~$
```

Note how the parent process disappeared and the child became the parent again, but also note how at least one LED on the low-order (0-10) LEDs is still on. If you don't have any, restart and try again. I want you to see this. SIGKILL ignores any handlers. The kernel just pulls the rug out from under the process. Files get left open, LEDs get left on, and hardware may be left in an unknown state. kill -9 or kill -SIGKILL is a weapon of last resort.

Could you use kill to send signals to processes you don't own? Absolutely, and in fact it's a standard tool for Linux/UNIX system administration, but you'll need to use sudo (remember sudo?), or you won't have permission to send the signal. If you want to try sending SIGKILLs to system components like systemd, I'd suggest waiting until you're done with this book, in case you have to rebuild the SD card.

Conclusion

We've covered a lot of unfamiliar ground in this chapter, and it's really starting to show that the Pi is not just a glorified Arduino. It's a miniature Linux box with GPIO pins. You can do more with it, but there's a lot more complexity under the hood as a result. You might want to reread this chapter and play with signals more, and perhaps read man kill for more details.

You may be starting to realize that UNIX/Linux has three or four ways to do any given thing. It does. UNIX is *old*. Even the Linux kernel is old enough to vote in the United States. The mechanisms things use change over time, and new tools get added, but old ones don't go away, and so on. That's just how Linux and UNIX are. You get used to it.

In the next chapter, we'll look at a similar mechanism for executing two or more code streams at the same time. These are called *threads*.

CHAPTER 8

One Process, Multiple Threads

The ability to add processes, especially to load different applications in them (which you can with commands we didn't talk about last chapter), is a useful capability. But there are some downsides. Getting one process to communicate with another, for example, involves an outside mechanism. You can write to a file and have the second process read that file in, so long as you have some kind of file locking in place, so reads and writes don't happen at the same time. You can use a standard UNIX/Linux tool called a pipe, which looks like a file that is write-only to one process and read-only to the other. There are ways around the communication problem, many well established from the dinosaur UNIX days.

There are other issues. In these times of multi-gigabyte memories, it may seem like a small thing to copy the entire memory footprint of a process to the child process, but it could get very expensive very fast if your parent process has gigabytes of RAM allocated. It may not be obvious that all these functions are kernel-intensive, and that any time you wake up the kernel, you take a performance hit. As you may have guessed from the title of this chapter, there is another way. They're called threads.

© James R. Strickland 2018
J. R. Strickland, *Raspberry Pi for Arduino Users*,
https://doi.org/10.1007/978-1-4842-3414-3_8

Processes and Memory

In order to understand what threads are, we need to understand what's in a process a little better. To do that, in turn we need to understand memory in a virtual memory system like Linux a little better. You don't need to understand the exact anatomical details unless you're doing assembly programming—the compiler and linker take care of most of this for you—but it's helpful to know what's going on.

Linux is, among other things, a virtual memory system. This means that as far as each process is concerned, its memory starts at address 0. The kernel maintains a map of which physical pages of RAM are mapped to which process, and some of those pages may even be stored on the microSD card (in our case on the Pi), but from the process's point of view, it's the only thing running; it is always running, and its addresses are real hardware RAM addresses, just like it would be in the Arduino.

So here's what's in that virtual memory address space. Since Raspbian (as of this writing) is still a 32-bit operating system (even though the CPU cores are 64-bit machines), its processes can be a maximum of 4GiB in size. Few, if any, processes ever get that big, especially on the Pi with its 1GiB of physical RAM, but that's how much address space a process could have.

Kernel Space

Starting at virtual address 0, there can be up to a GiB of kernel space. This memory is part of the kernel itself, and it's where kernel-calling routines are stored. It can't be written to or read from by the process, only called. If it sounds like that would make our process stop and the kernel wake up, you're right. It does. The kernel space in a process is roughly equivalent to the Arduino core—the functions and values the program can call to access hardware.

The Stack

Next is the stack. The compiler determines how big the stack can get, and you can set it in code (look up `getrlimit` and `setrlimit`, if you want to know more about that). The default is several MiBs.

The stack holds some interesting and important things. When you call a function, your previous location in the code is stored in the stack. When your function has local variables, they're stored in the stack. If you write a recursive function that calls itself over and over again until something breaks, what breaks will be the stack. Another good reason not to use function recursion outside academic settings is that once the stack grows, it never shrinks again until the process terminates. The stack begins a random offset from the end of kernel space, and as it expands, it goes from low addresses to higher addresses, or "down," where the top of memory is address 0.

Memory Mapping Segment

If you're using memory mapped file IO (remembering that everything in Linux is a file, more or less), here's where the mapped data will be. When you have a large file or something like a file (a chunk of video memory, perhaps), you can ask the kernel to map it here, and then read and write without making further kernel calls. Search on mmap for more information. Like the stack, the memory mapping segment expands down.

The Heap

The heap is where all the dynamic data structures live. If you've called new (assuming you're writing C++), the memory pointer new returns points to memory in the heap. And so on. In C and C++, most of the memory your program uses will be in the heap. Unlike the stack, the heap expands upward, from high addresses to lower addresses. If the heap and the stack meet, your program will crash.

The BSS Segment

Static members are a special case in C++. They're essentially a class global, so that every object in a given class shares one and only one copy of that member. When you create one, and before you set its value to something, it's stored here. The BSS segment is all zeros and NULLs.

The Data Segment

Another memory section for the explicit handling of static members, the data segment holds the values of statics once they've been set to something.

The Text Segment

Your code—the binary machine code generated by the compiler and linker for your program—lives here.

Threads at Last

Now that we've waded through the basics of what's in a Linux process, it's a lot easier to understand what a thread is. When a process is forked, it copies (at least conceptually) all those different segments to the child. (From the child's perspective, it has a copy of the parent's memory segments. With modern fork() calls, the segments aren't actually copied until the child tries to write to them, but this is handled by the kernel and virtual memory systems, and is invisible to the process itself.)

A thread, by contrast, only has a copy of the stack. All the threads in a process use the same memory mapping, heap, bss, and data segments. Because there's less shifting of memory and fewer kernel calls, they are faster to start and faster to task-switch between. Threads really shine on multicore or multiprocessor systems, where a single process can use more cores and speed up computing.

Whole books have been written about pthreads, the POSIX standard threads we're using here, but the basics are fairly straightforward. I'll show you how to create thread functions, declare thread IDs, create threads, cancel threads, control the flow of the parent process while threads run, and protect memory (variables, objects, etc.) so that threads always get their data in a known state. If you want to know more about threads in C++ and Linux, a good website on the subject is here: `http://www.bogotobogo.com/cplusplus/multithreading_pthread.php`. For good measure, I'll also show how to write the project to use WiringPi's thread mechanism, which is only slightly different.

Thread Functions

As you've already seen many times, I like to declare my functions first, before `main()`, and thread functions are no exception, so we'll cover declaring the functions first. As always with modern C++/C, you can declare a prototype for the function and put the actual function code last. You can also put all the function prototypes in your own `.h` file and include them, and have the prototype declaration check to see if you've pulled in the function's actual code using the C preprocessor. In any case, a `pthread` function must return a `void` pointer and be able to take a `void` pointer for an argument. You can pass any pointer you want as an argument for your thread function, so long as you cast it to a `void` pointer first. Something to bear in mind is that a `pthread` function, like an ISR, must return a pointer to something, even if that something is nothing. As with ISRs, we have to return a `NULL` pointer.

```
void *upper(void *vp){
    scan(false,true);
    return(NULL);
}
```

Looks a lot like a WiringPi ISR, doesn't it? There's a reason for that. Linux doesn't let user space programs touch hardware interrupts. That's what signals are for. Instead, WiringPi hooks our "ISRs" up to a thread that fires the "ISR" at the right time. So the truth is we've already written a multithreaded program, and we didn't even know it.

Thread IDs

As with most things POSIX, there's a custom data type for thread IDs. In this case, it's pthread_t. Usually these happen because different implementations of UNIX and UNIX-like operating systems couldn't agree on a data type. It's an integer, but how long an integer varies depending on the platform. Typically this is done in main(), where the threads are launched.

```
pthread_t upper_thread;
```

Creating Threads

To start a thread with the POSIX thread library (pthreads), you just call pthread_create() with a pointer to the thread's ID number, a pointer to any attributes you want to set on the thread, a call to the function you want to use, and a pointer to any arguments you want to pass that function. The pthread_create() function will return 0 if the thread is created properly, and error codes otherwise. You can throw this data away, but it's a good idea to make sure your threads actually get started, so here's how I do it. If the result of the pthread_create() call is true (i.e., it's not zero or false), throw an error message and return from main with an error message.

```
if(pthread_create(&upper_thread,NULL,upper,NULL)){
    cout<<"Error Creating thread.\n"<<flush;
    return 1;
}
```

Cancelling Threads

Unlike processes, there are lots of ways to terminate threads. The easiest is to terminate the process they're attached to. All the threads go along for the ride. The thread's function can simply exit and reach `return()`. Or the thread can be cancelled. Cancelling a thread is very straightforward: call `pthread_cancel()` with the thread ID.

```
pthread_cancel(upper_thread);
```

Flow Control

It's not really accurate of me to call the process the "parent" process. Threads are not child processes. They're part of the same process. It does get at an important concept, though. The parent thread—the process's original thread—doesn't stop just because we started a thread, or a dozen threads, assuming we don't run out of memory. If the process needs to wait until a given thread is done, instead of writing a delay loop, we can tell the kernel not to schedule the process until the threads exit. This is called blocking, and with pthreads, it's done with the `pthread_join()` function. Joining a thread means that whatever thread called the join will block—not be scheduled to run—until the joined thread exits. You can have join capture the thread's status on exit by passing it yet another pointer to yet another variable, but for brevity and simplicity's sake, we'll just pass it a NULL.

```
pthread_join(lower_thread,NULL);
```

Note   Some platforms require you to pass an attribute to `pthread_create()` to tell the system that this thread can be joined. Raspbian is not one of those platforms.

Protecting Memory: Mutexes

Once upon a time, I built combat robots on a microcontroller with pthreads. I had a sense thread that looked for the enemy robot ahead, another sense thread that looked for the edge of the combat board so the robot didn't fall off, and an action thread that controlled the motors. All three threads shared one variable that they communicated through. If that variable had the value "target acquired," set by the first sense thread, the motor thread was to go straight ahead as fast as possible. If the variable contained "edge detected," from the second sense thread, the motor thread was to stop and back up immediately, lest the robot be disqualified.

You can undoubtedly see the problems I had. If both sense threads wrote at the same time, the value in that variable would be indeterminate. If I added a priority variable so that the edge thread overrode the target acquired thread, it would actually make things worse, since the status value and the priority value might well get out of sync if both sense threads were trying to write at the same time. I could wind up with a high priority message of "enemy detected," even though the edge of the board was detected too. Whether the priority would even be handled correctly is also a question. That robot didn't do very well in combat, because I didn't know that the threads might interrupt each other mid-write.

What that program needed was some way to protect the variables each thread tried to write to, so that they all remained in sync, and they all had determinate values, set by one or the other thread. That's what a mutex, or MUtual Exclusion, does.

A mutex is simply this: a way to set a "lock" on a variable, so that if one thread is reading or writing it, other threads checking the lock can't access the variable until the first thread is done. Mutexes go surprisingly deep into the Linux kernel and have to be supported by the CPU itself, but from our perspective as programmers, they're pretty simple.

Creating Mutexes

To create a mutex, declare a global variable of the type pthread_mutex_t, then pass the address of that variable to the pthread_mutex_init() function to set it up. As always, there's a parameter data structure we could pass through a pointer to pthread_mutex_t. As usual, for brevity, we'll just pass it a NULL:

```
pthread_mutex_t running_lock;
pthread_mutex_init(&running_lock,NULL);
```

Using Mutexes

Nothing is automatic about mutexes. If we touch a global variable from a thread without explicitly checking its mutex, then the mutex doesn't help us. We have to explicitly wrap any access to the variable we want to protect in code to lock and unlock the mutex. The simplest is just that, locking and unlocking. If a thread locks the mutex, and another thread tries to lock the same mutex, the second thread will block—not get scheduled for processor time by the kernel—until the first thread unlocks the mutex.

```
pthread_mutex_lock(&running_lock);
running=false;
pthread_mutex_unlock(&running_lock);
```

In some cases, it might be perfectly fine for the second thread to try the lock, and if it's locked go on and do something else, or perhaps try again later. By now, it's hardly a surprise to find a function for that too. It's called pthread_trylock(); If the mutex is not locked, trylock will lock it.

You have to be careful and make sure that you don't try to unlock an unlocked mutex. The results are undefined, and that's usually bad. Also, some types of mutexes don't check to make sure that the thread trying to unlock them is the thread that locked them. You need to keep straight for yourself who locked what and whether the mutex was unlocked or not. Mutexes can hang threads if you have a thread lock a mutex and die, and the other threads are trying to mutex_lock() the mutex and waiting until it's unlocked. Worse is a situation, where your second thread is using pthread_mutex_trylock() waiting for another thread to unlock the mutex, and the locking thread has exited or died. This is called a spinlock, and the surviving thread can chew up a lot of system resources waiting for an unlock that never comes.

In any case, here's a simple example of trylock.

```
if (!pthread_mutex_trylock(&running_lock)){
    local_running=running;
    pthread_mutex_unlock(&running_lock);
}
```

POSIX versus WiringPi Threads

Up until now, I've talked about threads in terms of POSIX standard threads, or pthreads. They're primarily used in C programming, rather than C++, and since Larson.cpp doesn't need any objects to make it understandable, that's fine for us. The truth is, there are many different libraries, particularly for C++, to create with multi-threaded applications. I know pthreads, so that's what I use to talk about them. They're not the only game in town.

The author of WiringPi has also given us a thread-management system, called WiringPi threads. He freely admits that WiringPi threads are just wrappers of code around pthreads to make them easier to use. I'm not going to spend any time talking about WiringPi threads. If you've understood pthreads, WiringPi threads will be pretty obvious. I'll put the WiringPi thread version of the code at the end of the chapter.

Larson_pthread

The first version of this program we're going to create is Larson_pthread. As the title implies, we'll do this one the POSIX thread way.

The Plan

Copy Larson_multiprocess.cpp to a new project and name it Larson_pthread.cpp. Name the project Larson_pthread so we're all on the same page.

Larson_multiprocess.cpp has nearly everything we need in it already. We need to take the fork() call out, as well as the logic that depends on it. We need to take out the unistd.h library, since we're not using it, and put the pthread.h library in instead. We also need to add -l pthread to the build instructions, just as we do with WiringPi, and for the same reason. We need to create the thread functions, which will just call scan() with various parameters, then declare their thread ID variables and start the threads in main(). We also need to create the mutex to protect running init in main(), modify the signal handler to lock and unlock the mutex during writes, and modify the scan() function to trylock and unlock the mutex during reads. Finally, we need to use pthread_join and pthread_cancel to control the original thread while the threads we create run.

Everything else is the same.

The Modifications

In the #includes area, remove #include <unistd.h> and put in #include <pthreads.h>. Then declare a mutex in the global variables section like this:

```
int pins[LEDs]={2,3,4,14,15,18,17,27,22,23,24,10,9,11,25,8,7,1,0,5};
volatile bool running=true;
pthread_mutex_t running_lock;
```

Next, in the scan function, we need to declare local_running as a boolean and set it true, so the variable declarations look like this now:

```
int c=0;
int localLEDs;
int localzero;
bool localstart_low=start_low;
bool local_running=true;
```

Change the while(running) loop to test local_running instead. Try the running_lock mutex. If it's true, set local_running to running and unlock running_lock. Otherwise carry on. Everything else in scan() is unchanged.

```
while(local_running){
    if (!pthread_mutex_trylock(&running_lock)){
        local_running=running;
        pthread_mutex_unlock(&running_lock);
    }
```

Next, declare two simple thread functions: upper and lower. Both return void pointers and take a void pointer as a parameter. Upper calls scan with the low_order_LEDs flag false, and the start_low flag true. This means that this scan function will scan from LED 10 to LED 19 and that it will begin on LED 10.

Lower calls scan with low_order_LEDs true and start_low false. This means that the scan function will scan from LED 0 to LED 9, and begin on LED 9. Note that we don't use *vp for anything.

```
void *upper(void *vp){
    scan(false,true);
    return(NULL);
}
void *lower(void *vp){
    scan(true,false);
    return(NULL);
}
```

Next, we need to modify the SIGINT_handler function so that it locks the running_lock mutex before it sets running to false, then unlocks the mutex. It only takes a couple extra lines of code. Note that we have to pass the address of the running_lock mutex using &. This lets the function change the value of running_lock. Otherwise, when you pass a function a variable, the function gets a copy of the value in the variable.

```
void SIGINT_handler(int signal_number){
    pthread_mutex_lock(&running_lock);
    running=false;
    pthread_mutex_unlock(&running_lock);
}
```

Main() is where the bulk of the changes are. We need to remove the pid_t process_id=fork() line completely and remove the logic that checks the result of fork() to determine whether to initialize the pins. Instead, we declare our pthread IDs (pthread_t variables), upper_thread and lower_thread, so we can keep them straight, initialize the running_lock mutex with pthread_mutex_init() and initialize the pins every time. Our extra threads don't exist yet.

```
int main(void){
    signal(SIGINT,SIGINT_handler);
    wiringPiSetupGpio();

    pthread_t upper_thread;
    pthread_t lower_thread;

    pthread_mutex_init(&running_lock,NULL);

    for (int c=0;c<LEDs;c++){
        //cout<<"Setting pin "<<pins[c]<<"to output\n"<<flush;
        pinMode (pins[c],OUTPUT);
        digitalWrite(pins[c],HIGH);
    }
```

Next, we take out the scan(true,false) call. We'll have a separate thread for that. Speaking of the threads, we'll need to put in two calls to pthread_create to start the upper and lower threads. Like I said earlier, it's a very good idea to make sure your threads actually start, so wrap the calls in an if-then and call return 1 (return from main with an error) if they

271

don't. We can't communicate with the threads directly, so it would be good to send some text messages to tell the user (us) that we tried to start the threads and additionally if they didn't start.

```
cout<<"Creating Thread Upper\n"<<flush;
if(pthread_create(&upper_thread,NULL,upper,NULL)){
    cout<<"Error Creating thread.\n"<<flush;
    return 1;
}
cout<<"Creating Thread Lower\n";
if(pthread_create(&lower_thread,NULL,lower,NULL)){
    cout<<"Error Creating thread.\n"<<flush;
    return 1;
}
```

Before we reach the cleanup loop at the end of the program, we need to attach to one of the threads, so we block the main() thread of the process from cleaning up and shutting down until the threads we created are done. For neatness and to demonstrate the use of pthread_cancel, let's cancel whichever thread we don't join. Make sure to do this *after* the join. Everything before the pthread_join call will happen immediately at runtime.

```
pthread_join(lower_thread,NULL);
pthread_cancel(upper_thread);
```

And that's it. When we fall out the bottom of the join, we cancel the other thread, turn all the LEDs off, and return 0—exit without an error.

The Code

```
/* Larson_pthread.cpp
 *
 * Copyright 2017 Jim Strickland <jrs@jamesrstrickland.com>
 *
 * Standard GNU boilerplate:
 * This program is free software; you can redistribute it and/
 * or modify it under the terms of the GNU General Public
 * License as published by the Free Software Foundation;
 * either version 2 of the License, or (at your option) any
 * later version.
```

```
/*
 * Larson_pthread
 * This program implements the classic "Larson (Memorial)
 * Scanner", albeit a 20 pin Raspberry Pi version, with two
 * "eyes," each running inits own pthread It //requires// a Pi
 * with a 40 pin GPIO bus, or it won't call the right pins in
 * wiringPi. It's a pthread demo, basically.
 */

/* Iostream gives us cin and cout, which we might need for
 * debugging. WiringPi is the star of this show, the software
 * interface to the GPIO pins. pthread.h gives us the Linux
 * thread library. It's included in WiringPi too, so we don't
 * //technically// have to include it here,but it's bad
 * business to depend on declarations in other libraries.
 *
 * We define LEDs as 20, both to set the index of the pins
 * array, and as the maximum index value of the loop that reads
 * it. Likewise delaymils is a constant value of how many
 * milliseconds to wait between changing LEDs.
 */

#include <iostream>
#include <csignal>
#include <wiringPi.h>
#include <pthread.h>
#define LEDs 20
#define delaymils 40

/*
 * We're only using one namespace in this program, so it's safe
 * to set this program's default namespace to std.
 */
using namespace std;
```

273

```
/*
 * There's no good reason to use an object here, so we'll use a
 * global variable instead. This is the array that maps the pin
 * numbers in the order they're plugged into the LED arrays to
 * its own index value (from 0 to LEDs).
 */
int pins[LEDs]={2,3,4,14,15,18,17,27,22,23,24,10,9,11,25,8,7,1,0,5};
volatile bool running=true;
pthread_mutex_t running_lock; //declare our mutex.

/* void scan(bool low_order_LEDs, bool start_low)
 * Parameters:
 *     low_order_LEDs is a boolean that tells scan whether it's
 *         from the 0th LED to 10. If this parameter is false,
 *         we're scanning from LED 10 to LED 20.
 *     start_low is a boolean that tells scan whether to start
 *     at the lowest LED and scan up, or the highest LED and
 *     scan down.
 *         This only affects the //first// scan.
 * Returns nothing.
 *
 * How it Works:
 * -------------
 * Basically the guts of main() in Larson.cpp, but we have to
 * do some processing of local variables first.
 * Initialize c at 0 for safety.
 *
 * Declare localLEDs and localzero. These are the maximum and
 * minimum LEDs this particular instantiation of scan should
 * scan between.
 *
 * Initialize localstart_low to start_low. If it's false, we
 * start high on the first scan.
 *
 * Set up localzero and localLEDs.
 * If we were passed low_order_LEDs as true,
 *         set localzero to 0 and localLEDs to LEDs divided
 *         by 2. (This value is probably 10, but who knows
 *         how many LEDs those wily users have hooked up?)
 * Otherwise (low_order_LEDs is false),
 *         set localzero to LEDs divided by 2 and localLEDs
 *         to LEDs.
 *
```

```
 * Loop as long as running is true. It's set false by the
 * signal handler.
 * (This means we may get as much as one full scan between the
 * signal being caught and scan exiting. That's ok.)
 *          If localstart_low is TRUE
 *                Scan Low to High LED #. Starting with localzero,
 *                    turn the LED on,
 *                    wait delaymils,
 *                    then turn the previous LED off.
 *          else set localstart_low TRUE.
 *                (start_low and localstart_low only affect the
 *                first scan.)
 *                Scan from high to low
 *                    Switch the current LED on,
 *                    Wait delaymils,
 *                    then switch the previous LED off.
 */
void scan(bool low_order_LEDs,bool start_low){
    int c=0;
    int localLEDs;
    int localzero;
    bool localstart_low=start_low;
    bool local_running=true;

    //set up localzero and localLEDs
    if (low_order_LEDs){
        localzero=0;
        localLEDs=(LEDs/2);
    }else{
        localzero=(LEDs/2);
        localLEDs=LEDs;
    }

    while(local_running){ //loop forever as long as local_running is true.
        if (!pthread_mutex_trylock(&running_lock)){
            local_running=running;
            pthread_mutex_unlock(&running_lock);
        }
        if (localstart_low){
            //if localstart_low is true, loop from localzero to
            // localLEDs - "scan" from low LED # to high.
```

```
                for (c=localzero;c<localLEDs;c++){
                    //cout << "switching" << pins[c] <<"\n"<< flush;
                    digitalWrite(pins[c],LOW);
                    delay(delaymils);
                    if (c>localzero) digitalWrite(pins[c-1],HIGH);
                }
            }else{
                //if localstart_low was false, we skipped the low-to-high
                //part of the scan and came here. We only want this to
                //happen on the first scan, so when we GET here, set
                //localstart_low true. Then do the high-to-low part
                //of the scan as usual.
                localstart_low=TRUE;
            }

            //loop from localLEDs to localzero - scan from high LED # to low.
            for (c=localLEDs-1;c>=localzero;c--){
                //cout << "switching" << pins[c] <<"\n"<< flush;
                digitalWrite(pins[c],LOW);
                delay(delaymils);
                if (c<localLEDs)digitalWrite(pins[c+1],HIGH);
            }
        }
    }
}

/* void *upper(void *vp)
 * Parameters:
 *      void *vp, a void pointer called vp.
 *      Not used for anything, but the pthreads call requires it.
 * Returns:
 *          a void pointer.
 *          Note bene: void pointers are not void, so we do
 *          actually have to return a NULL pointer.
 *
 * These are here so the pthread functions can pass parameters
 * to and return the end status of the thread.
 *
 * How it works:
 * -------------
 * call scan, tell it to use the low order LEDs, and to start high.
 * return a NULL pointer.
 */
void *upper(void *vp){
    scan(false,true);
    return(NULL);
}
```

```
/* void *lower(void *vp)
 * Parameters:
 *     void *vp, a void pointer called vp.
 *     Not used for anything, but the pthreads call requires it.
 * Returns:
 *         a void pointer.
 *         Note bene: void pointers are not void, so we do
 *         actually have to return a NULL pointer.
 *
 * These are here so the pthread functions can pass parameters
 * to and return the end status of the thread.
 *
 * How it works:
 * -------------
 * call scan, tell it to use the high order LEDs, and to start low.
 * return a NULL pointer.
 */
void *lower(void *vp){
    scan(true,false);
    return(NULL);
}

/* SIGINT_handler
 * Parameters:
 * signal_number, an integer
 * Returns: nothing.
 *
 * How it works
 * ------------
 * Very much like a wiringpiISR interrupt handler,
 * signal_handler is called by a system event, namely a signal
 * being raised. In this case we're looking for SIGINT, a macro
 * for the signal we get when Ctrl+C is pressed in the Geany
 * run window. This handler only fires if SIGINT is raised,
 * so no decoding logic is needed.
 */
void SIGINT_handler(int signal_number){
    pthread_mutex_lock(&running_lock);
    running=false;
    pthread_mutex_unlock(&running_lock);
}
```

```
/*
 * Main()
 * Parameters: none
 * Returns: an integer to tell the system its exit status.
 * We're actually using this status when we test to make sure
 * the pthreads started properly.
 *
 * How it works:
 * -------------
 * Set up wiringPi to use BCM GPIO numbers
 *
 * Declare two pthread IDs, upper_thread and lower_thread.
 *
 * Initialize the GPIO pins as outputs and set them HIGH (off)
 *
 * Tell the user we're creating the upper thread, then call
 * pthread_create and create the thread. Notify the user and
 * exit if we fail. This thread will light the LEDs from 10-20.
 *
 * Tell the user we're creating the lower thread, then call
 * pthread_create and create it, too. As before, if we fail, tell
 * the user and exit. This thread will light the LEDs from 0-10.
 *
 * Make a pithy comment to the users so they know the main
 * thread is proceeding on its own.
 *
 * For our main thread, loop as long as running is true. Not
 * much else for the main thread to do. We could have processed
 * one of the "eyes" here, obviously.
 * Check running every 100ms as long as it's true. If it's
 * false, go through all the pins again and set them HIGH to
 * turn them off. Then exit the process which will take the
 * pthreads we created with it.
 */

int main(void){
    //hook up the SIGINT signal handler.
    signal(SIGINT,SIGINT_handler);

    //Initialize wiringPi
    wiringPiSetupGpio();

    //Declare our pthread ID data structures
    pthread_t upper_thread;
    pthread_t lower_thread;
```

```
//Initialize the running_lock mutex
pthread_mutex_init(&running_lock,NULL);

//Initialize Pins.
for (int c=0;c<LEDs;c++){
    //cout<<"Setting pin "<<pins[c]<<"to output\n"<<flush;
    pinMode (pins[c],OUTPUT);
    digitalWrite(pins[c],HIGH);
}

//Start the upper thread.
cout<<"Creating Thread Upper\n"<<flush;
if(pthread_create(&upper_thread,NULL,upper,NULL)){
    cout<<"Error Creating thread.\n"<<flush;
    return 1;
}

//Start the lower thread.
cout<<"Creating Thread Lower\n";
if(pthread_create(&lower_thread,NULL,lower,NULL)){
    cout<<"Error Creating thread.\n"<<flush;
    return 1;
}

//Send a message to the user from the main thread (this thread)
cout<<"It's really hard to see like this...\n"<<flush;

//Join the lower thread and block (sit here) until it exits. Then we
//cancel the upper thread explicitly and fall through to the LED
//cleanup code. Could we have just monitored running from the main
//thread and canceled both upper_thread and lower_thread from here
//when it changed? Yes. But it makes a better demo this way.
pthread_join(lower_thread,NULL);
pthread_cancel(upper_thread);

//Turn off all the LEDs by setting their pins HIGH.
for (int c=0;c<LEDs;c++){
    digitalWrite(pins[c],HIGH);
}

//Tell the user we're done and exit the whole process,
cout<<"Done.\n"<<flush;
return 0;
}
```

Larson_wiringPithread

Larson_wiringPithread is a modification of Larson_pthread so you can try WiringPi threads for yourself. It does exactly the same thing as Larson_ pthread, and from the system's perspective, the program works the same way. WiringPi threads don't have a non-blocking trylock function, so we'll have to use a blocking piLock() instead. It's exactly equivalent to pthread_mutex_lock, although its parameters are simpler. The equivalent of pthread_mutex_unlock is piUnlock(). The piLock() and piUnlock() functions don't have complex data structures to pass. You pass them an integer from 0 to 3, and WiringPi handles the rest.

Pay special attention to the differences in the global variable and mutex declarations, and to main(), where the threads are set up. We're done making Larson scanners at this point, but don't take the circuit apart on the breadboard yet. We're going to use it for a completely different project in the next two chapters.

The Code

```
/* Larson_wiringPithread.cpp
 *
 * Copyright 2017 Jim Strickland <jrs@jamesrstrickland.com>
 *
 * Standard GNU boilerplate:
 * This program is free software; you can redistribute it
 * and/or modify it under the terms of the GNU General Public
 * License as published by the Free Software Foundation;
 * either version 2 of the License, or (at your option) any
 * later version.
 *
 * This program is distributed in the hope that it will be
 * useful, but WITHOUT ANY WARRANTY; without even the implied
 * warranty of MERCHANTABILITY or FITNESS FOR A PARTICULAR
 * PURPOSE. See the GNU General Public License for more details.
 *
```

```
 * You should have received a copy of the GNU General Public
 * License along with this program; if not, write to the Free
 * Software Foundation, Inc., 51 Franklin Street, Fifth Floor,
 * Boston, MA 02110-1301, USA.
 *
 */

/*
 * Larson_wiringPithread
 * This program implements the classic "Larson (Memorial)
 * Scanner", albeit a 20 pin Raspberry Pi version, with two
 * "eyes," each running inits own thread. It //requires// a Pi
 * with a 40 pin GPIO bus, or it won't call the right pins
 * in wiringPi. It's a wiring pi thread demo, basically.
 *
 */

/* Iostream gives us cin and cout, which we might need for
 * debugging. WiringPi is the star of this show, the software
 * interface to the GPIO pins.
 * We define LEDs as 20, both to set the index of the pins array,
 * and as the maximum index value of the loop that reads it.
 * Likewise delaymils is a constant value of how many
 * milliseconds to wait between changing LEDs.
 */

#include <iostream>
#include <csignal>
#include <wiringPi.h>
#define LEDs 20
#define delaymils 40

/*
 * We're only using one namespace in this program, so it's safe
 * to set this program's default namespace to std.
 */
using namespace std;

/*
 * There's no good reason to use an object here, so we'll use a
 * global variable instead. This is the array that maps the pin
 * numbers in the order they're plugged into the LED arrays to
 * its own index value (from 0 to LEDs).
 */
int pins[LEDs]={2,3,4,14,15,18,17,27,22,23,24,10,9,11,25,8,7,1,0,5};
volatile bool running=true;
```

```
/* void scan(bool low_order_LEDs, bool start_low)
 *      Parameters:
 *      low_order_LEDs is a boolean that tells scan whether it's scanning
 *          from the 0th LED to 10. If this parameter is false,
 *          we're scanning from LED 10 to LED 20.
 *      start_low is a boolean that tells scan whether to start
 *      at the lowest LED and scan up, or the highest LED and
 *      scan down.
 *          This only affects the //first// scan.
 * Returns nothing.
 *
 * How it Works:
 * -------------
 * Basically the guts of main() in Larson.cpp, but we have to
 * do some processing of local variables first.
 * Initialize c at 0 for safety.
 *
 * Declare localLEDs and localzero. These are the maximum and
 * minimum LEDs this particular instantiation of scan should
 * scan between.
 *
 * Initialize localstart_low to start_low. If it's false, we
 * start high on the first scan.
 *
 * Set up localzero and localLEDs.
 * If we were passed low_order_LEDs as true,
 *          set localzero to 0 and localLEDs to LEDs divided by 2.
 *          (This value is probably 10, but who knows how many
 *          LEDs those wily users have hooked up?)
 * Otherwise (low_order_LEDs is false),
 *          set localzero to LEDs divided by 2 and localLEDs to LEDs.
 *
 * Loop as long as running is true. It's set false by the signal handler.
 * (This means we may get as much as one full scan between the
 * signal being caught and scan exiting. That's ok.)
 *          If localstart_low is TRUE
 *              Scan Low to High LED #. Starting with localzero,
 *                  turn the LED on,
 *                  wait delaymils,
 *                  then turn the previous LED off.
```

```
*            else set localstart_low TRUE.
*                (start_low and localstart_low only affect the
*                first scan.)
*                Scan from high to low
*                    Switch the current LED on,
*                    Wait delaymils,
*                    then switch the previous LED off.
*/
void scan(bool low_order_LEDs,bool start_low){
    int c=0;
    int localLEDs;
    int localzero;
    bool localstart_low=start_low;
    bool local_running=true;

    //set up localzero and localLEDs
    if (low_order_LEDs){
        localzero=0;
        localLEDs=(LEDs/2);
    }else{
        localzero=(LEDs/2);
        localLEDs=LEDs;
    }

    while(local_running){ //loop forever as long as local_running is true.
        piLock(0); //try to lock a mutex for running.
        local_running=running;
        piUnlock(0);
        if (localstart_low){
            //if localstart_low is true, loop from localzero to
            // localLEDs - "scan" from low LED # to high.
            for (c=localzero;c<localLEDs;c++){
                //cout << "switching" << pins[c] <<"\n"<< flush;
                digitalWrite(pins[c],LOW);
                delay(delaymils);
                if (c>localzero) digitalWrite(pins[c-1],HIGH);
            }
        }else{
            //if localstart_low was false, we skipped the low-to-high
            //part of the scan and came here. We only want this to
            //happen on the first scan, so when we GET here, set
            //localstart_low true. Then do the high-to-low part
            //of the scan as usual.
            localstart_low=TRUE;
        }
```

```
            //loop from localLEDs to localzero - scan from high LED # to low.
            for (c=localLEDs-1;c>=localzero;c--){
                //cout << "switching" << pins[c] <<"\n"<< flush;
                digitalWrite(pins[c],LOW);
                delay(delaymils);
                if (c<localLEDs)digitalWrite(pins[c+1],HIGH);
            }
        }
    }
}

/* PI_THREAD (upper)
 * Parameters: None
 *
 * Returns:
 *          a void pointer.
 *          Since we're really dealing with pthreads inside
 *          wrappers, and since pthreads return a void pointer,
 *          we return NULL to keep the pthread library happy.
 *
 * How it works:
 * -------------
 * We're passing a name (upper) to the PI_THREAD function to
 * create a pthread with that name for us, so we don't have to
 * handle void pointers. Except that we have to return //
 * something// (a NULL pointer) or the compile will barf.
 * call scan, tell it to use the low order LEDs, and to start high.
 * return a NULL pointer.
 */
PI_THREAD(upper){
    scan(false,true);
    return(NULL);
}

/* lower
 * Parameters: None
 *
 * Returns:
 *          a void pointer.
 *          Since we're really dealing with pthreads inside
 *          wrappers, and since pthreads return a void pointer,
 *          we return NULL to keep the pthread library happy.
 *
 *
```

```
* How it works:
* -------------
* We're passing a name (lower) to the PI_THREAD function to
* create a pthread with that name for us, so we don't have to
* handle void pointers. Except that we have to return //
* something// (a NULL pointer) or the compile will barf.
* call scan, tell it to use the high order LEDs, and to start low.
* return a NULL pointer.
*/

PI_THREAD(lower){
    scan(true,false);
    return(NULL);
}

/* SIGINT_handler
 * Parameters:
 * signal_number, an integer
 * Returns: nothing.
 *
 * How it works
 * ------------
 * Very much like a wiringpiISR interrupt handler, signal_handler
 * is called by a system event, namely a signal being raised.
 * In this case we're looking for SIGINT, a macro for the
 * signal we get when Ctrl+C is pressed in the Geany run window.
 * This handler only fires if SIGINT is raised, so no decoding
 * logic is needed.
 */

void SIGINT_handler(int signal_number){
    piLock(0); //try to piLock a mutex for running.
    running=false;
    piUnlock(0);
}

/*
 * Main()
 * Parameters: none
 * Returns: an integer to tell the system its exit status.
 * We're actually using this status when we test to make sure
 * the threads started properly.
 *
```

```
* How it works:
* -------------
* Set up wiringPi to use BCM GPIO numbers
*
* Initialize the GPIO pins as outputs and set them HIGH (off)
*
* Tell the user we're creating the upper thread, then call
* piThread_Create and create the thread. Notify the user and
* exit if we fail. This thread will light the LEDs from 10-20.
*
* Tell the user we're creating the lower thread, then call
* piThread_Create and create it, too. As before, if we fail, tell
* the user and exit. This thread will light the LEDs from 0-10.
*
* Make a pithy comment to the users so they know the main
* thread is proceeding on its own.
*
* For our main thread, loop as long as running is true. Not
* much else for the main thread to do. We could have processed
* one of the "eyes" here, obviously.
* Check running every 100ms as long as it's true. If it's
* false, go through all the pins again and set them HIGH to
* turn them off. Then exit the process which will take the
* pthreads we created with it.
*/

int main(void){
    //hook up the SIGINT signal handler.
    signal(SIGINT,SIGINT_handler);

    //Initialize wiringPi
    wiringPiSetupGpio();

    //Initialize Pins.
    for (int c=0;c<LEDs;c++){
        //cout<<"Setting pin "<<pins[c]<<"to output\n"<<flush;
        pinMode (pins[c],OUTPUT);
        digitalWrite(pins[c],HIGH);
    }

    //Start the upper thread.
    cout<<"Creating Thread Upper\n"<<flush;
    if(piThreadCreate(upper)){
        cout<<"Error Creating thread.\n"<<flush;
        return 1;
    }
```

```
//Start the lower thread.
cout<<"Creating Thread Lower\n";
if(piThreadCreate(lower)){
    cout<<"Error Creating thread.\n"<<flush;
    return 1;
}

//Send a message to the user from the main thread (this thread)
cout<<"It's really hard to see like this...\n"<<flush;

//Test running every 100ms to make sure it's still true.
//When it's not, the signal handler must have fired,
//so let the program exit gracefully. We could also have
//called scan directly from here in place of one of the
//threads we started.
while(running) delay(100);

//Turn off all the LEDs by setting their pins HIGH.
for (int c=0;c<LEDs;c++){
    digitalWrite(pins[c],HIGH);
}

//Tell the user we're done and exit the whole process,
//including this thread and the two threads we created.
cout<<"Done.\n"<<flush;
return 0;
}
```

Conclusion

In this chapter, we discussed threads, their similarities and differences from processes, and how to write multi-threaded programs. We wrote two programs that give the Larson (Memorial) Scanner two "eyes," scanning at the same time—one using POSIX threads, or pthreads, and one using WiringPi's own wrapper around pthreads. Threads and processes tap into the strength of UNIX/Linux operating systems and reach far beyond what AVR-based Arduinos can do. Next up: networking.

## CHAPTER 9

From Pi to the World: Network Sockets

Gadgets on the Internet

The public, capital I Internet, at its heart, is a mechanism for moving data from one computer to another. The World Wide Web is a combination of servers, clients (web browsers), and code that use the Internet to move data (web pages) from servers anywhere in the world to the web browser on your phone or on your desktop computer. Email is a different application that also uses the Internet to deliver its content. The Web is not the Internet. Email is not the Internet. The web and email are applications that use the Internet.

See the distinction? It can be easy to miss. It's important, because we're about to write our own application that uses the Internet.

First, we should talk a little bit about how the Internet really works, because the project in this chapter will, when it's done, reach out onto the public Internet and pull data from a server out there into your Pi and use that data to change the state of the LEDs we hooked to the Pi in for the Larson (Memorial) Scanner. Internet, Pi, GPIO. This is how the Internet of Things is built.

© James R. Strickland 2018
J. R. Strickland, *Raspberry Pi for Arduino Users*,
https://doi.org/10.1007/978-1-4842-3414-3_9

Some Words on Security

Once upon a time, when the Pi first came out, I built a sprinkler system timer that would have been web accessible. I got the hardware working and was just starting to think about the software, when it dawned on me (my wife pointed it out) that if someone broke into the Pi while we were away, they could turn our yard into dirt soup, and run us a multi-thousand-dollar water bill in the process. Ultimately I scrapped the project, because she was right. You wouldn't think something so simple and banal as a sprinkler system would be a security problem, but these things matter.

Think before you expose your gadget to the Internet. Internet connected door locks could be exploited to rob your house. Internet connected pet feeders could malfunction, and your pet could suffer. The list goes on and on. It's not just hobbyists like us with this problem, either. The average Internet of Things manufacturer knows little and cares less about security. As a result, there are bot-nets to take advantage of security cameras, refrigerators, and so on. If it still seems like a good idea, do your security homework.

A Quick Introduction to Networking

TCP/IP, the network protocol that underlies the public Internet and most other computer networks today, is a fairly complex beast. Whole books are written on the subject, and there are even professional training certifications on the subject. There's no way I can cover the whole story of how it works in this chapter, or even the next one, and for what we're doing, it's not that important. What's important for us here is that your Pi is talking to your network, whether it's using WiFi or (if you have a Raspberry Pi 3 Model B) wired 802.3 Ethernet. If your Pi's web browser can reach Google, we're good. All the lower level stuff is working. We don't have to touch it. The only other really important things to know are that data is sent over TCP/IP as "packets." These are data structures (surprised?) that have the address the packet came from, the address where it's going, the port it's going to, and a checksum (data error checking), among other things.

TCP/IP is made up of two parts: TCP and IP. IP is the "network layer." It provides a way to address all the nodes on the network (and on the Internet, that's a lot). It provides mechanisms for forwarding packets of data from one computer to the next until they get where they're supposed to be. The packet will have a checksum done to make sure the data hasn't been mangled, but because the routing (the list of machines a given packet goes through) may be different from one packet to the next, there's no guarantee about the order the packets come in, nor whether anything received them at the other end. An IP packet has, among other things, the sending and receiving address of the packet, and some number of bytes of payload it can carry, which is called it's transmission unit. It's not a fixed number. Packets can carry from 68 bytes to 64KiB. You can optimize your IP for a given network's own maximum transmission unit (MTU) size. Wired Ethernet (802.11) has a maximum transmission unit of 1500 bytes, for example. It's less work for a given network to send complete packets in one transmission unit, although IP can break them apart into fragments and put them back together again.

IP is all about making sure *this* packet got through in one piece. It does not guarantee that this packet came in any particular order, and given that the list of computers forwarding the packet along may vary between packets, it's entirely possible for packets to come out of order. IP also makes no guarantee that anything is listening for those packets when they get there.

TCP, by contrast, is connection based. It ensures that both sides are actively communicating, that packets will be delivered in the right order, to the right application, and so on. TCP does this by having its own header, inside the data area of the IP packet it's traveling in, that has the source and destination ports, a packet sequence number, and so on. TCP deals in streams of data. TCP is what we use most of the time on the Internet these days. And it's what we'll be using in this chapter.

TCP/IP Ports and Sockets

It's important to understand the differences between a socket and a port. A port number is part of a TCP header that tells the destination computer what application to send this packet to. There is a list of "well known port numbers," maintained by The Internet Corporation for Assigned Names and Numbers (ICANN), that determines which ports should be attached to which servers. Web browsers listen on port 80, unless they're secure servers, in which case they listen on 443. Email servers listen on port 25. DNS servers listen on port 53. And so on. So if a TCP/IP packet lands on Google's web server, the TCP header will direct it to port 80 or port 443, and the mighty Google web server system will answer. Likewise, when you make a connection to another system, your system allocates you a port. Your port number doesn't matter the way server port numbers do. It is, after all, included in the TCP packet header, so the server already has what it needs to talk back to you.

A socket is an endpoint of a connection (we're dealing with TCP here; some protocols don't care about connections). Since we're using a UNIX-like operating system, for us, a socket is a file. We can open them, read and write to them, and close them. A socket is bound to a specific IP address and a specific port. Clear as mud? Here's an example.

Imagine your Pi is on the public Internet, and you want to use it as a web server. The server creates a socket and calls `bind()` to connect that socket to port 80, then calls `listen()` to wait for connection requests.

My browser tries to connect on port 80. The server process calls the `accept` function, which creates a new socket, listening on the same server port, connected to the originating port on my computer at my IP address.

My browser and your server can now exchange data.

This is what ports do. A port is an endpoint for a communication link. It's a number between 0 and 65535 included in the TCP packet header. IP doesn't know about ports, but TCP does. Like addresses in IP, the port number you're sending from and the port number you're sending to are both in the TCP header. The Internet Corporation for Assigned Names and Numbers (ICANN) maintains a list of well known ports. Web browsers listen on port 80, unless they're secure servers, in which case they listen on 443. Email servers listen on port 25. DNS servers listen on port 53. And so on. So if a TCP/IP packet lands on Google's web server, the TCP header will direct it to port 80 or port 443, and the mighty Google web server system will answer.

Don't take my word for it. Try it. Open your favorite browser and type in http://www.google.com:80. Looks the same as usual, right? What we did is specify that we want to use port 80. The Google server knows to send data to your IP address, and your port, because its own socket (created by accept() or something similar) points to them. You can send Google data; it can send you data. Now you can look up cute cat pictures.

Socket programming isn't terribly hard to get your head around, but finding good documentation on how it's done with the modern libraries can be tricky. Be choosy. The older versions of the socket() library and related libraries were harder to use and much harder to understand.

IPv4 and IPv6

There is, of course, another wrinkle. You may have heard the drama a few years ago about how the "Internet is going to run out of addresses." IPv4, the protocol most used on the Internet, has only 32 bits of address space. That's 2^{32} -1 addresses, (0.0.0.0 doesn't work normally) or 4,294,967,295 addresses total. For the whole Internet. Worldwide. One for your phone, one for your desktop computer, one for your Pi, and so on, it's easy to see how that will run out. There are a number of sneaky ways around this, most commonly Network Address Translation. NAT basically assumes that since all or most of the connections on my home network will be out bound, it doesn't matter if they all appear (to the outside world) to come from my router's address. As long as the router knows which connection is which and translates the address to one on my home network, nobody cares. This is why, on most home networks, your actual IP address is 192.168.whatever.whatever. The 192.168.255.255 (32,766 usable addresses) is reserved for private networks.

NAT, and other workarounds, are why the Internet hasn't rolled over and died, and won't any time soon. The real fix for the problem is IPv6. In addition to a few nicer touches, IPv6 has 128 address bits and can have (on the face of it) 2^{128} addresses. This would allow us to assign an address to every atom on the surface of the Earth. It should hold us for a while, even in a world where your fridge, your car, your watch, and probably your clothes, shoes, and lunch all have addresses. The IPv6 network stack is out there, and it's *mostly* compatible with IPv4. TCP doesn't notice the difference, since it's encapsulated inside IP regardless of the version. But since our program will be using addresses, and I have no idea how far in the future you're reading this book, we'll write our program to deal with both. The modern socket library actually makes it easier to do both than to do it the old (IPv4) way.

Domain Name Service

Almost nobody types web addresses like this: http://172.217.11.238, and even fewer like this: http://[2607:f8b0:400f:801::200e]. They both lead to Google's home page. Domain name service means that you don't have to. You give domain name service (DNS) a word address, like http://www.google.com, and it turns www.google.com into either of the other two addresses, depending on whether your system is set up for IPv4 or IPv6. We'll want to build our program with domain name service, for sure, not least because the domain name service will also tell us whether we're dealing with an IPv4 or IPv6 address, and save us a lot of tinkering. The downside to this is it makes our program completely dependent on DNS working.

Client or Server

I've thrown these words around quite a bit, but we should really be clear on exactly what they mean. These two terms define the roles two computers take in network communication. Most of the communication we do on the network is in the client-server model.

In its pure form, clients are consumers of outside resources, and servers share their resources. The most common interactions with the Internet—email, web, and DNS—are all client-server models. Your computer asks the DNS server for the IP address for a given name. The DNS server provides it. Your computer connects to google.com and asks Google's search engine to find you cute cat pictures. Google sends a list of links back to your computer to click on. And so on. Of course, with modern web pages where JavaScript can run on your client computer, this model is a little more fuzzy.

A given computer can be both a client and a server. If, for example, you ran a web server on your Pi, and connected the Pi's own browser to it, the Pi would be both client and server. There are other relationships computers can have than client-server, such as peer to peer, but they're beyond the scope of this chapter.

The Program

What we're going to write is a reasonably secure mechanism (in my non-expert opinion) for a program on the Pi to go to a website on the public Internet and exchange data with it. This is how my thermostat and the commercial sprinkler timer I finally did buy do it. Instead of listening for connections and turning the device into a standing target for hacking, and instead of requiring a static IP address, which is complicated in a NAT environment, they reach out to a server operated by their manufacturers to get their settings, software updates, and whatever. When I want to control these devices from my computer chair, or my phone halfway around the planet (true story), I connect to the commercial website. In exchange for a few minutes of lag time between polls by my sprinkler system or thermostat, the website (and its operators) handle security. The worst you can (theoretically) do to my thermostat or sprinklers is keep them from talking to the web server, which means they go on with the programs they are already running.

Since we're not setting up an external website, we won't do the code that actually filters the data we want out of the website. But I do want to demonstrate that data from the outside world can be used to trigger GPIO pins, so what we'll do is reuse the Larson project's hardware setup and display the binary value of the characters we download from whatever website you point the software at. The point is you could have any of the GPIO lines do whatever you want based on that data.

The Plan

There are basically five things this program has to do: Ask the user for an address and how many lines to display, do a DNS lookup, create a socket and connect it to the numeric address we get back from the DNS server, exchange data with the server, and display it on the GPIO pins. If you were writing a program to control a gadget from a remote website, only the last stage would be different. You'd probably connect to a specific location inside the web page, where a CGI script would give your program the data it needs, so you'd process that data in the last step and determine what to do with the GPIO pins that way.

The modern socket() and netdb.h libraries allow us to declare a pointer to an addrinfo data structure, pass that pointer to the DNS routines, and directly use that data structure to create the socket and connect it. DNS does most of the heavy lifting for us—figuring out address families, decoding DNS results, all of that. In the process, it lets our program be IP version agnostic. It will work just as well for IPv4 and IPv6. In exchange for this, if DNS isn't working, our program won't work either. This isn't a problem, just something to keep in mind when you're designing your program.

This program's going to have two distinct groups of functions, one for the GPIO side of things, and one for the socket side of things. If those sound like good uses for objects in this code, you've got a good ear. We'll have two classes, and ultimately we'll have one object from each one. If we had multiple devices connected to the GPIO system, or if we were connecting to multiple websites, we might want more, but let's keep it simple. You can make it more complex when you do your own projects.

gpio_class

The first class of objects is `gpio_class`. It does what you think: encapsulates a lot of the code we've already written for the various iterations of `Larson.cpp` (it's based on the version from `Larson_pthread.cpp`, actually).

What's in it?

Private Members

We'll get to the private members of the class first. These, if you'll recall, can only be touched by other members of the same object.

The `pins[]` array should be private. Nothing outside the object has any business touching it.

We'll also need a function to write to a byte to the first eight pins (from the left) of the LED array. Yes, we could have done a port write, and let the WiringPi library do this for us, but we'd have had to rearrange the LEDs a bit, and frankly this is easier. We'll go ahead and make this private too, since it's called by another method of the class. Let's call it `gpio_write()`. It takes a single `uint8_t` variable as a parameter. Why `uint8_t` instead of of a char? Because we're assuming that every character is 8 bits only. I've been bitten before by traditional types (chars, ints, etc.) not being the length I expected. A `uint8_t` will be 8 bits, every time. If our chars actually are 8 bits long (they are in Raspbian, at least today), then a `uint8_t` will accept the char without trouble.

Public Members

From the perspective of our program's `main()` function, outside the objects, these methods are all objects of this class can do. There are only two public methods (also called member functions) in objects of this class: `gpio_write_string()` and `clear_pins()`. The `gpio_write_string()` function will take a `std::string` object (I'll cover those shortly), break it down character by character, and feed it to `gpio_write()`, one character at a time, with a delay between characters so we can actually see the LEDs light up. If you suspect this code will also respect a `SIGINT` handler, you're right. The `clear_pins()` function does what you'd expect: sets all the pins `HIGH` to turn the LEDs off.

Complications

The methods of this class should, by now, be old hat to you. But there are a couple of wrinkles. You might, for example, be tempted to put the `wiringPiSetupGpio()` function call in the constructor for this class. I certainly was, until I thought about it. A class can be instantiated more than once. If you or I reuse this class at some later date, it will call `wiringPiSetupGpio()` once for each time the object is instantiated and that, as you will recall, is a bad idea. Pedantically speaking, that call probably should be in the constructor, but the code to ensure it only happens once, despite the fact that multiple instantiations of gpio_class objects would be messier and harder to understand than putting the call in main() where it belongs.

socket_class

Objects of this class allow the user to create and manage one socket and one TCP/IP connection. They can do the DNS lookup, make the connection, read and write to the socket, and close the socket. The class handles IPv4 and v6 both, depending on what type of address the DNS server gives back. They're neat, tidy packages for dealing with sockets in C++.

So, what's in it?

Private Members

We'll need a variable for the socket itself. Since a socket is a file descriptor, and since file descriptors are integers, our file descriptor will be an int. We'll call it file_descriptor, just for clarity.

Next is a method called exit_error(). There are a lot of places a connection across a network can fail, and we'll be testing for at least some of them. If any of them happen, the whole program needs to end, right now, and it'd be nice if we were told why. That's what exit_error does. It takes a std::string object, prints it, and then terminates the program using the exit() system function.

The last private method is dns_lookup. It takes a std::string object and an integer port number and returns a pointer. The data structure that pointer points to will contain the numeric PI address, port number, IP version, and all the rest of the information we need to make the connection. If there's more than one address returned (say, an IPv6 and IPv4 address, for starters) the pointer will point to a linked list nodes that contain that information for each address. I'll go over linked lists briefly too. They're not complicated, at least conceptually. We won't have to gather the data, nor create the data structure itself. All that's part of a library we'll pull in.

Public Members

A socket_class object, from the perspective of main() does more than gpio_class objects do. It has four public methods—connect_socket(), read_socket(), write_socket(), and close_socket(). Each of these, in turn, ties together multiple functions from multiple libraries that make up the socket and DNS systems in Linux.

The connect_socket() member takes a std::string object address and an integer port and calls dns_lookup() on that string and port number. It takes the data structure it gets back, creates a socket, and tries the address and port number. If the connection fails, it goes on to the next address in the linked list (if there is one) and tries that. When a connection succeeds, it hands control back to whoever called it. Regardless of its status when it exits, it cleans up the data structure returned by the dns_lookup() function.

The read_socket() function reads data from the socket and returns a std::string containing the data. The strings are limited by the buffer_length macro, which we'll define at the beginning of the program.

The write_socket() function takes a std::string parameter and writes it to the socket, and thereby to the remote system.

The close_socket() function closes the socket. We only get so many on a system, so we need to close sockets we're not using. It's also polite not to use up the remote system's socket resources by making it try to determine if we're still connected.

main()

Main needs to do a few things. It needs to set up the SIGINT signal handler, get an address and a number of lines to read but not a port number) from the user, then build up a proper HTTP request (which I'll also cover as we dig into the code). It also needs to instantiate a gpio_class object, clear its pins, then instantiate a socket object and try to connect it. If the connection doesn't succeed, the program will terminate without returning to main(), so main() only need concern itself with successful connections. On a successful connection, main() sends the HTTP request, then reads the number of lines the user asked for and feeds them to the gpio_class object's gpio_write_string() method. The read loop will also respect the SIGINT handler.

Some Words on std::string

C++ has a string object. It's not entirely different from the Arduino string class, which may, in fact, be a superset of std::strings. A std::string object is a C string (a char[] array) with quite a few additional functions for niceties like computing string length, accessing strings character by character, searching and replacing in strings, iterating through the string, finding the beginning and the end of the string, and so on. When necessary, the object can cough up a char array pointer (a C string) and several other types. The std::string object type assumes ASCII strings, aka UTF-8, so if you're coding for non-English systems, be aware of that. C++ std::strings are well documented here: http://www.cplusplus. com/reference/string/string/.

Note that when we declare that we're using the std namespace, we no longer have to call them std::strings in the code. It's a term I'll go on using for clarity, so they don't get mixed up with C string character arrays. (Which we'll use, because some of the socket and related library functions refuse to play ball with std::strings.)

Some Words on Pointers

I've mentioned pointers before. We don't use them a whole lot in Arduino programming. We most certainly will use them in this program, so we should talk about them.

A pointer is a variable that contains the *address* of a chunk of data in memory. The data type of the pointer tells C++ how the data is laid out there. A pointer to a `uint8_t` tells C++ that there is one byte at that location. A pointer to a complex data structure says "There are <however many> bytes there. These bytes are a string, that next byte is a `uint8_t`, those bytes are an integer, and so on."

To dereference a pointer—that is, to access the data the pointer points to—you put an asterisk (*) at the beginning of the variable name. To declare one, you do the same thing. To get the address of some other variable so you can point a pointer at its data, you use the & prefix for that other variable. So for example, you might declare a pointer `int *my_int_pointer` and `int some_other_integer=4`. If you set `my_int_pointer` (note the lack of the dereference *) to `&some_other_integer`, `my_int_pointer=&some_other_integer` C++ won't complain. If you then use `cout << *my_int_pointer<<endl`, C++ will dutifully print out 4, since `my_int_pointer` points to the same data as `some_other_integer`. So far, pretty straightforward.

Where this gets complicated is scope. If I have a function called `myfunction`, and it declares its variable `int myfunction_variable`, and you have `myfunction` return a pointer to `myfunction_variable`'s address, you have a problem. By the time some other code tries to use the pointer `myfunction` returned, `myfunction_variable` no longer exists, and what's in that memory space is undefined. Worse, you might sometimes get what you expect, if that memory hasn't been recycled yet, which makes it harder to debug.

You can go the other way safely enough. If main declares int my_main_integer and declares an int pointer int *my_int_pointer, set it my_int_pointer=&my_main_integer and pass that to a function. The function will be able to modify the contents of my_main_integer, which it could not otherwise do.

You can also do math on pointers. Digest that for a moment. You can do math on integers if you are careful. First, like any other variable, you *must not* assume that when you declare your pointer, it's initialized at NULL. (The pointer equivalent of zero.) Adding 1 to a pointer means "go ahead the size of whatever this pointer points at." So on a pointer to a uint8_t, it would go ahead one byte (plus whatever overhead C++ incurs and takes care of for itself). If that's memory you haven't allocated, your program will probably crash. If it doesn't, there's no way to say what you'll be pointing at.

One other wrinkle. The way C and C++ do arrays is this: pins[0] is a pointer, equivalent to *pins. So if you use pins+1 in a function, you get the address of pins[1]. You can dereference that by using *(pins+1), the dereference of pins+1, which gives you the value of pins[1]. Pointers are the biggest single way C and C++ programmers get ourselves in trouble, and they can be devilishly hard to debug. If you see a segmentation fault or *segfault* error, it means your program's process has tried to access memory that doesn't belong to it. It's a good indicator you've got a pointer running amok someplace. You can do some incredibly elegant and fast code with pointers, but with great power comes great responsibility, along with complicated debugging.

Writing the Code

Go ahead and open a Geany instance from the terminal window with Geany &. This tells Geany to run in the background. Open the Larson_pthread project with this instance. Open a second Geany instance the same way, create the project Socket, and create the file Socket.cpp. We'll be cutting and pasting code from the Larson.pthread.

Libraries

The first thing we'll need are all the libraries. Some of them will be familiar. Some won't. I'll mention what each one does just the same.

- `#include <iostream>`: The usual C++ IO functions and objects, especially `cout`.

- `#include <wiringPi.h>`: The WiringPi library. So we can talk to the GPIO pins.

- `#include <math.h>`: The `math.h` library's a new one. It gives us advanced math functions. It's not part of the standard C/C++ library (since it has the `.h`). These are often platform specific. An 8-bit Arduino has a different (and more limited) `math.h`.

- `#include <string>`: The `std::string` class is in this library.

- `#include <csignal>`: In order for our signal handler to work, we need this one.

- `#include <sys/socket.h>`: This is the socket library. Obviously, it's not part of C++, but it's a pretty standard tool.

- `#include <netdb.h>`: This is the library we need to talk to DNS. It declares the `addrinfo struct`, which we'll use extensively. It also #defines a lot of useful constants, like IP address types and bit widths.

- `#include <unistd.h>`: Using a NULL pointer? Any time you deal with linked lists, you probably will. Among many, many other things, they're defined in `unistd.h`.

Preprocessor Macros (#defines)

We have a few #defines of our own. Most of them we've used before in some fashion, so they're nothing new.

```
#define LEDs 20
```

As always, we only have 20 LEDs.

```
#define delaymils 100
```

This is the delay between bytes displayed on the LEDs. To my eye, 100ms is about as short a time as you can see "yep, that's a separate byte." It's not long enough to read them. If you want to verify that they work right, set this longer.

```
#define buffer_length 150
```

The buffer length is where we tell the socket how long to make our C-style char array, and how many bytes (minus 1) to read from the socket at a time. A buffer is just an area in memory to put data so systems that run at different speeds can do so without holding each other up. We could read the socket one byte at a time, but the only reason to do it like that might be for better security. Overflowing buffers is a time-honored technique to cause security problems.

```
#define debug_messages 1
```

By now, you've noticed that I habitually have debug code in programs, and I usually just comment it out. That's fine for small programs without a lot of debug code, but it gets tedious quickly when you have to find and comment out (or in) a lot of code. For this program, I've changed tacks. We define debug_messages to *something, anything*. In the code, if we surround our debug code with #ifdef debug_messages and #endif, they will be compiled in. If we comment out the #define debug_messages 1 line, the debug code won't be compiled in at all. We'll leave it in for this program. It's easier to understand what the program does when it runs if we leave all the chatty debug code in. If we reuse this code (like we have with Larson.cpp for the last few chapters), we might want to turn the debug code off later.

Global Functions and Variables

You can cut and paste these out of Larson_pthreads.cpp if it seems worth it. They're exactly the same; I just moved them to the top of the program.

```
bool running=true;
```

The global variable the SIGINT handler uses.

```
void SIGINT_handler(int signal_number){
    running=false;
}
```

The signal handler itself.

```
using namespace std;
```

Not really a global variable or function, but it's a namespace setting we're using globally, so this seemed like a good place to put it.

The gpio_class Declaration

This is the class with the most code cut and pasted from Larson_pthread.cpp. It abstracts all the GPIO-related code except for wiringPiSetupGPIO(), as I mentioned in the plan. Go ahead and copy the int pins[LEDs] array declaration and declare it as a private member of the class gpio_class. You don't have to break it into two lines, as I did. That was to make the typesetter's job easier for this book.

```
class gpio_class {
    private:
        int pins[LEDs]={2,3,4,14,15,18,17,27,22,23,24,10,9,11,25,8,7,1,0,5};
```

Next, we'll declare `gpio_write`. This private method accepts an 8-bit value (usually a character) and lights the appropriate LEDs (from right to left). For parameters, it takes an 8-bit unsigned integer as a parameter. (A char would probably work, but they're not explicitly 8-bit unsigned data types, and this code assumes that our chars are exactly 8 bits, no more, no less.) It returns nothing.

```
void gpio_write(uint8_t data){
    uint8_t mask=0;
```

We're going to use bitwise-anding, so we declare an `uint8_t` called `mask` to use as a mask and set all its bits to 0.

```
    clear_pins();
```

Call `clear_pins()` to clear anything already displayed on the GPIO LEDs. We haven't written this method yet, because it's public. These are private.

```
    for (int c=0;c<8;c++){
        mask=(uint8_t)pow(2.0,(float)c);
        if (data & mask){
            digitalWrite(pins[8-c],LOW);
        }
    }
}
```

Here's where all the assumptions about 8-bit characters happen. We iterate on C from 0 to 7. Then we cast C to a float (because pow() is a floating point function) and use that as the exponent in 2^c using the pow() math function, and then cast the result back to a `uint8_t`. This converts C to one of these values: 1,2,4,8,16,32,64,128,255. We then set `mask` to that value, turning on exactly one bit in mask. We bitwise the data and mask together, and if we get anything other than zero, that bit was set in data, so we turn that LED on with `digitalWrite()`. Actually, since our LEDs are numbered left to right, and binary numbers go right to left from lowest to highest, we subtract C from 8 and turn on *that* LED.

We're done with the private members of the gpio_class class. Next up: the public members, of which there are two, both of them methods (aka member functions). They are gpio_write_string() and clear_pins(). We'll do gpio_write_string() first.

```
void gpio_write_string(string the_string){
```

This method returns nothing and takes a std::string called the_string as its parameter.

```
int string_length=the_string.length();
```

Call the_string's method length() to get the number of characters in the_string. Since we're going to use this number a lot, we store it in an integer called string_length. The compute-overhead of calculating that length every time is probably not significant on the Pi, but I've found that Arduino coding habits for conserving processor power die hard.

```
#ifdef debug_messages
    cout<<"Writing this string: "<<the_string<<endl;
#endif
```

If debug_messages is #defined anywhere before this point, we cout the value of the_string.

```
for (int c=0;c<string_length;c++){
    if (!running) return;
```

Iterate on C from 0 to the string length (-1). Check to see if running is set to TRUE. If it's not, our SIGINT handler has fired and we exit from the method so we can do a controlled shutdown and turn all the LEDs off.

```
#ifdef debug_messages
    cout<<"C is: "<<c<<" Character is: "<<the_string.at(c)<<endl;
#endif
```

Another debug message. Write out the value of C and the character in the string at that position.

```
gpio_write(the_string.at(c));
delay(delaymils);
```

Call the gpio_write() private method of this object with the character in the_string at position C. Then (using WiringPi's delay() function) delay for however many milliseconds we set delaymils to.

```
    }
};
```

That's it for gpio_write_string. Next up is clear_pins().
The clear_pins method takes no parameters and returns nothing.
Just cut and paste the Initialize Pins code out of main() in Larson_
pthread.cpp, although you can take the cout out. I did. Yes, this means
every time we clear the pins we set them all as outputs. It doesn't hurt
anything. We iterate on C from 0 to LEDs -1, set the pinMode of that pins[c]
to OUTPUT, and digitalWrite that output HIGH, turning the LED off.

```
void clear_pins(void){
    for (int c=0;c<LEDs;c++){
        pinMode (pins[c],OUTPUT);
        digitalWrite(pins[c],HIGH);
    }
};
```

After that, we reach the end of the gpio_class class. Classes can
be lengthy. It's a good idea to put a comment to remind yourself (and
others) that the class ends here. Also, the semicolon at the end of a class
declaration is mandatory. It's not required at the end of functions or
methods (although I tend to put them in anyway).

```
};//end of gpio_class
```

The socket_class Declaration

The socket class has six methods total: two private (exit_error() and
dns_lookup()) and four public (create_socket(), read_socket(),
write_socket(), and close_socket()). Of these, create_socket() and

dns_lookup() do almost all the work and contain most of the code, and naturally create_socket() calls dns_lookup(). This is the hard part. Once we're through here, it's all downhill. Let's dive in.

We start by declaring the class. I'll mention it again, even though you're probably tired of reading it: classes do not declare objects. They're patterns for objects you'll declare (instantiate) later. I've already said we'll have a couple of private methods, and it shouldn't be a surprise that we have a private member variable either, so we declare the class and start the private section.

```
class socket_class {
    private:
    int file_descriptor=0;
```

I've said over and over again that everything in Linux is a file. Here's where that really becomes important. A socket, in UNIX-like operating systems, is a file descriptor. That means it points to something that can be written to and read from like a file. The variable type that points to it is called a file descriptor, and they're represented by integers. To make it clear what this int is, I called it file_descriptor. Just as you can have multiple files open at the same time, you can have multiple sockets open at the same time. We'll get into files a little more in chapters to come. The beauty of everything being a file in Linux is that your system security model only has to understand files. So a socket has permissions, owners and groups, and access control. In this case, it's a file your program creates, so the user your program is running under owns the socket.

The first method is called exit_error(). It takes a std::string parameter of an error message and returns nothing. Nor should it return anything. It couts the string it took as input, then calls exit() with a 1 parameter. This *terminates the whole program* with an error status of other than zero, meaning there was an error. This isn't the most robust way to error-check a connection, but the bottom line is with this program, if we have an error looking up DNS, connecting, or transferring data, the program can't do anything useful anyway. If we were writing a web browser, it'd be different. The exit_error function is a wrapper around exit() that lets it at least tell us why the program terminated.

```
void exit_error(string msg){
    cout <<msg<<endl;
    exit(1);
}
```

The dns_lookup() function returns a *pointer* to an adderinfo data structure. Here's what's in an adderinfo.

```
int             ai_flags      Input flags.
int             ai_family     Address family of socket.
int             ai_socktype   Socket type.
int             ai_protocol   Protocol of socket.
socklen_t       ai_addrlen    Length of socket address.
struct sockaddr *ai_addr      Socket address of socket.
char            *ai_canonname Canonical name of service location.
struct addrinfo *ai_next      Pointer to next in list.
```

If you assumed that the values in ai_flags, ai_family, ai_socktype, and ai_protocol are all #defined in netdb.h, you catch on fast. For our purposes with this program, we only care about ai_socktype, and that only when it's set to SOCK_STREAM. That gives us TCP connections. We'll use that later. The sockaddr struct is defined in socket.h. (It's conceptually safe to assume netdb.h includes socket.h, but unsafe to assume it in code. We need to include socket.h for ourselves.) *ai_cannonname is a pointer to a C character string. And there's *ai_next, which points to another addrinfo struct. This means our addrinfo struct can really be a linked list of structs. Which it can.

Socket programming the old way involved building up sockaddrs manually in code, plugging them into a sockaddr_in (or sockaddr_in6 for IPv6), moving things in and out of the big endian byte order used by IP, and so on. With the modern libraries, we don't have to do any of that. We call getadderinfo() from the netdb.h library, and it returns a linked list of adderinfos. We have all that stuff already set.

So dns_lookup returns a pointer to an addrinfo linked list and takes a string and an integer for the text address and port number, respectively.

```
addrinfo *dns_lookup(string text_address,int port){
    addrinfo *server_info_ptr;
```

We need our own pointer to use internally and return the value of, so we create a pointer to an addrinfo called server_info_ptr.

```
addrinfo hints;
hints.ai_socktype=SOCK_STREAM;
hints.ai_family=0;
hints.ai_protocol=0;
hints.ai_flags=0;
```

One of the arguments of the getaddrinfo function is the hints structure, which is also an addrinfo. The hints argument essentially acts as a filter, so we don't get information back from the DNS server that we don't need. Anything set to 0 in the hints structure is ignored, and we set hints. ai_socktype to SOCK_STREAM, so the getaddrinfo function only tells us about TCP addresses. The UDP addresses are usually duplicates anyway. Note that hints is not a pointer. Rather, it's a variable of the addrinfo type.

```
string text_port=to_string(port);
```

Next, we fix a small design error on my part. I brought the port number in as an integer, whereas getaddrinfo wants it as a character array. So we declare the std::string text_port and use the to_string function of the strings library to convert the port number integer to a string value.

```
#ifdef debug_messages
    cout<<"Using port# "<<text_port<<endl;
#endif
```

Here's another one of those debug messages that is not compiled in if debug_messages isn't #defined somewhere. We need to know that the port number was set correctly.

```
if (getaddrinfo(text_address.c_str(),
                text_port.c_str(),
                &hints,
                &server_info_ptr)==0){
```

We actually call getaddrinfo() in this if statement.

```
#ifdef debug_messages
    addrinfo temp_addr;
    char host[256]; //buffer for host names.

    for (addrinfo *ptr=server_info_ptr;
            ptr!=NULL;
            ptr=(*ptr).ai_next){
        temp_addr=*ptr;

        getnameinfo(temp_addr.ai_addr,
            temp_addr.ai_addrlen,
            host,
            sizeof(host),
            NULL,
            0,
            NI_NUMERICHOST);

        cout<<"Found SOCK_STREAM address: "<<host;
        if (temp_addr.ai_family==AF_INET6){
            cout <<" IPv6";
        }else{ //equal to AF_INET
            cout<<" IPv4";
        }
        cout<<"."<<endl;
    }
#endif
```

Here's where the #ifdef debug_messages makes a big difference.
If it's not defined, this whole loop disappears. If it is defined, we
declare an addrinfo called temp_addr. Then we declare a 256-char
array (getnameinfo is one of those routines that won't play nice with
std::strings). And then we have our for loop.

This for loop is different from every other for loop we've written.
Instead of iterating on an integer (almost always C, by my habit) through
some enumerated list of data (nearly always an array), we iterate on *ptr
(a pointer to an addrinfo struct) through the linked list starting at

server_info_ptr, ending when ptr is NULL (note that when comparing to NULL, you don't dereference ptr). If ptr is not NULL, we set ptr to the dereference of ptr's ai.next and go on looping. We're using a for loop to traverse a linked list.

What we're doing in that linked list is printing out the results of the DNS lookup we just did.

Set temp_addr to the data pointed at by *tmp (note the dereference). This is to simplify the notation, more than anything. In my opinion, code that's easier to read is valuable. Having set temp_addr to *temp, we can now access temp_addr's elements with ease and feed them to the various parameters of getnameinfo. Note that we pass getnameinfo host, which contains the address of host[0] and is an implied pointer to the whole char array. Pointers can be tricky. NI_NUMERICHOST is yet another macro, #defined by either netdb.h or socket.h, that tells getnameinfo() we want the host's numeric IP address, whether the name could be found or not. After all. We know what the name was.

We also do a quick check to see if temp_addr.ai_family is AF_INET6, yet another macro defined for us by the libraries we've loaded. If the ai_family is AF_INET6, we have an IPv6 address. Otherwise, it's IPv4. Tell the user the address and what kind of address it is.

```
        return server_info_ptr;
    }else{
        exit_error("DNS Failed.");
        return server_info_ptr;
    }
}; //end of dns_lookup.
```

Whether we did or did not do the debug_messages code, we return server_info_ptr if our lookup was successful, or exit_error if it wasn't. The return after the exit_error call should never happen, but C++ will complain if there's no return there.

That's the last of the private members. Next we start with the public ones, and we jump right in with connect_socket, which does the other half of the heavy lifting for us. It returns nothing and takes a std::string with the text address and an integer with the port as arguments.

```
public:
void connect_socket(string address,int port){
    #ifdef debug_messages
        char host[256];
    #endif
```

If debug_messages is set, we'll need another char array. We'll call it host, again.

```
addrinfo *dns_results_ptr = dns_lookup(address,port);
addrinfo temp_addr;
```

Declare a pointer to point at the addrinfo linked list and point it at the linked list that dns_lookup returns. We call dns_lookup here with the std::string address and the integer port.

Declare temp_addr to contain the data of an individual addrinfo struct, just as we did in dns_lookup.

```
for (addrinfo *ptr=dns_results_ptr;
                ptr!=NULL;
                ptr=(*ptr).ai_next){
    temp_addr=*ptr;

    //Text-ify the address and tell the user we're trying it.
    #ifdef debug_messages
        getnameinfo(temp_addr.ai_addr,
                    temp_addr.ai_addrlen,
                    host,
                    sizeof(host),
                    NULL,
                    0,
                    NI_NUMERICHOST);
        cout<<"Trying: "<<host<<endl;
    #endif
```

This works exactly the same way as printing the addresses did in dns_lookup. To be honest, the code was copied and pasted from there. However, this loop does a lot more, as you can see.

```
file_descriptor=socket(temp_addr.ai_family,
                 SOCK_STREAM,
                     0);
if (file_descriptor==-1){
    exit_error("Unable to create socket.");
}
```

Create the socket. This shouldn't ever fail unless we've run your system out of sockets completely, which isn't likely. If it does fail, call exit_error.

```
if (connect(file_descriptor,
        temp_addr.ai_addr,
        temp_addr.ai_addrlen)==0){

    #ifdef debug_messages
        cout<<"Connected!"<<endl;
    #endif

    break;
```

Try to connect the socket to the ai_addr and ai_addrlen currently in temp_addr. If connect returns 0, it succeeded. If we're sending debug messages, send one. Then break. Break exits from the loop without further iterations. It's a simple (if not very elegant) technique that saves a lot of complexity in the for loop declaration. We exit from the loop right there and execute the next line of code.

```
}else{ //connect returns -1 on failures.
    close(file_descriptor);
}
```

If we get this far, connect returned a -1 on failure to connect. We close the file descriptor and then loop around and try the next address. If your system isn't set up to use IPv6, but DNS returned an IPv6 address as well as an IPv4 address, this should connect you to the IPv4 address on its next cycle.

```
}
freeaddrinfo(dns_results_ptr);
```

When we exit the loop, release the memory allocated in getaddrinfo(). Hint for future reference: malloc and free are what you'd use for your own linked lists. Freeaddrinfo is a specialized version of free, presumably, that traverses the linked list and frees each addrinfo struct.

```
};
```

And...we're done. Connect_socket ends here. Everything is easier from here on. Take read_socket() for example. It returns a string with the data you read from the socket and takes no arguments.

```
string read_socket(){
    char from_server[buffer_length]="";
    int bytes=0;
```

Declare a char array from_server of buffer_length (remember buffer_length?) length. Because recv hates std::strings. Also, declare an integer to hold the number of bytes we actually read.

```
    bytes=recv(file_descriptor,from_server,
               buffer_length-1,0);
    if (bytes<0){ //recv returns -1 on fails.
        exit_error("Error on Receive.");
    };
```

Call recv on the socket's file_descriptor. Pass it the implicit pointer from_server (remember, from_server is equal to &(from_server[0]) so recv can write to the from_server character array. Pass it buffer_length-1 so it knows where to stop. Recv takes flag values. We don't care. We pass it a 0.

```
    #ifdef debug_messages
        cout<<"Received "<<bytes<<" bytes from server."<<endl;
    #endif
```

If debug_messages is defined, tell the user how many bytes we got from the server. If not, that code won't even be here.

```
    return string(from_server);
```

Here's a wrinkle. We're returning a std::string. We don't know its name, but we can call the constructor of a std::string class object and load it with the char array that from_server points to and return that. I suspect this kind of thing is what confuses people badly on whether a class instantiates objects or not. What's really happening is that a temporary std::string is being created *but not named*. We use its constructor and pass it to return (which returns its value). The fact that it's not named doesn't matter, since we're returning and all the memory it used will be cleared when the method exits.

```
}; //end of read_socket
```

The write_socket method is almost as simple. It takes a std::string object as a parameter and returns nothing.

```
void write_socket(string text){
    int bytes = send(file_descriptor,
            text.c_str(),
            text.length(),0);
    if (bytes<0){
        exit_error("Error on Send.");
    };

    #ifdef debug_messages
        cout<<"Sent "<<bytes<<" bytes to server."<<endl;
    #endif
}; //end of write_socket
```

We declare an integer for number of bytes, then set it to the output of the send() function, which is the opposite of recv. Send needs the file descriptor of the socket, the char array of data to send, which we get from the std::string text's c_str method, the length of the char array, which we get from the std::string text's length() method, and flags, which we ignore and set to 0.

If bytes is less than 0, the send failed, and we call exit_error with a message. Otherwise we fall through and, if we have debug_messages #defined, we tell the user how many bytes were sent.

And then we exit.

The last method of the socket_class is close_socket. It returns nothing and takes no parameters. Since only one file descriptor is included in a socket_class object, we don't need to pass it as a parameter. We just call close() on file_descriptor and exit.

```
void close_socket(){ //just a wrapper for the close() function.
    close(file_descriptor);
}; //end of close_socket.
}; //end of socket_class.
```

Remember, semicolons are required at the end of classes.

The main() Function

At last, we reach the main function. Its job is (mostly) to instantiate objects and call their functions, but it does talk to the user a little too.

```
int main(void){
    string message="";
    int number_of_lines=0;
    string target_address;
    string http_request="";
```

First, we declare some variables—a std::string called message to hold strings we read from the server, an integer called number_of_lines, so we can tell main() how much data we really want to display on the LEDs, one byte every 100ms (the novelty does wear off quickly), and two other std::strings, one to hold the net address we're going to (target_address), and one to hold the HTTP request line to ask the web server to talk to us (http_request).

```
    wiringPiSetupGpio();
    signal(SIGINT,SIGINT_handler);
```

Set up WiringPi and hook up the SIGINT handler, just as we did in Larson_pthread.

```
cout<<"What address should I connect to?"<<endl;
getline(cin,target_address);
cout<<"How many lines should I read?"<<endl;
cin>>number_of_lines;
```

Ask the user, in a series of couts and cins, what address to connect to and how many lines to read.

```
//http requests have to be sent quickly, or the server times out.
//here, we're building a simple request to send us the website's
//top level index file. You could put any path in here, however.
cout <<"Building HTTP request."<<endl;
http_request="GET http://"+target_address+"/index.html";
http_request+=" HTTP/1.1\r\nhost:"+target_address+"\r\n\r\n";
```

Web servers (aka HTTP servers) communicate in plain text, but they're fussy about timing. By the time we type in the request, the server will have timed out on us. So this code generates the request for us. It uses std::string addition (concatenation) to put the pieces together around the variables we've already set.

We're asking the server to GET the website http://<address>/index. html, telling it we want HTTP version 1.1, then a carriage return (\r) and a linefeed (\n). We also want it to use the host address, followed by two more pairs of carriage returns and linefeeds. I didn't make this up. I looked up the spec and knocked it together from some examples. For your application, you'll want to tailor this to your server more, and to which web page you want your application to connect to. /cgi-bin/<your cgi script> seems like a likely choice.

```
cout<<"Setting up GPIO bus object."<<endl;
gpio_class gpio;
cout<<"Clearing GPIO pins."<<endl;
gpio.clear_pins();
```

Tell the user we're setting up the GPIO bus object and instantiate an object called gpio of gpio_class. Then tell the user and call the clear_pins() method of the gpio object to clear the pins.

```
cout<<"Setting up socket object."<<endl;
socket_class socket;
```

Tell the user and instantiate an object called socket of socket_class.

```
cout<<"Connecting socket to "<<target_address<<"on port 80."<<endl;
socket.connect_socket(target_address,80); //connect our
//socket object to the target address the user specified,  on port 80.
//port 80 is the standard for http (web) servers.
```

Tell the user, then connect the socket to the target address on port 80 (where HTTP servers listen for unsecured traffic).

```
cout <<"Sending HTTP request: "+http_request<<endl;
socket.write_socket(http_request);
socket.write_socket("\r\n");
```

Tell the user, then send our HTTP request. Send another carriage-return/linefeed pair after that.

```
for (int c=0;c<number_of_lines;c++){
    if (!running) break;

    message=socket.read_socket(); //read from the socket into message
    cout<<"Received: "<<message<<"."<<endl; //show message
    gpio.gpio_write_string(message);
};
```

Iterate on C for number_of_lines times. Check to see if running is true. If it's not, exit from the loop with break. Otherwise, set message to socket.read_socket(), display the the message string, and call gpio_write_string on message. Repeat this for each line.

```
socket.close_socket();
gpio.clear_pins();
return 0;
```

Whether we exited from the loop because of the signal handler or because we ran out of lines, close the socket, clear the pins, return 0, and exit.

```
}; //End of program
```

Running the Code

Now for the moment of truth. Run the code. It's one of those slightly magical moments when code you write suddenly starts receiving data from afar, and the LEDs start displaying it. It wears off, especially as you debug things, but when it works that first time, do enjoy it.

```
pi@PiOW:~/projects/Socket$ ./Socket
What address should I connect to?
www.apress.com
```

I pointed the program at the address of the publisher of this fine book. This program, if it works right, should generate a trivial amount of traffic. Connect, read two lines, and exit. I'd point it at your own website until you know it works correctly, just to be safe. Note that you want only the address, not http:// <yadda>. The http:// part of a URL is to tell your web browser what it's looking for, as opposed to file:///home/pi/projects/Socket/Socket.cpp. You knew it would do that, right? Carrying on...

```
How many lines should I read?
2
Building HTTP request.
Setting up GPIO bus object.
Clearing GPIO pins.
Setting up socket object.
Connecting socket to www.apress.com on port 80.
Using port# 80
Found SOCK_STREAM address: 151.101.0.250 IPv4.
Found SOCK_STREAM address: 151.101.64.250 IPv4.
Found SOCK_STREAM address: 151.101.128.250 IPv4.
Found SOCK_STREAM address: 151.101.192.250 IPv4.
Trying: 151.101.0.250
Connected!
Sending HTTP request: GET http://www.apress.com/index.html HTTP/1.1
host:www.apress.com

Sent 70 bytes to server.
Sent 2 bytes to server.
Received 149 bytes from server.
Received: HTTP/1.1 301 Moved Permanently
```

I'm not very fluent in HTTP messages, but if I read this right, it means the server has been moved permanently. I'm sure if we loaded more lines, we'd get the new URL. Interesting to note that (as it says) they're using an Apache server, just like we will be in the next chapter.

```
Server: Apache
Set-Cookie: springercomcountry=US; path=/; domain=.apress.com
Location: https://www.apress.com/index.
Writing this string: HTTP/1.1 301 Moved Permanently
Server: Apache
Set-Cookie: springercomcountry=US; path=/; domain=.apress.com
Location: https://www.apress.com/index
C is: 0 Character is: H
C is: 1 Character is: T
C is: 2 Character is: T
C is: 3 Character is: P
```

Lots of lines deleted as we go through all 149 characters. Your LEDs should be merrily blasting out each byte.

```
Received 149 bytes from server.
Received: .html
Content-Type: text/html; charset=iso-8859-1
x-wl-v: prod-sgw-web-3
Via: 1.1 varnish-v4
Set-Cookie: BIGipServer~SPRCOM~pl-sgw-live_80=412739.
Writing this string: .html
Content-Type: text/html; charset=iso-8859-1
x-wl-v: prod-sgw-web-3
Via: 1.1 varnish-v4
Set-Cookie: BIGipServer~SPRCOM~pl-sgw-live_80=412739
C is: 0 Character is: .
C is: 1 Character is: h
C is: 2 Character is: t
C is: 3 Character is: m
C is: 4 Character is: l
```

More lines deleted...

```
C is: 146 Character is: 7
C is: 147 Character is: 3
C is: 148 Character is: 9
```

That's how it ends. The LEDs should all turn off, and the program should exit.

This isn't the most useful of programs, in and of itself. It's little more than a demo, much like the Larson series of programs. But what it's demonstrating is a huge capability—to have your programs on your Pi exchange data with an Internet server and act on that data with GPIO action as well as code.

The Code

As always, here's the complete code for this project. As usual, the comments are longer than the code. They need to be. The classes get a little complicated in spots. Also, I've learned over the years that invariably someone will want me to revise code I haven't touched in a year, or ten, by which time I don't remember anything useful about it. Comment your code. Your future self will thank you.

```
/*
 * socket.cpp
 *
 * Copyright 2017 Jim Strickland <jrs@jamesrstrickland.com>
 *
 * Standard GNU boilerplate:
 * This program is free software; you can redistribute it and/
 * or modify it under the terms of the GNU General Public
 * License as published by the Free Software Foundation;
 * either version 2 of the License, or (at your option) any
 * later version.
 *
 * This program is distributed in the hope that it will be
 * useful, but WITHOUT ANY WARRANTY; without even the implied
 * warranty of MERCHANTABILITY or FITNESS FOR A PARTICULAR PURPOSE.
 * See the GNU General Public License for more details.
 *
 * You should have received a copy of the GNU General Public
 * License along with this program; if not, write to the Free
 * Software Foundation, Inc., 51 Franklin Street, Fifth Floor,
 * Boston, MA 02110-1301, USA.
 *
 */
```

```
/*
 * Socket.cpp
 * This program lets you connect your Pi to a remote website on
 * the public internet, reads a number of lines from its front
 * page, and displays them in binary on the larson.cpp LED array.
 * It implements two classes: a GPIO class that does most of
 * what larson.cpp did, and a socket_class class that contains
 * the socket itself and all the code we need to go from an
 * internet address to reading and writing from a socket.
 * The socket_class class assumes we will only ever want
 * SOCK_STREAM connections (tcp), but it is compatible with
 * IPv4 and IPv6 both. We're using the modern addrinfo struct
 * instead of the old school ipv4 and ipv6 specific structs,
 * and this means that getaddrinfo() does most of the heavy
 * lifting for us determining what version of IP we're talking
 * to and so on.
 */

#include <iostream> //gives us cout, especially.
#include <wiringPi.h> //access to the GPIO pins.
#include <math.h> //exponent function pow() lives here.
#include <string> //std::strings
#include <csignal> //signal handlers need this.
#include <sys/socket.h> //the socket library.
#include <netdb.h> //addrinfo struct, plus a bunch of defines.
#include <unistd.h> //NULL pointer definition, general POSIX compliance.

#define LEDs 20
#define delaymils 100
#define buffer_length 150

#define debug_messages 1

bool running=true;

void SIGINT_handler(int signal_number){
    running=false;
}

/*
 * We're only using one namespace in this program, so it's safe
 * to set this program's default namespace to std.
 */
using namespace std;
```

```
/* gpio_class declaration
 * ----------------------------------------------------------------
 * Objects of this class represent the GPIO port with a public
 * function called "write" which lets outside functions send
 * c++ strings to the GPIO port for display on the LEDs.
 * ----------------------------------------------------------------
 * Private members:
 * ================================================================
 * int pins[]        :Variable
 *                    This private variable is an array
 *                    that maps the GPIO numbers to their
 *                    position in the 20 LED array we built
 *                    for the Larson project, from LED[0] to
 *                    LED[LEDs -1]. Assuming LEDs is defined
 *                    as 20, that's LED0 to LED19.
 * ----------------------------------------------------------------
 * gpio_write()
 * This private method accepts an 8-bit value (usually a
 * character), and lights the appropriate LEDs (from right to left).
 * Takes an 8-bit unsigned integer as a parameter. (A char would
 * probably work, but they're not explicitly 8-bit unsigned
 * data types.)
 * Returns nothing.
 * How it Works:
 * Take an 8 bit value in "data".
 *
 * Declare a local 8 bit unsigned integer (uint8_t) called "mask."
 *
 * Clear the pins by calling the clear_pins() public function.
 *
 * Iterate on c from 0 to 7.
 *         Set mask equal to 2^c - that is, the cth power of 2.
 *         (We're actually using the floating point pow
 *         function, and casting the inputs and results back
 *         and forth to ints.) Since a bit is a power of two,
 *         this sets one and only one bit in mask to 1.
 *
 *         If the value of data bit-wise anded with the value
 *         of mask is not 0 (false) then data must have that
 *         bit set. Turn on the appropriate LED.
```

```
*  -------------------------------------------------------------
*  Public Members:
*  =============================================================
*  We use the default constructor and destructor. We don't want
*  to initialize WiringPi in the constructor because if we have
*  multiple instances of this class, we put WiringPi in an unknown
*  state. (It SHOULD do nothing, but if the protection code
*  fails to account for our call, it's a fatal error.)
*
*  gpio_write_string()     :Method
*                           This public method takes a
*                           std::string called the_string,
*                           iterates through its data one
*                           character at a time and calls
*                           gpio_write() with each character,
*                           pausing after each one
*                           for delaymils milliseconds.
*                           It also prints out the string's
*                           data and each letter as it's sent
*                           to gpio_write.
*                           This method takes a std::string and
*                           returns nothing.
*  How it works:
*  ------------
*  Take a C++ string //object// called "the_string" as a parameter.
*  Declare an integer string_length and set it to the length
*  attribute of the_string.
*  Print the string to the terminal.
*  Iterate on c from 0 to string_length-1
*          Print the character returned by the at() method of
*          the_string at position c.
*          Call gpio_write() with the character returned by the
*          at() method of the_string.
*          delay delaymils milliseconds.
*  -------------------------------------------------------------
*  clear_pins()        :Method
*                       This public method iterates through the
*                       pins[] array attribute and switches all
*                       the pins HIGH, turning the LEDs off.
*                       This method returns nothing and takes no
*                       parameters.
```

327

```
 * How it works:
 * ------------
 * Iterate on c from 0 to LEDs -1 (from 0 to 19 most likely).
 *        Call pinMode with the value of pins[] at the c
 *        position to set the pin as an output. Only needs to
 *        be done once, but additional calls won't hurt anything.
 *        Call digitalWrite with the value of pins at the c
 *        position to set the pin HIGH, which raises the
 *        negative side of the LED to 3.3v, equal with the
 *        positive side, thus switching it off.
 * ----------------------------------------------------------------
 */
class gpio_class {
    private:
// =============================================================
    int pins[LEDs]={2,3,4,14,15,18,17,27,22,23,24,10,9,11,25,8,7,1,0,5};
//       --------------------------------------------------------
    void gpio_write(uint8_t data){ //send data to the GPIO pins.
        uint8_t mask=0;   //all the bits of mask start off as 0s.
        clear_pins(); //make sure nothing is displayed already.
        for (int c=0;c<8;c++){ //for 8 bits, we'll get 2^c.
            mask=(uint8_t)pow(2.0,(float)c); //and switch on one bit only.
            if (data & mask){ //and that one bit with data
                digitalWrite(pins[8-c],LOW);  //if data had that bit set
            }                                 //turn on that led.
        }
    }
//   ------------------------------------------------------------
    public:
// =============================================================
    void gpio_write_string(string the_string){ //Write strings LEDs.
      int string_length=the_string.length();//store this number in an int so
                                  //we don't call the function as much.

        #ifdef debug_messages

                cout<<"Writing this string: "<<the_string<<endl;
        #endif

        for (int c=0;c<string_length;c++){
            if (!running) return; //if our sigint handler fired, exit.
```

```
            #ifdef debug_messages
                    cout<<"C is: "<<c<<" Character is: "<<the_string.
                    at(c)<<endl;
            #endif

            gpio_write(the_string.at(c)); //send each character to
                                          //gpio_write().
            delay(delaymils);             //wait between characters.
        }
    };
// --------------------------------------------------------------
    void clear_pins(void){
        for (int c=0;c<LEDs;c++){ //iterate through all the pins.
            pinMode (pins[c],OUTPUT); //set them as OUTPUTS
            digitalWrite(pins[c],HIGH); //And turn
        }
    };
// --------------------------------------------------------------
};//end of gpio_class

/* socket_class declaration
 * --------------------------------------------------------------
 * The class socket_class contains the entire mechanism for
 * connecting to and exchanging data with an Internet host.
 * It makes a few assumptions: first, that we'll always be
 * creating TCP connections (SOCK_STREAMS).
 * Second, it assumes that DNS always works.
 * This class does understand IPv6 as well as IPv4 and implements
 * as neat a class as possible to do both.
 * --------------------------------------------------------------
 * Private
 * ==============================================================
 * file_descrptor      : Variable.
 *                       An integer, the file descriptor of
 *                       whatever socket we use.
 * --------------------------------------------------------------
 * exit_error          : Method.
 *                       Accepts an error message, displays
 *                       it, and terminates the program with
 *                       error status.
 *                       Accepts a std::string. Returns nothing.
```

```
* How it works
* ------------
*     Accept a std::string into the variable msg.
*     Display the string with cout.
*     Call the exit function with a status of 1.
* -------------------------------------------------------------
* dns_lookup          : Method
*                       Accepts a string containing an
*                       Internet address and an integer with
*                       a port number. Returns a pointer to
*                       an addrinfo linked list containing
*                       address information, IP version
*                       information, port information, and
*                       so on. Everything connect() needs to
*                       function.
*                       Accepts a string and an integer.
*                       Returns an addrinfo *.
* How it works
* ------------
*
*     Declare a pointer called server_info to an adderinfo
*     data structure.
*
* Declare an adderinfo datastructure called hints.
* (Hints is used to filter the output of the DNS lookup.)
*
* Set the hints.ai_socktype member to SOCK_STREAM.
* We only want to see TCP addresses.
*
* Set all other fields in hints to 0, which will cause no
* filtering on those fields.
*
* call the to_string function with port as its parameter and
* set the string text_port to the result. We need the port
* as a string containing the letters "80" rather than the
* integer value 80.
*
* Send output to the user telling them what text_port is set to.
*
* Do the actual DNS lookup with getaddrinfo. Pass that
* function the c string version of text_address and text_port,
* and the address of the hints addrinfo struct. Also pass in
* the address of the pointer server_info_pointer, so the
* //value// of server_info_pointer can be set to point at the
* linked list returned by getaddrinfo.
*
```

```
* If the dns lookup is successful,
*           declare an addrinfo pointer temp_addr,
*           and a char array host, with 256 chars of space.
*           It would have been nice to use a string here, but
*           getnameinfo absolutely refused to deal with them.
*
*           Iterate through the linked list that getaddrinfo
*           returned with a for loop on the ptr, a pointer to
*           adderinfo structs. When ptr is NULL, stop. Iterate
*           ptr by setting it to the .ai_next field of the
*           addrinfo struct ptr currently points at.
*
*               Because dereferencing pointers complicates
*               reading the code, we declare temp_addr as an
*               adder_info struct, and set that to the struct.
*               that ptr is currently pointing at.
*
*               Next, we call getnameinfo on tempaddr,ai_
*               adr,temp_addr.aiaddrlen, pass it the host char
*               array so it can fill it in, tell it how big the
*               host array is, decline to pass it flags, and
*               tell it we want the numeric hostname.
*
*               Display the hostname with cout. Don't pass endl yet.
*               There's more that goes in this output line.
*
*               If tempaddr_aifamily is AF_INET6,
*                   then we must be dealing with an IPv6
*                   address. Tell the users so.
*                   Otherwise tell them it's an IPv4 address.
*
*               Now write the endl.
*
*           Go back to the top of the for loop unless we're done.
*
*               Having exited the for loop, return server_info_ptr,
*               exiting the method.
*
* If we reach this point, the getaddrinfo call returned
* something besides 0. Remember we tested that clear up at the
* top? If it did that we had a DNS error, and can't proceed.
* Call the exit_error() function and tell the user DNS failed.
* Terminate the whole program.
```

```
*
* We can't ever get here, but we have to tell C++ that we're
* returning data, or it will complain.
* --------------------------------------------------------------
*
* Public
* ==============================================================
* connect_socket        :Method:
*                        This method takes a std::string
*                        address and an integer port, then
*                        does a DNS lookup on the address and
*                        uses the information that returns to
*                        create a socket with the right
*                        configuration and connect it to the
*                        address. This method takes a
*                        std::string address and an integer
*                        port and returns nothing.
* How it Works
* ------------
*     Take the string parameter address and the int parameter port.
*
*     Declare a 256 char array to hold text addresses, since
*     getnameinfo refuses to work with std::strings.
*
*     Declare a pointer named dns_results and point it to the
*     results returned by dnslookup on the address and port we
*     were given.
*
* Declare an addrinfo struct called temp_addr, because
* dereferencing pointers constantly is a nuisance.
*
* As with dnslookup, iterate on the adderinfo pointer ptr from
* dns_results to NULL.
*
*         Set temp_addr equal to the struct pointed at by ptr.
*         Saves a lot of dereferencing pointers.
*
*         Call getnameinfo on temp_addr.ai_addr,temp_addr.
*         ai_addrlen, host, the size of host, no flags, and
*         request a numeric host.
*
*         Now that host[] is set, use it to tell the user
*         which address we're trying.
*
```

```
*          Create the socket by setting file_descriptor to the
*          output of the socket() function called with
*          temp_addr.aifamily, SOCK_STREAM, and 0.
*          temp_addr.aifamily will be AF_INET for IPv4 and
*          AF_INET6 for IPv6. So our socket() call will work for
*
*          either one. If file_descriptor is -1, the socket
*          didn't create.
*              exit program on error.
*
*          Call connect() on the socket by passing connect the
*          socket's file_descriptor, the address as stored in
*          temp_addr.ai_addr (which includes the port), and the
*          address length stored in temp_addr.aiadderlen.
*
*          If we're successful (connect returns 0),
*              tell the user and
*              exit the for loop with break.
*
*          Otherwise close the socket.
*       Go back to the top of the for loop and try the next address.
*
* When we get here, either the for loop has exited and we've
* had no successful connections, or we've exited the for loop
* with the break on a successful connection. Either way, free
* the linked list that dns_lookup originally returned so as
* not to waste memory.
* ----------------------------------------------------------------
* read_socket()         :Method
*                        This method reads up to buffer_length
*                        characters from the socket, which were
*                        received from the remote host, and
*                        returns them in a std::string.
*                        It takes no parameters and returns a
*                        std::string.
* How it works
* ------------
* Declare a char array of buffer_length called from_server,
* because recv doesn't like std::strings.
*
* Declare an integer called bytes, and set it to the output of
* the recv() function, which we pass the socket's id
* (file_descriptor), the from_server char array, buffer_length -1
* (because strings always have a null terminator attached) and
* no flags.
*
```

```
* If bytes is less than zero
*          exit on error. Receive has failed.
*
* If we reach this point, the recv call worked. Tell the user
* how many bytes we got from the server.
*
* Load from_server into a std::string and return that
* std::string.
* This contains the buffer_length characters the remote host sent.
* ----------------------------------------------------------------
* write_socket()          :Method
*                          This method takes a std::string and
*                          writes its contents to the socket,
*                          sending them to the remote host.
*                          It takes a std::string parameter and
*                          returns nothing.
* How it Works
* ------------
* Accept a std::string into the variable text.
*
* Declare an integer, bytes, and set it to the output of a
* call to the send() function, which we pass the socket's
* file_descriptor. We next pass the results of the std::string
* text's c_str() member function, the results of the std::string
* text's length() function, and 0 flags.
*
* If bytes is less than zero
*          exit on error - the write failed.
*
* If we reach this point, tell the user how many bytes we sent.
* ----------------------------------------------------------------
* close_socket()          :Method
*                          Closes the socket.
*                          Takes no parameters, returns nothing.
* How it Works
* ------------
* Call the close function with our socket's file descriptor,
* set in the class private variable file_descriptor.
* ----------------------------------------------------------------
*/
```

```
class socket_class {
    private:
// ============================================================
    int file_descriptor=0;            //The all-important name of our socket.
// ------------------------------------------------------------
    void exit_error(string msg){ //display the message and terminate
        cout <<msg<<endl;         //the program. Something's gone wrong.
        exit(1);
    }
// ------------------------------------------------------------

    //look up the text address and return critical data: the IP address,
    //what kind of address it is, etc., in an adderinfo struct.

    addrinfo *dns_lookup(string text_address,int port){
        //declare variables
        addrinfo *server_info_ptr;

        //declare and set up hints
        addrinfo hints;
        hints.ai_socktype=SOCK_STREAM;
        hints.ai_family=0;
        hints.ai_protocol=0;
        hints.ai_flags=0;

        //declare and load the text_port string.
        string text_port=to_string(port);

        #ifdef debug_messages
            cout<<"Using port# "<<text_port<<endl;
        #endif

        if (getaddrinfo(text_address.c_str(),
                        text_port.c_str(),
                        &hints,
                        &server_info_ptr)==0){
            #ifdef debug_messages
                addrinfo temp_addr;
                char host[256]; //buffer for host names.

                for (addrinfo *ptr=server_info_ptr;ptr!=NULL;ptr=(*ptr).
                ai_next){
                    temp_addr=*ptr;
                    getnameinfo(temp_addr.ai_addr,
```

```
                              temp_addr.ai_addrlen,
                              host,
                              sizeof(host),
                              NULL,
                              0,
                              NI_NUMERICHOST);

            cout<<"Found SOCK_STREAM address: "<<host;
            if (temp_addr.ai_family==AF_INET6){
                cout <<" IPv6";
            }else{ //equal to AF_INET
                cout<<" IPv4";
            }
            cout<<"."<<endl;
        }
    #endif

    return server_info_ptr;
}else{
    exit_error("DNS Failed.");
    return server_info_ptr;
}
}; //end of dns_lookup.
// ------------------------------------------------------------

public:
// ============================================================
void connect_socket(string address,int port){ //creates and connects socket.
    #ifdef debug_messages
        char host[256]; //buffer for host address text.
    #endif

    addrinfo *dns_results_ptr=dns_lookup(address,port);
    addrinfo temp_addr;

    for (addrinfo *ptr=dns_results_ptr;ptr!=NULL;ptr=(*ptr).ai_next){
        temp_addr=*ptr;

        //Text-ify the address and tell the user we're trying it.
        #ifdef debug_messages
            getnameinfo(temp_addr.ai_addr,
                        temp_addr.ai_addrlen,
                        host,
                        sizeof(host),
                        NULL,
                        0,
                        NI_NUMERICHOST);
```

```cpp
            cout<<"Trying: "<<host<<endl;
        #endif

        //create socket.
        file_descriptor=socket(temp_addr.ai_family,
                               SOCK_STREAM,
                               0);
        if (file_descriptor==-1){ //socket returns -1 on fail.
            exit_error("Unable to create socket.");
        }

        //connect socket.
        if (connect(file_descriptor,
                    temp_addr.ai_addr,
                    temp_addr.ai_addrlen)==0){

            #ifdef debug_messages
                cout<<"Connected!"<<endl;
            #endif

            break;
        }else{ //connect returns -1 on failures.
            close(file_descriptor);
        }
    }
    freeaddrinfo(dns_results_ptr); //clear memory used by dns results.
}; //end of connect_socket.
// -------------------------------------------------------------
string read_socket(){
    char from_server[buffer_length]=""; //recv hates std::string.
    //also, as with all arrays, from_server is implicitly a pointer.
                            // like here.
    int bytes=0;            // VVV
    bytes=recv(file_descriptor,from_server,buffer_length-1,0);
    if (bytes<0){ //recv returns -1 on fails.
        exit_error("Error on Receive.");
    };

    #ifdef debug_messages
        cout<<"Received "<<bytes<<" bytes from server."<<endl;
    #endif

    return string(from_server); //calls the constructor of an unnamed
    //std::string.
}; //end of read_socket
```

```cpp
// ----------------------------------------------------------------
    void write_socket(string text){
        int bytes=send(file_descriptor,text.c_str(),text.length(),0);
        if (bytes<0){ //send returns -1 on fails.
            exit_error("Error on Send.");
        };

        #ifdef debug_messages
            cout<<"Sent "<<bytes<<" bytes to server."<<endl;
        #endif
    }; //end of write_socket
// ----------------------------------------------------------------
    void close_socket(){ //just a wrapper for the close() function.
        close(file_descriptor);
    }; //end of close_socket.
// ----------------------------------------------------------------
}; //end of socket_class.

int main(void){
    string message="";  //declare our message string
    int number_of_lines=0; //how many lines to read.
    string target_address; //what address should we use?
    string http_request=""; //what should we send the HTTP server?
    wiringPiSetupGpio(); //Set up the GPIO system to use GPIO pin #s.

        //Connect the signal handler to fire on SIGINT.
    signal(SIGINT,SIGINT_handler);

    cout<<"What address should I connect to?"<<endl;
    getline(cin,target_address);
    cout<<"How many lines should I read?"<<endl;
    cin>>number_of_lines;

    //HTTP requests have to be sent quickly, or the server times out.
    //Here, we're building a simple request to send us the website's
    //top level index file. You could put any path in here, however.
    cout <<"Building HTTP request."<<endl;
    http_request="GET http://"+target_address+"/index.html";
    http_request+=" HTTP/1.1\r\nhost:"+target_address+"\r\n\r\n";

    cout<<"Setting up GPIO bus object."<<endl;
    gpio_class gpio; //instantiate our gpio_class object.

    cout<<"Clearing GPIO pins."<<endl;
    gpio.clear_pins(); //use the gpio_class method clear_pins().

    cout<<"Setting up socket object."<<endl;
    socket_class socket; //instantiate our socket_class object.
```

```
cout<<"Connecting socket to "<<target_address<<"on port 80."<<endl;
socket.connect_socket(target_address,80); //connect our
//socket object to the target address the user specified, on port 80.
//port 80 is the standard for http (web) servers.

cout <<"Sending HTTP request: "+http_request<<endl;
socket.write_socket(http_request);
socket.write_socket("\r\n"); //send our request and an extra linefeed
//to the http server at that address.

for (int c=0;c<number_of_lines;c++){ //iterate on c for all the lines
    if (!running) break; //if our sigint handler fired, break.

    message=socket.read_socket(); //read from the socket into message
    cout<<"Received: "<<message<<"."<<endl; //show message
    gpio.gpio_write_string(message); //gpio_write_string message
    //so all the bytes of the lines wind up displayed on the LEDs.
};
socket.close_socket(); //close the socket. You only get so many,
//so clean up after yourself.

gpio.clear_pins(); //turn all the LEDs off.
return 0; //exit normally.
}; //End of program
```

Conclusion

In this chapter, we talked about what the Internet is, a little about how it works. Then we dove headlong into writing our own socket program to pull data from a remote web server for processing (also called scraping, in some circles) by the Pi, and ultimately displayed that data in binary on the LEDs of the Larson (Memorial) Scanner. We talked some about security, and why this method of polling a remote website might be safer than running a server on the Pi itself. Despite this, in the next chapter, we'll set up exactly that—a network server running on the Pi and using Apache and cgi-bin programming.

CHAPTER 10

Serving Pi: Network Servers

If you've read any tutorials other than the preceding chapter on socket programming, the next example they inevitably include is using socket programming to write your own server. If that's what you really want to do, go ahead. With what you've learned last chapter, it shouldn't be too hard. Server programming is easy enough to do, but writing a secure server is not. Think twice again before connecting a homemade server to the public Internet. It may take an infinite number of monkeys with typewriters an infinite amount of time to produce the works of Shakespeare, but even Internet trolls are smarter than monkeys, so it takes somewhat fewer of them much less time to figure out how to break your server.

If you're just looking for a way other than polling an outside web server to control your Pi from some other computer connected to the Internet, there's a better, easier, faster way than writing your own server, and that's what this chapter is about. We'll load the Apache web server onto our Pi. This server is maintained by people who are experts at security, and it's well tested by the near-infinite number of network trolls. It's a much harder target. We'll write a CGI program that controls the LED array left over from the various Larson projects, then write the HTML code we need to let a web browser communicate with the CGI, and thus, with our Pi. Along the way, we'll dispel some myths about GPIO programs needing to run as root, practice some of the filesystem knowledge we worked on a few chapters

© James R. Strickland 2018
J. R. Strickland, *Raspberry Pi for Arduino Users*,
https://doi.org/10.1007/978-1-4842-3414-3_10

back, and generally come around to the UNIX/Linux way of doing things. Also, if you're getting tired of projects based on the Larson (Memorial) Scanner LED array, you'll be pleased to know that this is the last one.

Running Your Own Programs

Up until now, we've run all of our programs inside the test window in Geany, for convenience's sake. In this project, we'll be running them in other accounts and testing them outside of Geany, so here's how that's done.

Open a terminal window on your Pi and cd to ~/projects/ Larson_pthread. If you type ls, you'll see Larson_pthread.cpp, Larson_pthread.o, and Larson_pthread. The .o file is an object file. It's the compiled output of Larson_pthread.cpp and nothing else. The file simply called Larson_pthread is the .o file linked with all the libraries we included in that program—iostream, csignal, WiringPi, and pthread. This is your executable. This is a program that can run directly on your Pi. Here's what that looks like.

```
pi@PiOW:~$ cd ~/projects/Larson_pthread
pi@PiOW:~/projects/Larson_pthread$ ls
Larson_pthread  Larson.pthread  Larson_pthread.cpp  Larson_pthread.o
pi@PiOW:~/projects/Larson_pthread$ ./Larson_pthread
Creating Thread Upper
Creating Thread Lower
It's really hard to see like this...
```

The LEDs should run with both eyes.

```
^CDone.
pi@PiOW:~/projects/Larson_pthread$
```

When you press Ctrl+C, it should exit and clear the LED array, thanks to the SIGINT handler.

The Apache Web Server

The Apache HTTP server, as it's formally called, is an open source, modular, cross-platform web server. It sits on socket 80 (for non-encrypted communications), answers requests, and serves web pages with the HTTP protocol. Fully half the web pages on the Internet as of January 2018, are served by Apache servers. It's robust, easy to work with, and well tested in terms of security. Conveniently, it's also available in the Debian software repositories Raspbian uses. In short, we can install it with apt-get.

Installing with Apt-Get

It's been a while since we last touched apt-get, so let's do a little review. Any time we install software, but particularly when we're installing a major package with security implications like Apache, it's a good idea to update the repository catalog, then update the operating system completely. We do want kernel upgrades, as they often have security implications too. It's a good idea to reboot after upgrading the operating system, to make sure all the new stuff is running. I'll just list the commands. (Also, yes, I switched Pis to get one I haven't already done this to. All this works on the Raspberry Pi Zero W, too.)

```
pi@Pi3:~$ sudo apt-get update
pi@Pi3:~$ sudo apt-get dist-upgrade
pi@Pi3:~$ sudo systemctl reboot
```

Once that's done, go ahead and install the Apache server. Once upon a time, this was a painful, drawn-out process that I got paid to write documentation for. Now it's a one-line command.

```
pi@Pi3:~$ sudo apt-get install apache2
Reading package lists... Done
```

Lots of information from apt-get was deleted.

```
Need to get 1,948 kB of archives.
After this operation, 6,263 kB of additional disk space will be used.
Do you want to continue? [Y/n] y
```

Once you press Y, apt-get will get chatty again, and I've cut all that out of this log. It will end with something like this, although your version number will likely be different:

```
Processing triggers for systemd (232-25+deb9u1) ...
pi@Pi3:~$
```

That's all there is to it. Apache is now installed and running. Go ahead and try it. You should be able to reach your Pi by putting its name in your web browser, followed by .local, to tell your system to use the zeroconf nameservice (aka Bonjour in the Mac world). Like this:

```
http://Pi3.local
```

Make sure to include http://, or your browser may "helpfully" throw your query to your search engine of choice, which won't know what you're talking about.

You can use the browser on your Pi, or another Pi if you like. Raspberry Pis running Raspbian have zeroconf installed by default, as do Macs and most Linux distributions, so the .local address should work properly. Windows users, your computer doesn't have zeroconf installed by default, but if you've installed Skype, iTunes, or any recent version of Photoshop, they all install it for you, so go ahead and try connecting. If the <your pi name>.local address doesn't work, Adafruit has an excellent page on installing zeroconf at https://learn.adafruit.com/bonjour-zeroconf-networking-for-windows-and-linux/overview.

If everything works as advertised, you should get a web page that looks something like Figure 10-1.

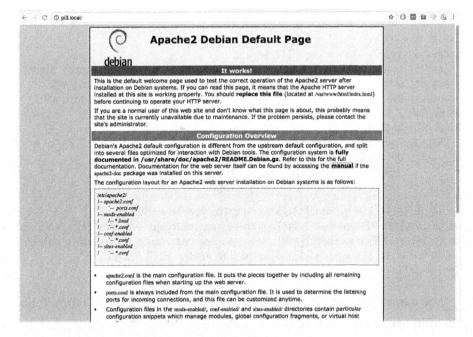

Figure 10-1. *Apache2 Debian default page*

Troubleshooting Apache

If you don't get a web page like the one shown in Figure 10-1, the most likely culprit is the address you used. Check your Pi's name by choosing the Raspberry Menu ➤ Preferences ➤ Raspberry Pi Configuration ➤ System. Make sure you used whatever name is in the Hostname box with .local appended to the end. If you can't reach it from your desktop computer, try it from the Pi's own browser. If that works, check your Pi's network connection and make sure your desktop has zeroconf or Bonjour running. You can check to make sure Apache is running by typing sudo systemctl status apache2. This tells systemd to check the status of the Apache server for you.

You should get this:

```
pi@Pi3:~$ sudo systemctl status apache2
apache2.service - The Apache HTTP Server
   Loaded: loaded (/lib/systemd/system/apache2.service; enabled; vendor preset:
   Active: active (running) since Wed 2018-01-10 16:55:37 MST; 57min ago
  Process: 398 ExecStart=/usr/sbin/apachectl start (code=exited, status=0/
  SUCCESS
 Main PID: 464 (apache2)
   CGroup: /system.slice/apache2.service
           ├─464 /usr/sbin/apache2 -k start
           ├─465 /usr/sbin/apache2 -k start
           └─466 /usr/sbin/apache2 -k start

Jan 10 16:55:37 Pi3 systemd[1]: Starting The Apache HTTP Server...
Jan 10 16:55:37 Pi3 apachectl[398]: AH00557: apache2: apr_sockaddr_info_get() fa
Jan 10 16:55:37 Pi3 apachectl[398]: AH00558: apache2: Could not reliably determi
Jan 10 16:55:37 Pi3 systemd[1]: Started The Apache HTTP Server.
lines 1-14/14 (END)
```

You can also try restarting Apache with the following in case something just didn't get started correctly:

```
sudo systemctl restart apache2
```

To debug deeper than this, take a look at the text file /var/log/apache2/error.log. We need Apache to be working for the project in this chapter. If you can't communicate with it, back up and fix Apache first.

Anatomy

Apache is, as I said previously, modular. This means it has a lot of configuration options. All of these are turned on and off and configured in /etc/apache2. Change to that directory in your terminal window and have a look around.

```
pi@Pi3:~$ cd /etc/apache2
pi@Pi3:/etc/apache2$ ls
apache2.conf    conf-enabled  magic          mods-enabled  sites-available
conf-available  envvars       mods-available  ports.conf    sites-enabled
pi@Pi3:/etc/apache2$
```

Configuring Apache is another one of those subjects that entire books have been written about, but the configuration system is pretty straightforward.

- `apache2.conf` is the main configuration file for the server.

- `conf-enabled` is a directory full of symbolic links to the configuration files in `conf-available` that are actually being used.

- `magic` (poorly named, in my opinion) is the configuration for the MIME typing system. In short, the system that sorts out what kind of file you're sending, marks it, and sends it so the browser understands.

- `mods-enabled` is a directory of simlinks to scripts in `mods-available` that loads specific modules of Apache when it is started. So if we were installing a module, we'd install it, then create a simlink (`ln -l`) in `mods-enabled` that links to the loading script for the module in `mods-available`. If there are config files for the modules, they must also be simlinked from `mods-available` to `mods-enabled`.

- The `sites-available` directory lists the websites we can host. On bigger installations, it's not uncommon for one Apache server to serve many, many URLs, and they'll be configured here. Ours just contains `000-default.conf`. The `sites-enabled` directory contains simlinks to files in `sites-enabled`.

- The `envvars` file sets the environment variables for the Apache server, mostly making sure that Apache knows what paths to find its files in.

- The `ports.conf` file is where the Apache server is configured with the ports it can use. Ours lists port 80, obviously, and port 443, for encrypted (secure socket layer) communication.

- The actual HTML (web page) files live in `/var/www/html`.

- CGI files live in `/usr/lib/cgi-bin`. Like with `/var/www/html`, you'll need root permissions (`sudo`) to modify these directories or their contents.

Configuring for CGI

Our Apache setup is going to be pretty simple. We're not adding a database or enabling any of a dozen web scripting languages like PHP or Python. We're just enabling CGI so we can drop an executable in `/usr/lib/cgi-bin` and have Apache call it. It takes two commands, plus one more to restart the server.

CD into the `/etc/apache2/mods-enabled` directory and create a symlink to `/etc/apache2/mods-available/cgi.load` called `cgi.load`. You can do an `ls` to make sure the link came out right if you like.

```
pi@Pi3:~$ cd /etc/apache2/mods-enabled
pi@Pi3:/etc/apache2/mods-enabled$ sudo ln -s ../mods-available/cgi.load cgi.load
pi@Pi3:/etc/apache2/mods-enabled$ ls cgi.load
cgi.load
pi@Pi3:/etc/apache2/mods-enabled$
```

The next thing you have to do is restart the server. I've used cd to go back to the pi account's home directory. You don't have to.

```
pi@Pi3:~$ sudo systemctl restart apache2
pi@Pi3:~$
```

That's it. That's all you have to do to the Apache server. Now you just need to write the program and the web page. Don't worry. They're short.

The Program: DisplayPost.cgi

CGI programs run under the auspices of the HTTP server, which is Apache in this case. Our web page will call the CGI program and send data to it via the HTML POST method. Apache will take the data the user put in the web page and put it in stdin, then call our CGI program, which will read stdin, send a text message to the user through the browser, and display the message the user sent on the Larson LED array. We'll deal with the CGI program first. It's easiest to test. Despite the .cgi extension we'll give it so Apache will load it when the time comes, it's written in C++, like everything else we've done in this book.

The Plan

Displaypost is derived from Socket.cpp. All the socket code is taken out, and we just read from stdin.

Of course, it's not quite that simple. Apache (and HTML) add a lot of information to the data sent with the POST command, so we'll need to strip that out to reveal the text the user sent. In your application, this data might be important, especially to verify that the web page you think called the CGI program is the one that actually did.

Once the text message is stripped of its HTML POST add-ons, display it to the user and write the text message to the LED array using the gpio_class from Socket.cpp.

Some Words on stdin

Most operating systems have several IO streams connected to a given program by default. Most of the time these are called the same things: stdin, stdout, and stderr. When we read "from the keyboard" with cin, we're reading from stdin. When we cout, we're writing to stdout. If our program throws errors that we don't explicitly send to cout, they go to

349

stderr. Since we're in a UNIX-like operating system, these all masquerade as files. This is useful to know, because you can redirect files in UNIX/Linux with the > and < operators. So if you want to log the output of a program, you type `program-name > my-output-file.txt`. To redirect a file to stdin for your program, you type `program-name <my-input-file.txt`. These are different from command-line parameters (for example, `nano test.txt`, where `nano` is the program name and `test.txt` is the file you want to edit), which are handled by the shell and read differently, and not something we'll be using in our programs.

Some Words on the HTML POST Method

Each field in an HTML form, which requests data from the user, has a name. When the POST method hands control to the CGI program, it prepends that field name, with an equals sign, to the value the user sent. Also, POST replaces every blank space in the posted data with a +. I cover the HTML side of this project more when we get to it, but we're about to spend some effort stripping all that stuff back out of the line we read from stdin.

Modifying Socket.cpp to Displaypost.cpp

Go ahead and create the `Displaypost` project. Now open `Socket.cpp`, choose File ➤ Save As, and save the file as `Displaypost.cpp` in the `/home/pi/projects/Displaypost` directory. Let's get started.

In the `#includes`, take out these lines:

```
#include <sys/socket.h>
#include <netdb.h>
```

`Displaypost.cpp` doesn't handle sockets for itself. Also comment out or remove this line:

```
#define debug_messages 1
```

All the output that Displaypost sends to stdout (anything with a cout, basically) will wind up transmitted to the browser. Having debug_messages turned on will either confuse the browser or the user.

The gpio_class remains the same, but the entire socket_class can be cut out. We're not using it. Also cut out everything between the declaration of the main() function and the end of main(). We'll be writing a completely new main().

Add the parse_cgi Function

For all that it does a simple job, strip out all the extra data that the HTML POST method put in our data stream, the parse_cgi function we're about to add is the most complicated in the program. We're going to dig a lot deeper into std::strings than we have previously.

```
string parse_cgi(string instring,string field_name){
```

Declare the function and take two std::strings as parameters— instring and field_name. instring is the raw HTML POST from stdin, and field_name is the name of the field from the form. Since we'll define that in the HTML file, we can hard-code it in main() and pass that hard-coded value here.

```
string temp=instring;
```

Declare a third string local to parse_cgi and copy instring into it.

```
if (temp.find(field_name)!=temp.npos){
```

The std::string object temp has a number of useful constants and methods we're going to use. The first is find(). Remembering that the find() method is part of a string object (like temp), if you call temp. find("some string"), it will return the location of the leading s in "some string" if the words "some string" occur in temp. If they don't, it returns some other value. That other value is not an integer. Fortunately, that value is defined in a constant in the `temp` object, called `temp.npos`. So, if `temp.find(field_name)` does not equal `temp.npos`, it means `"some string"` does occur in `temp`.

```
temp.replace(temp.find(field_name+"="),
             field_name.length()+1,
             "");
}
```

Here, we're using even more of the `std::string` goodness. First, we add an `=` to the end of fieldname with the `+` method of the `field_name` `std::string` object and send the result to `temp.find()`. `Temp.find()` returns the position of the first letter in whatever the `field_name` `std::string` contains, along with the `=` sign. Then we call the `replace()` method of the `temp` object. `Replace` takes three parameters: starting position, length of text to be replaced, and the replacement text. We use the results of our `find()` call as the starting position, the results of the `length()` method of the temp object (+1) as the length, and an empty string as the replacement string. This replaces the `<some field name>` `=` that the HTML `POST` method inserted with nothing, therefore getting rid of it. But we're not done yet.

```
for (string::iterator c=temp.begin();c<=temp.end();c++){
    if(*c=='+'){
        *c=' ';
    }
}
```

We've come a long way in our programming lives to get here. There's a lot going on in these three lines of code. Obviously, we're doing a `for` loop, and if looks like the kind of loop you've done to traverse linked lists before, you've got a good eye. That's exactly what's going on. We've talked a lot about the `std::string` class, but remember we included it as a library. There's more to it than just the class. It has its own datatype for iterating through a `std::string` contents. It's a pointer datatype, and we need one. To get at that datatype, we tell C++ to use the `string::` namespace and let us define `c` as a `string::iterator` type. We initialize it at `temp.begin()`, which returns a `string::iterator` type. After that, we compare `c` to `temp.end()`, which also returns a `string::iterator` type. If it's lower we do... what?

Yes. Pointer arithmetic. I said previously that I don't like pointer arithmetic—that it's a great way to wind up poking at memory you don't own—and I stand by that. But in this object's data structures, we're tightly constrained between two good values that the object has set for us. We can do it here. The `c` iterator gets advanced to the next correct memory address, and we loop on through.

Remember, `c` is a pointer. It points to the characters in the `std::string` temp, between `temp.begin()` and `temp.end()`. So if we dereference it, we get a character at that position in the `temp` string object. If that character is +, we replace it with an empty space.

```
return temp; //return the modified string.
}
```

Once we're done modifying `temp`, return it.

A Few Words on Double and Single Quotes

In C++, as in C, double quotes contain a constant `char` array value. You can compare it to other character arrays, move it into strings, and so on. Single quotes contain a single `char`.

Rewriting the main() Function

Compared to the `parse_cgi` function, the `main()` function is simple and direct. It declares a `std::string` called message, sets up WiringPi, hooks up the `SIGINT` handler (probably unnecessarily), instantiates a `gpio_class` object called `gpio`, clears the pins, reads the line from stdin, feeds it to `parse_cgi`, sends the results as a text message to the browser, and feeds the results to `gpio.writestring()`. Once that's all done, it clears the LEDs and exits. There is one new command that I'll note when we get there.

```
int main(void){
    string message;
    wiringPiSetupGpio();

    signal(SIGINT,SIGINT_handler);
```

Declare a std::string called message, set up WiringPi, and hook up the SIGINT handler.

```
gpio_class gpio;
gpio.clear_pins();
```

Instantiate a gpio_class object called gpio, and use it to clear the LED array by setting the pins high.

```
getline(cin,message);
```

Read the first line from cin, which is the STDIN file descriptor. Put the results in the message std::string. getline is a specialized form of read.

```
message=parse_cgi(message,"in_text");
```

Send the message string object to parse_cgi(), along with the field name "in_text", which is the same one we use in the HTML file. Set message equal to the result.

```
cout << "Content-type:text/html\n\n"<<endl;
```

The first time this program talks to the browser, it must send the content type information, or the browser will throw an error message.

```
cout <<"<p>Wrote: \""<<message<<"\" to GPIO.</p>"<<endl;
```

Send the contents of the message string object to the browser, mostly so we can make sure parse_cgi did its job. We surround it with the HTML <p> and </p> tags so HTML will treat this little blob of text as a paragraph.

```
gpio.gpio_write_string(message);
```

Send the message string object to the gpio_write_string method of the gpio object, which displays the bytes of that string to the Larson LED array.

```
gpio.clear_pins();
```

Turn all the LEDs off by setting the pins high using the clear_pins() method of the gpio object.

```
return 0;
```

Exit normally.

```
}; //End of program
```

Testing the Program

We'll need a short text file to feed Displaypost to make sure it works. Use cd to get into the /usr/pi/projects/Displaypost directory and use your editor of choice to create a text file. The text can be anything you want that will fit in one line. I used the nano editor, as shown in Figure 10-2. You can call the file whatever you like. I called mine test.txt.

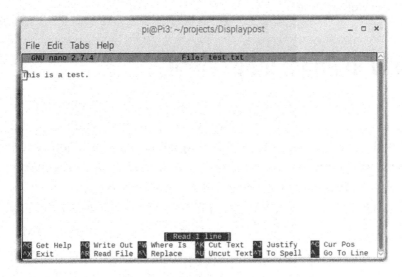

Figure 10-2. *Creating the text test file*

Okay, we have the pieces, so let's test. Make sure you (and your `test.txt` file) are in the `/home/pi/projects/Displaypost` directory. (You can do it otherwise, but putting the pathnames in gets tedious quickly.) Then call the `Displaypost` program with `./` (because bash doesn't have this directory on the list of directories it searches for programs) and redirect `test.txt` to its `stdin`. Like this:

```
pi@Pi3:~/projects/Displaypost$ ./Displaypost < test.txt
```

You should get output that looks a lot like what follows, and your LED array should flash out the bytes of your `test.txt` file.

```
Content-type:text/html

<p>Wrote: "This is a test." to GPIO.</p>
pi@Pi3:~/projects/Displaypost$
```

Note that the `Content-type` line is critical and must be followed with double carriage return/linefeeds. Note the `<p>` and `</p>` tags. These are the two lines that `Displaypost` will send to `stdout`, which will be sent to the web browser. The last line of this output is bash talking. Apache won't send that to the web browser.

The Web Page: index.html

If you're going to do this kind of project for real, I strongly encourage you to learn some HTML. It's far, far beyond the scope of this book, and I'm by no means an HTML expert, so I'm only going to cover the minimum you need to make a page that works. Obviously, HTML is a big topic, the subject of many books and websites. Pick your favorite.

Go ahead and create a new document in Geany and save it as `index.html`. Geany does a reasonable job editing and syntax-coloring HTML. If this is your first exposure to HTML, the biggest single thing you must remember is that HTML tags (anything in <> marks) nearly always come in pairs. For every <p> there will be a </p>. And so on. The first tag opens the area, the second with the slash closes it. Because HTML is kind of a sloppy spec, it's not always true, but nearly enough for our purposes.

An HTML document is a text file with four major parts, and some of them are nested inside each other.

DOCTYPE Declaration

This data is not displayed, but it tells the browser what kind of data it's about to receive. This is not actually an HTML tag, it's an instruction to the browser. You can tell because it begins with <! and has no closing tag. At a minimum, for web browsers to load your document reliably, you should declare it like this:

```
<!DOCTYPE html>
```

The <html> and </html> Tags

The next required part of a web page are the <html> and </html> tags. The <html> tag is the root of the HTML document, and </html> closes it. These should surround the rest of the document. Without </html>, the browser never knows for sure when to stop trying to read more data from the server.

The <head> and </head> Tags

Inside the <html> tags are the <head> and </head> tags. This data is also not displayed, but it can be used to set the title that shows at the top of your browser, among many, many other things. Make sure to use the </head> tag when you're done with the head information, otherwise the browser will be confused about what to display and what not to.

The <body> and </body> Tags

Also inside the <html> tags, after the closing head tag (</head>), is the body. Its opening tag is <body>, and its closing tag is </body>. This is where everything else in the web document goes. So a minimal document skeleton would look like this:

```
<!DOCTYPE html>
<html>
        <head>
        </head>

        <body>
        </body>
</html>
```

It doesn't do anything, but at least your browser shouldn't choke on it.

The index.html Web Document

Since we haven't touched HTML until now, let's walk through this file in some detail.

```
<!DOCTYPE html>
<html>
```

Declare the doctype and open the HTML document root.

```
<head>
        <title>Displaypost Test</title>
</head>
```

Declare the head of the HTML document, and set the title to Displaypost Test with the <title> and </title> tags. This should appear somewhere at the top of your browser, or in the tab name if your browser is so equipped.

```
<body>
        <h1>Displaypost Test</h1>
        <p>This page is here to test the displaypost cgi-bin program.
        To use it, type some text in the form below and hit the "post" button.
        </p>
```

Open the <body> tag of the document. (Remembering that the <html> tag is still open as well.) Keeping track of what tags are open will make debugging web pages much, much less painful. They're rather like open and close braces { } in C++. If you lose count, nothing works.

```
<form action="/cgi-bin/displaypost.cgi" method="post">
```

Tags can take arguments. In this case, the tag is <form>, but we're giving it an action to take. That action is to go to the cgi-bin directory set up in the web server and call displaypost.cgi using the POST HTML method. If you think Displaypost (the executable) will wind up being displaypost.cgi, you're right. If you think POST is what causes the browser to send data to the web server for the web server to send to displaypost.cgi, you're right again.

HTML is case insensitive, but the Linux filesystem is most certainly case sensitive, so it's best to keep your CGI and HTML filenames lowercase.

```
Type Text Here: <input type="text" name="in_text"> <br>
```

Inside a form, the <input> tag gives the user a line to type information in. Remember how I said that not all tags have closing tags? Input is one of them. The <br> tag is another.

```
<input type="submit" value="Press Here to Send">
```

This line creates a button called "Press Here to Send." You can just press Return, or you can click the nice button if you want to.

```
</form>
```

That's all there is in our form. It can have as many input values as you want, but in our case we only want one. That's all Displaypost knows how to deal with anyway, and more would definitely make our parse_cgi function choke.

```
    </body>
</html>
```

Make sure, absolutely sure, that you have </body> and </html> tags. There are no guarantees that your document will display at all without them. As for the indentation, it's customary to indent items that are nested inside each other in HTML this way, exactly the same way we do in C++. This isn't for the browser's benefit—the browser ignores extra spaces—it's to make the HTML human-readable. I've found that making code human-readable is always a good idea, since I'm usually the human who has to read it and fix it. The full code of the HTML document is listed later in this chapter, underneath the source code for Displaypost.

If you click execute on Geany, the file should come up in the web browser on your Pi. Also, be aware that Geany will automatically fill in the close tags when you write an open tag. So <body> will have </body> appended to it. Geany's smart enough to know not to do that with browser instructions starting with < !

Hooking Everything Up

Okay. We have Displaypost working, and we have a web page that should call it. Let's hook everything up. Use cp and sudo to copy Displaypost to /usr/lib/cgi-bin and call it displaypost-cgi.

Next, take a quick look in /var/www/html to see if there's an index. html document already there. There should be. You can take a look at the file if you want, but you've already seen what it looks like in your web browser. If not, the beginning of it is in Figure 10-1. We don't want it anymore. We're going to copy our index.html file right over top of it with sudo and cp. Altogether, these commands look like this:

```
pi@Pi3:~/projects/Displaypost$ sudo cp Displaypost /usr/lib/cgi-bin/displaypost.cgi
pi@Pi3:~/projects/Displaypost$ ls /var/www/html/index.html
index.html
pi@Pi3:~/projects/Displaypost$ sudo cp index.html /var/www/html/index.html
pi@Pi3:~/projects/Displaypost$
```

All the pieces are now in place, but if you've jumped ahead and tried the web server, you'll find that the cgi-bin doesn't work. In fact, you'll find that Apache throws an internal server error message to the browser. The file is there—it was set executable by Geany when we created it—but Apache can't run it.

Adding the GPIO Group to the www-data Account

If you've run in Raspberry Pi circles much, you may have been told that you have to run gpio programs as root. Nothing could be further from the truth, and in fact, this is a really bad idea. You most certainly do not want Apache running as root, nor any script callable from the outside world. The problem is that the GPIO pins require a special group to access. The pi account is a member of that group by default. The account that owns Apache, www-data, is not. So here's where the knowledge about groups that I went over way back in Chapter 3, "Survival Linux," comes into play. If we can add the gpio group to the user www.data, the Apache server will be able to access the gpio pins just fine.

You do that with the usermod command, like this: sudo usermod -a -G gpio www-data. Be careful with usermod. It's one of those commands that if you feed it a typo or two, it can really wreak havoc. Here's what we're doing. The usermod program modifies system users. You can change virtually any aspect of the user's information in the system. We chose the –a flag to append a user to a group. –G specifies the list of supplementary groups (everyone has their own file group) that the user is part of. We're telling usermod to append the group gpio to the user www.data. Reloading the web page now still won't work. We have to restart Apache for the changes to be applied to it.

```
pi@Pi3:~$ sudo usermod -a -G gpio www-data
pi@Pi3:~$ sudo systemctl restart apache2
pi@Pi3:~$
```

Running the Project

Finally. Here we are. Ready to run. Apache has the permissions it needs to access the gpio pins because its owning account, www-data, is a member of the gpio group. We've set up Apache's mods-enabled directory with a link to cgi.load. The displaypost.cgi program is in /usr/lib/cgi-bin, and the index.html file is in /var/www/html.

Go ahead and feed your web browser the address: http://<your pi name>.local/index.html. Fill in the form and either press Return or click the button. The LEDs should light and you should get your message back on your web browser. Figure 10-3 shows what that looked like before pressing Return.

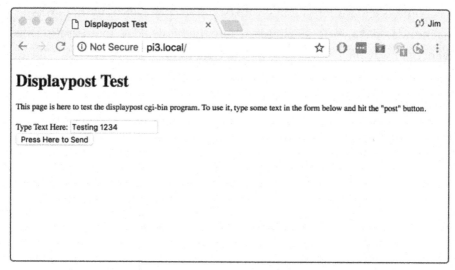

Figure 10-3. *Web page loaded*

As you can see, the page loaded and gave me the form. I filled it in with Testing 1234. Note that if you put punctuation in, it will be escaped into the appropriate HTML codes. Our parse_cgi function doesn't handle those. Figure 10-4 shows the result.

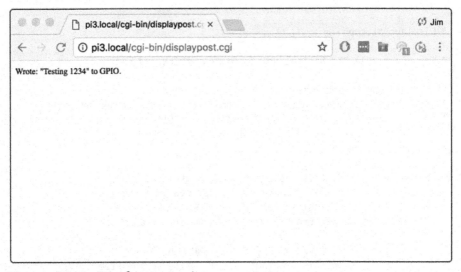

Figure 10-4. *Displaypost.cgi run*

Note that the results page doesn't load until the LED array is done flashing, when displaypost.cgi exits. This is important. Your CGI programs should, like interrupt service routines, get in, do what they need to do, and get out.

I can't stress enough that Socket.cpp and displaypost.cgi (combined with Apache) are powerful tools. They give your gadget enormous reach and invite the whole world (if you set it up that way) to come play with your gadget.

The Code: displaypost.cgi

As always, here's the source code, in this case for displaypost.cgi. It's also known as Displaypost.cpp. As is often true, my comments are longer than the code.

```
/*
 * Displaypost.cpp
 *
 * Copyright 2017 Jim Strickland <jrs@jamesrstrickland.com>
 *
 * Standard GNU boilerplate:
 * This program is free software; you can redistribute it and/or modify
 * it under the terms of the GNU General Public License as published by
 * the Free Software Foundation; either version 2 of the License, or
 * (at your option) any later version.
 *
 * This program is distributed in the hope that it will be
 * useful, but WITHOUT ANY WARRANTY; without even the implied
 * warranty of MERCHANTABILITY or FITNESS FOR A PARTICULAR
 * PURPOSE.  See the GNU General Public License for more details.
 *
 * You should have received a copy of the GNU General Public
 * License along with this program; if not, write to the Free
 * Software Foundation, Inc., 51 Franklin Street, Fifth Floor,
 * Boston, MA 02110-1301, USA.
 *
 */

/*
 * Displaypost.cpp
 * This program lets you connect your Pi to a remote website on
 * the public internet, reads a number of lines from its front
 * page, and displays them in binary on the larson.cpp LED array.
 * It implements two classes: a gpio class that does most of what
 * larson.cpp did, and a socket_class class that contains the
 * socket itself and all the code we need to go from an internet
 * address to reading and writing from a socket. The socket_class
 * class assumes we will only ever want SOCK_STREAM connections
 * (tcp), but it is compatible with IPv4 and IPv6 both. We're
 * using the modern addrinfo struct instead of the old school
 * ipv4 and ipv6 specific structs, and this means that
 * getaddrinfo() does most of the heavy lifting for us
 * determining what version of IP we're talking to and so on.
 */
```

```
#include <iostream> //gives us cout, especially.
#include <wiringPi.h> //access to the GPIO pins.
#include <math.h> //exponent function pow() lives here.
#include <string> //std::strings
#include <csignal> //signal handlers need this.
#include <unistd.h> //NULL pointer definition, general POSIX compliance.

#define LEDs 20
#define delaymils 100
#define buffer_length 150

//#define debug_messages 1
//We don't want the debug messages this time around. We have to be
//much more careful with our output lest we confuse the server,
//the browser, or both.

bool running=true; //clear the flag our SIGINT handler uses for
//cleaning up the LEDs after use when we terminate the program.

void SIGINT_handler(int signal_number){
        running=false;
        //handle when we throw the program a SIGINT. Which we probably
        //can't in this version.
}

/*
 * We're only using one namespace in this program, so it's safe to set
 * this program's default namespace to std.
 */
using namespace std;

/* gpio_class declaration
 * ----------------------------------------------------------------
 * Objects of this class represent the GPIO port with a public
 * function called "write" which lets outside functions send
 * c++ strings to the GPIO port for display on the LEDs.
 * ----------------------------------------------------------------
 * Private members:
 * ================================================================
 * int pins[]             :Variable
 *                        This private variable is an array
 *                        that maps the GPIO numbers to their
 *                        position in the 20 LED array we built
 *                        for the Larson project, from LED[0] to
 *                        LED[LEDs -1]. Assuming LEDs is defined
 *                        as 20, that's LED0 to LED19.
 * ----------------------------------------------------------------
```

```
* gpio_write()
* This private method accepts an 8 bit value (usually a
* character), and lights the appropriate LEDs (from right to
* left). Takes an 8 bit unsigned integer as a parameter. (A char would probably
* work, but they're not explicitly 8 bit unsigned datatypes.)
* Returns nothing.
* How it Works:
* Take an 8 bit value in "data".
*
* Declare a local 8 bit unsigned integer (uint8_t) called "mask."
*
* Clear the pins by calling the clear_pins() public function.
*
* Iterate on c from 0 to 7.
*           Set mask equal to 2^c - that is, the cth power of 2.
*           (We're actually using the floating point pow
*           function, and casting the inputs and results back
*           and forth to ints.) Since a bit is a power of two,
*           this sets one and only one bit in mask to 1.
*
*           If the value of data bit-wise anded with the value
*           of mask is not 0 (false) then data must have that
*           bit set. Turn on the appropriate LED.
* --------------------------------------------------------------
* Public Members:
* ==============================================================
* We use the default constructor and destructor. We don't want
* to initialize wiringPi in the constructor because if we have
* multiple instances of this class, we put wiringPi in an
* unknown state. (It SHOULD do nothing, but if the protection
* code fails to account for our call, it's a fatal error.)
*
* gpio_write_string()        :Method
*                            This public method takes a std::string
*                            called the_string, iterates through its data
*                            one character at a time and calls
*                            gpio_write() with each character, pausing
*                            after each one for delaymils milliseconds.
*                            It also prints out the string's data and
*                            each letter as it's sent to gpio_write.
*                            This method takes a std::string and returns
*                            nothing.
```

```
* How it works:
* ------------
* Take a C++ string //object// called "the_string" as a parameter.
* Declare an integer string_length and set it to the length attribute
* of the_string.
* Print the string to the terminal.
* Iterate on c from 0 to string_length-1
*           Print the character returned by the at() method of
*           the_string at position c.
*           Call gpio_write() with the character returned by
*           the at() method of the_string.
*           delay delaymils milliseconds.
* -----------------------------------------------------------------
* clear_pins()          :Method
*                       This public method iterates through the
*                       pins[] array attribute and switches all the
*                       pins HIGH, turning the LEDs off.
*                       This method returns nothing and takes no
*                       parameters.
* How it works:
* ------------
* Iterate on c from 0 to LEDs -1 (from 0 to 19 most likely).
*           Call pinMode with the value of pins[] at the
*           c position to set the pin as an output. Only needs
*           to be done once, but additional calls won't hurt anything.
*           Call digitalWrite with the value of pins at the c
*           position to set the pin HIGH, which raises the
*           negative side of the LED to 3.3v, equal with the positive side,
*           thus switching it off.
* -----------------------------------------------------------------
*/
class gpio_class {
      private:
// =============================================================
      int pins[LEDs]={2,3,4,14,15,18,17,27,22,23,24,10,9,11,25,8,7,1,0,5};
// -------------------------------------------------------------
      void gpio_write(uint8_t data){ //send data to the GPIO pins.
            uint8_t mask=0; //all the bits of mask start off as 0s.
            clear_pins(); //make sure nothing is displayed already.
            for (int c=0;c<8;c++){ //for 8 bits, we'll get 2^c.
                  mask=(uint8_t)pow(2.0,(float)c); //and switch on one bit only.
```

```
                if (data & mask){ //and that one bit with data
                        digitalWrite(pins[8-c],LOW);  //if data had that bit set
                }                                      //turn on that led.
            }
        }
// ------------------------------------------------------------
        public:
// ============================================================
        void gpio_write_string(string the_string){ //Write strings LEDs.
            int string_length=the_string.length();//store this number in an
                                                   //int so we don't call the
                                                   //function as much.
            #ifdef debug_messages
                    cout<<"Writing this string: "<<the_string<<endl;
            #endif

            for (int c=0;c<string_length;c++){
                    if (!running) return; //if our sigint handler fired, exit.

                    #ifdef debug_messages
                        cout<<"C is: "<<c<<" Character is: "<<the_string.
                        at(c)<<endl;
                    #endif

                    gpio_write(the_string.at(c)); //send each character to
                                                  //gpio_write().
                    delay(delaymils);   //wait between characters.
            }
        };

// ------------------------------------------------------------
        void clear_pins(void){
            for (int c=0;c<LEDs;c++){ //iterate through all the pins.
                pinMode (pins[c],OUTPUT); //set them as OUTPUTS
                digitalWrite(pins[c],HIGH); //And turn them OFF
            }
        };
// ------------------------------------------------------------
};//end of gpio_class

//clean out all the stuff the web server puts into a string during post.
string parse_cgi(string instring,string field_name){
        string temp=instring;
        if (temp.find(field_name)!=temp.npos){
```

```
        //if temp.find(field_name)!=string::npos, we found something.
        //We're using the string class's npos constant here. See below.
        temp.replace(temp.find(field_name+"="),
                        field_name.length()+1,
                        "");
    }
    //use the replace() function of std::strings to remove the field
    //name and the = sign that comes after it.

    for (string::iterator c=temp.begin();c<=temp.end();c++){
            //iterator is a datatype defined in std::strings. By using the
            //scope resolution operator, we can use the type here, outside
            //a string object (But it only makes sense in operations on
            //a string object.)
            if(*c=='+'){
                *c=' ';
            }
                //An iterator struct is a pointer.
                //If whatever address c points at contains a "+" character...
                //set whatever address c points at to contain a blank space.

    } //Ever wonder what pointer arithmetic is? We just did some.

    return temp; //return the modified string.
}
    //We could, and perhaps should, subclass std::string and make
    //parse_cgi part of it, but it doesn't really buy us much clarity-wise.
    //Basically it would allow us to attach our own member function to string
    //and use all its public members. Private members would still be off limits.

int main(void){
    string message;   //declare our message string
    wiringPiSetupGpio(); //setup the GPIO system to use GPIO pin #s.

        //connect up the signal handler to fire on SIGINT.
    signal(SIGINT,SIGINT_handler);

    gpio_class gpio; //instantiate our gpio_class object.
    gpio.clear_pins(); //use the gpio_class method clear_pins().

    getline(cin,message); //read stdin (Standard command line input) for
    //text to put into the std::string message. The http server puts any
    //messages sent from browser to server in posts into the cgi as on stdin.
```

```
    message=parse_cgi(message,"in_text"); //Grind out the stuff that post
    //put in our input string.

    cout << "Content-type:text/html\n\n"<<endl;
    cout <<"<p>Wrote: \""<<message<<"\" to GPIO.</p>"<<endl;
    //Display the text, along with a content type so the server knows what
    //it's sending the viewer.

    gpio.gpio_write_string(message);
    //GPIO_write the string, in binary, on the LEDs.

    gpio.clear_pins(); //turn all the LEDs off.
    return 0; //exit normally.
}; //End of program
```

The Code: index.html

As promised, here's the code for index.html. It contains no comments
whatsoever.

```
<!DOCTYPE html>
<html>
    <head>
        <title>Displaypost Test</title>
    </head>
    <body>
        <h1>Displaypost Test</h1>
        <p>This page is here to test the displaypost cgi-bin program.
        To use it, type some text in the form below and hit the "post"
        button.
        </p>
        <form action="/cgi-bin/displaypost.cgi" method="post">
            Type Text Here: <input type="text" name="in_text"> <br>
            <input type="submit" value="Press Here to Send">
        </form>

    </body>
</html>
```

Conclusion

In this chapter, instead of writing our own socket server, we installed the Apache web server and put our own code in a `cgi-bin` program, where the web server can call it. The code allows a remote webserver to type a string in and have that string displayed on the Larson (Memorial) Scanner LEDs. We also talked about how to start and stop Apache, wrote a little HTML to connect our `cgi-bin` to a website, and learned how to run WiringPi programs from unprivileged users, instead of running them as root, as many (outdated) tutorials recommend.

In the next chapter, we dig into filesystems and reading and writing files in them.

CHAPTER 11

Files and Filesystems

In case it wasn't obvious by now, UNIX-like operating systems are all about files. Files are one of the great strengths of the Raspberry Pi platform and are very difficult (but not impossible) to do with an Arduino. Files allow you to store data, and lots of it, with only a little code. We're going to discuss files and filesystems in Raspbian Linux a bit, and then add a second storage device (a USB flash drive) to the system and read and write some files on it.

Files

Conceptually, a file is a stream of data with a beginning and an end. You open the file to read it or write it, close the file when you're done, and you can seek to any point on the file. In the really old days, when you worked with data stored on magnetic tape, this is how files were laid out. There might be a directory file that told your program where to advance the tape in order to get to a specific file. More sophisticated tapes even had directories of directories, but you didn't want to hop around too much on the tape, because each time you did, you might have to wind a thousand feet of tape to get the file you wanted. Nine-track tapes went functionally extinct in 2003, so obviously that's not what's going on now, but the commands mount and umount were born in the days when you mounted and unmounted tapes. It's different today, and there are a lot of layers of abstraction that happen below the simple file.

© James R. Strickland 2018
J. R. Strickland, *Raspberry Pi for Arduino Users*,
https://doi.org/10.1007/978-1-4842-3414-3_11

Jargon

When you type ls, you are looking at the contents of a directory, which (one assumes) lists all the files in a directory. This may or may not be a mount point for an entire filesystem to connect it to the directory tree for the entire Linux filesystem. Clear as mud? Let's de-jargonize.

- *Directory tree:* The virtual tree of nested directories. / (root) contains them all, /home is a directory in / that contains all the system's users, /home/pi contains all of Pi's files, and so on. Don't confuse the filesystem root with the root account or root privileges. The root account owns /, and root privileges let you access anything as though you are the root account, but they're three separate concepts.

- *Device*: A hardware device, pointed to by a file in / dev. For example, /dev/sda. In the context of files and filesystems, a device will normally contain at least one partition and one filesystem. Modern Linux systems fill in devices in /dev for you when they detect that a device has been added. Devices have traditionally been called *drives*. I'll call them devices to try and avoid confusion.

- *Partition*: A subdivision of a device that becomes its own volume. Listed as a subdevice in /dev. For example, /dev/sda1. The main microSD card in our Pis has five separate partitions available in Linux. See for yourself with ls /dev/mmcblk0*, which is the device driver for microSD cards.

- *Volume*: A filesystem. Normally used in the context of the Logical Volume Manager (LVM) system, in which volumes can span multiple partitions or physical devices. Often used interchangeably with filesystem.

- *Filesystem*: One of two meanings. Either the entire file space available to the Linux system, or a formatted partition or volume. Filesystems are block devices, which means they are sent data in blocks rather than character streams as character devices are.

- *Mount point:* A directory on the directory tree where a new device can be mounted, making the directories in that device show up on the directory tree. So for example, if you mount a flash key to the mount point `/media/pi/stuff` and then `cd` to `/media/pi/stuff`, you will see what is on the flash key. Permissions and ownership apply.

The takeaway here is that these are all different levels of abstraction for physical devices containing data. A device gets you the driver for the hardware. A volume or a filesystem is the "formatting" that lives (usually) inside a partition on a device, and you mount it into the directory tree on a mount point.

Mount Points and Filesystem Types

The days are long past when you could just open a floppy drive and remove the media without telling the operating system. Modern operating systems like Linux will complain vociferously if you remove physical media (devices) without mounting them. You may well lose data, perhaps even all the data on the device. In Linux, to mount and unmount a filesystem, you need three things: the mount point, the filesystem type, and of course, a filesystem to mount.

Mount Point

The mount point is simply a directory somewhere in the existing directory tree. Here, let's make one.

```
pi@pi3plus:~$ mkdir myFlash
pi@pi3plus:~$ ls myFlash
pi@pi3plus:~$
```

Note that there's nothing in the mount point directory when the device (drive) is mounted there, and for sanity's sake (yours), you want it that way. If there are files in there, they won't be harmed, but you won't be able to access them while the filesystem is mounted. What you'll see instead is the outermost directory of the mounted filesystem.

Filesystem Types

Linux knows a lot of different filesystem types. Even a fairly basic setup like the Pi has at least three different types of filesystems mounted right now, as we speak. You can see them with the df command, for display filesystem. We'll pass it the h flag, so we get the size in mebibytes and gibibytes instead of bytes (h for human readable), and we'll pass it the T (capital T) flag for Type.

Unless they've drastically changed things in Raspbian between now for me and now for you, the results will look something like this:

```
pi@pi3plus:~$ df -Th
Filesystem      Type        Size  Used Avail Use% Mounted on
/dev/root       ext4        5.3G  3.8G  1.2G  76% /
devtmpfs        devtmpfs    460M     0  460M   0% /dev
tmpfs           tmpfs       464M     0  464M   0% /dev/shm
tmpfs           tmpfs       464M   13M  452M   3% /run
tmpfs           tmpfs       5.0M  4.0K  5.0M   1% /run/lock
tmpfs           tmpfs       464M     0  464M   0% /sys/fs/cgroup
/dev/mmcblk0p6  vfat         68M   22M   47M  32% /boot
tmpfs           tmpfs        93M     0   93M  v0% /run/user/1000
/dev/mmcblk0p8  ext4        488M  408K  452M   1% /media/pi/data
/dev/mmcblk0p5  ext4         30M  456K   28M   2% /media/pi/SETTINGS
pi@pi3plus:~$
```

As you can see, we have two ext4 filesystems mounted: /dev/root (a special name for partition 7 on the microSD card) mounted on / and /dev/mmcblk0p5 (the fifth partition on our microSD card), which is /media/pi/SETTINGS.

The rest are of the tempfs and devtempfs types, which means they're really pretend filesystems created by various parts of the system. Historically they were filesystems in their own partitions, but over time for speed and ease of use, they've been replaced by various system servers. We still see them as filesystems because we can still access them like filesystems.

There's another filesystem that lives in the sixth partition of the microSD card (/dev/mmcblk0p6). It is called /boot. It's a vfat filesystem, basically an MS-DOS disk. The /boot filesystem contains the binary firmware blob that the system chip needs to boot, as well as the Linux kernel and some configuration files. If you guessed that the system chip only speaks vfat, you're exactly right. Linux knows lots of filesystems, but until it's loaded, the system chip only knows the one. If you ever have to modify the system configuration files, this is where they live.

Your system might not have /dev/mmcblk0p8, mounted on /media/pi/data. This is the extra data partition we had the option to set up when we installed NOOBS. I chose to add it with this Pi.

Adding a USB Flash Device

We could use the pi account's home directory for this procedure, or we could use that data partition, but if you're logging large amounts of data, there are a several reasons you might not want to.

Try this:

```
pi@pi3plus:~$ pwd
/home/pi
pi@pi3plus:~$
```

You've seen pwd in action before, but it's telling us something important here. The pi account's home directory lives inside /home, which lives inside the root filesystem: /. Linux can have real problems booting and running if it can't write its logs, write temporary files, and so forth. If the data we gather exceeds the free space in the root filesystem, this will be a problem.

The second problem is more subtle. We could use, for example, the data partition we had the option to set up when we installed NOOBS. If that partition gets full, then certainly the rest of the system shouldn't have a problem. But consider this: flash has a limited number of write cycles. SSD flash drives have wear leveling firmware built in, and very high-quality flash memory, so you could likely write to them for years upon years without having a problem. Our microSD cards aren't necessarily made of the good stuff like that. They're cheap. They're meant for digital cameras, where they're expected to write large files, hold them, then be read, maybe a few hundred or a few thousand times. If your microSD card develops a fault, it takes your boot and root filesystems with it.

The third consideration is portability. You can't remove the microSD card with the Pi powered up. If you have some kind of remote data collection system, it might be nice to just unmount the data drive, remove it, plug in a new one, and start logging again.

Besides. This way we learn filesystems and how to set them up. So let's go ahead and add a whole new device. In this case a flash drive.

The Stuff You Need

- *Raspberry Pi Zero W users:* A USB hub, preferably with a micro-B input cable, preferably powered. I tried it with a small unpowered hub meant for laptop use, but that was pushing my luck quite a bit.

- *Everyone*: A USB to microSD card adapter and a microSD card, or some other USB flash drive.

Setting Up the USB Flash Device

Raspberry Pi Zero W users, you need to power your Pi down. The Pi Zero W does not take kindly to large changes in power demands from its USB port. Plug the hub into the USB socket on the Pi, with or without the micro-B USB to USB-A socket converter you've been using for your keyboard and mouse. Plug the keyboard and mouse into the hub. Put the microSD card into the microSD to USB adapter and plug that into the hub as well. Plug your hub's power supply into the wall, if you have one. Now power your Pi on.

Raspberry Pi 3 Model B+ users, you can just plug the USB drive into one of your USB ports without powering down. Your Pi has what amounts to a powered USB hub built in.

Device Drivers

In Arduinos, the Arduino core has code to control every piece of hardware built into the ATmega microcontrollers—the pins, the SPI interface, the I2C interface, USARTs, the works. If you want to add a device to an Arduino like that, you use one of those existing interfaces, and you write the code yourself. Arduinos don't have a concept of kernel space and user space (unless you're counting the Yun and similar models). All code can touch all hardware.

Linux, and thus Raspbian, are different. Drivers usually run in kernel space, with full privileges, and are linked to the kernel itself at runtime. You can use existing drivers to connect to other devices. We've been doing that right along with the Larson projects via WiringPi. But if we want to make a device available to the whole system, it needs to have a proper driver, linked to the kernel. Since we want to use the USB flash drive as a filesystem device, it needs a device driver. For us, that driver is /dev/sda. In the bad old days, we'd have had to find that code, drop it in the kernel, build the kernel for hours, and hope everything worked. Modern Linux kernels can load and unload drivers dynamically. For our USB drive, this is done automatically when the system detects the USB drive's connection. If you're connecting your drive by some other mechanism (such as SPI or over the GPIO pins), you may have to configure this manually, or even write your own device driver.

Unmounting the Flash Device

The system should have mounted your flash device automatically. This doesn't always work, and there are some types of devices where you must mount them manually. Also, we'd like to mount the device to our own mount point. So let's go ahead and unmount our flash drive so we can do this by hand. First, when the system asks to open the device in File Manager, tell it no. If the File Manager is already open, close it. Then type sudo umount /dev/sda1.

```
pi@pi3plus:~$ df -h
Filesystem          Size  Used Avail Use% Mounted on
/dev/root           5.3G  3.8G  1.2G  76% /
devtmpfs            460M     0  460M   0% /dev
tmpfs               464M     0  464M   0% /dev/shm
tmpfs               464M   13M  452M   3% /run
tmpfs               5.0M  4.0K  5.0M   1% /run/lock
tmpfs               464M     0  464M   0% /sys/fs/cgroup
/dev/mmcblk0p6       68M   22M   47M  32% /boot
tmpfs                93M     0   93M   0% /run/user/1000
/dev/mmcblk0p8      488M  408K  452M   1% /media/pi/data
/dev/mmcblk0p5       30M  456K   28M   2% /media/pi/SETTINGS
/dev/sda1            30G   45M   28G   1% /media/pi/flashkey
```

You can see my flash device is /dev/sda1, and it's mounted on /media/pi/flashkey. Linux/Raspbian did this all on its own when I plugged the flash filesystem in.

```
pi@pi3plus:~$ sudo umount /dev/sda1
pi@pi3plus:~$ df -h
Filesystem       Size  Used Avail Use% Mounted on
/dev/root        5.3G  3.8G  1.2G  76% /
devtmpfs         460M     0  460M   0% /dev
tmpfs            464M     0  464M   0% /dev/shm
tmpfs            464M   13M  452M   3% /run
tmpfs            5.0M  4.0K  5.0M   1% /run/lock
tmpfs            464M     0  464M   0% /sys/fs/cgroup
/dev/mmcblk0p6    68M   22M   47M  32% /boot
tmpfs             93M     0   93M   0% /run/user/1000
/dev/mmcblk0p8   488M  408K  452M   1% /media/pi/data
/dev/mmcblk0p5    30M  456K   28M   2% /media/pi/SETTINGS
pi@pi3plus:~$
```

After umount, you can see that /dev/sda1 is not mounted at all. It's possible that you may get something different, like this:

```
pi@pi3plus:~$ cd /media/pi/flashkey
pi@pi3plus:/media/pi/flashkey$ sudo umount /dev/sda1
umount: /media/pi/flashkey: target is busy
        (In some cases useful info about processes that
        use the device is found by lsof(8) or fuser(1).)
pi@pi3plus:/media/pi/flashkey$
```

I changed directory to /media/pi/flashkey and then tried to unmount the device out from under myself. The system told me it can't do that, saying the target is busy. This can happen if your shell is pointed at the target device, or if the file manager is, or some other program has files open in that filesystem.

Creating a Filesystem

Most flash drives come the factory with a vfat or FAT32 filesystem on them. We're going to put a Linux ext4 filesystem on ours. We do that with mkfs.

The mkfs command stands for make filesystem. It takes a large number of flags, of which we're going to use only one: the -t flag. It lets us specify the filesystem type. When you use mkfs, make sure to specify which partition you want to hit. If you don't, it will warn you. If you tell it to format the entire device with no partitions, it will, but that makes them hard to work with. If you do accidentally format the flash device without a partition table, you can read up on Parted/GParted or fdisk for Linux and fix it. It's no big deal. I'll assume that didn't happen to you, since I warned you. Above all, make sure you don't do anything to any of /dev/mmcblk0's partitions. That's a mess that only a reinstall will fix.

mkfs may also warn you that there's a vfat (or some other) filesystem on on your flash device. If you're sure you have /dev/sda1 selected for your device, go ahead and ignore this warning.

```
i@pi3plus:~$ sudo mkfs -t ext4 /dev/sda1
mke2fs 1.43.4 (31-Jan-2017)
/dev/sda1 contains a ext4 file system labeled 'flashkey'
        last mounted on /media/jim/flashkey on Fri Apr  6 18:47:50 2018
Proceed anyway? (y,N) y
Creating filesystem with 7814400 4k blocks and 1954064 inodes
Filesystem UUID: 45f32659-ec99-4ed7-88b7-24e8a85a16e7
Superblock backups stored on blocks:
        32768, 98304, 163840, 229376, 294912, 819200, 884736, 1605632, 2654208,
        4096000

Allocating group tables: done
Writing inode tables: done
Creating journal (32768 blocks): done
Writing superblocks and filesystem accounting information: done

pi@pi3plus:~$
```

Mount the New Filesystem

You can see your new filesystem with the parted command. Type sudo parted -l, and it will list all the file devices connected to the system and all the partitions on them.

```
pi@pi3plus:~$ sudo parted -l
Model: Lexar USB Flash Drive (scsi)
Disk /dev/sda: 32.0GB
Sector size (logical/physical): 512B/512B
Partition Table: msdos
Disk Flags:

Number  Start   End     Size    Type     File system  Flags
 1      1049kB  32.0GB  32.0GB  primary  ext4
```

Partitions from /dev/mmcblk0 were cut for brevity.

```
pi@pi3plus:~$
```

Parted's proper name is GNU Parted. It's a very powerful utility that lets you manipulate filesystems and partitions. We're only touching on its capabilities by using it to list our unmounted filesystems. There's also a graphical version called GParted, which I find much easier to use. You install that with sudo apt-get install gparted.

Now that we know our device and its filesystem are there, we can mount the filesystem.

Mounting is done with the mount command. As with mkfs, you specify the filesystem with the -t flag and tell it what device to mount. You also have to tell it the mount point. We created a directory for that earlier called myFlash. To mount the new filesystem to it, you'd type:

```
pi@pi3plus:~$ sudo mount -t ext4 /dev/sda1 myFlash
pi@pi3plus:~$
```

It should execute without further comment. A df -h call afterward should show that it mounted. You can see it in the last entry, mounted on /home/pi/myFlash, just like we told it to.

```
pi@pi3plus:~$ df -h
Filesystem      Size  Used Avail Use% Mounted on
/dev/root       5.3G  3.8G  1.2G  76% /
devtmpfs        460M     0  460M   0% /dev
tmpfs           464M     0  464M   0% /dev/shm
tmpfs           464M   13M  452M   3% /run
tmpfs           5.0M  4.0K  5.0M   1% /run/lock
tmpfs           464M     0  464M   0% /sys/fs/cgroup
/dev/mmcblk0p6   68M   22M   47M  32% /boot
tmpfs            93M     0   93M   0% /run/user/1000
/dev/mmcblk0p8  488M  408K  452M   1% /media/pi/data
/dev/mmcblk0p5   30M  456K   28M   2% /media/pi/SETTINGS
/dev/sda1        30G   45M   28G   1% /home/pi/myFlash
pi@pi3plus:~$
```

Testing

Let's test our new filesystem. First, cd to /home/pi/myFlash (or whatever you called your mount point) and type ls -l. You should get something like this:

```
pi@pi3plus:~$ cd /home/pi/myFlash
pi@pi3plus:~/myFlash$ ls -l
total 16
drwx------ 2 root root 16384 Apr  6 19:02 lost+found
pi@pi3plus:~/myFlash$
```

An ls -dl, which shows the directory itself and all its settings, will show an issue we need to take care of.

```
pi@pi3plus:~/myFlash$ ls -dl
drwxr-xr-x 3 root root 4096 Apr  6 19:02 .
pi@pi3plus:~/myFlash$
```

The . directory, shorthand for /home/pi/myFlash, is owned by root. The pi account can't write to it like this. Sound like a job for chown? You have a good ear. Type sudo chown -R pi . This will recursively descend the /home/pi/myFlash directory and chown it and everything in it to the pi account. The filesystem drivers will still be able to access lost+found as needed, because they run with root privileges.

```
pi@pi3plus:~/myFlash$ sudo chown -R pi .
pi@pi3plus:~/myFlash$ ls -ld
drwxr-xr-x 3 pi root 4096 Apr  6 19:02 .
pi@pi3plus:~/myFlash$
```

Now if you edit a file and save it in this directory, the activity LED should flash, and you should have access.

Modifying /etc/fstab

If you're going to the trouble of adding a USB flash device so you can record data on it over time, it would be really nice to make sure the filesystem mounts it (in the right place) at boot time. Linux, like UNIX before it, has a mechanism for this called /etc/fstab. Go ahead and cat it to see what's in it.

```
pi@pi3plus:~/myFlash$ cat /etc/fstab
proc              /proc  proc   defaults          0    0
/dev/mmcblk0p6 /boot  vfat   defaults          0    2
/dev/mmcblk0p7 /      ext4   defaults,noatime 0    1
# a swapfile is not a swap partition, no line here
# use dphys-swapfile swap[on|off] for that
pi@pi3plus:~/myFlash$
```

The devices and mount points should look familiar. The /boot and / filesystems are being mounted here, as well as proc, which is another special "filesystem" (procfs) that contains information from the kernel about processes in a file-like format. The left-most column is the device being mounted. The next column is the mount point. The third column is the filesystem type, and the fourth column contains mount options. You can see that the / (root) filesystem is mounted with noatime, which lets access to that filesystem not set the atime of every file every time it's accessed, to improve performance. (They get accessed a lot.)

We're going to add a new entry to mount /dev/sda1 to /home/pi/myFlash, a filesystem type of ext4, the default mount options, plus nofail. Why nofail? Something you should know about the fstab is that unless we tell it otherwise, if a filesystem doesn't mount at boot time, the system will stop booting there. The nofail parameter prevents an error from being reported if the filesystem is unavailable, and after 90 seconds (by default), the system will continue booting. The last two columns control archiving (which we're not doing, so 0 is fine) and what order the filesystems should be checked by fsck (filesystem check) at boot time. Our filesystem can be last, so we'll put a 3 there.

Go ahead and edit /etc/fstab with geany or your favorite UNIX/Linux editor. (You'll need to use sudo for this.) The spaces between columns can be spaces or tabs. Either one will work. Don't put spaces *in* a column entry though. After the modification, /etc/fstab should look like this:

```
pi@pi3plus:~$ cat /etc/fstab
proc                /proc            proc    defaults          0   0
/dev/mmcblk0p6  /boot            vfat    defaults          0   2
/dev/mmcblk0p7  /                ext4    defaults,noatime  0   1
/dev/sda1       /home/pi/myFlash ext4    defaults,nofail   0   3
# a swapfile is not a swap partition, no line here
# use dphys-swapfile swap[on|off]   for that
pi@pi3plus:~$
```

We could test this by rebooting, but it can be awkward if there's a problem. Let's go ahead and cd back to the pi account's home directory (cd ~) and unmount the device manually, then test the fstab.

To do this, type sudo umount /dev/sda1. You can also umount /home/pi/myFlash. Since the mount point and the device are associated by the mount, you can umount either one. Once unmounted, however, you have to use the device name to mount the device again. If umount gives you a target is busy error, you know what to do.

Now that it's unmounted, we can test our fstab by asking mount to mount everything in the fstab. This is done by passing mount the -a flag. The –a flag stands for *all*, and will mount every entry in the fstab that doesn't have a noauto option. Don't worry. You can't mount a filesystem twice, and mount will ignore the filesystems that are already mounted. You can see in the following output that mount -a has done the business, and the microSD card is once again mounted on /home/pi/myFlash. Now you can reboot, and the microSD card will always mount to the same place.

```
pi@pi3plus:~$ sudo umount /dev/sda1
pi@pi3plus:~$ sudo mount -a
pi@pi3plus:~$ df -h
Filesystem      Size  Used Avail Use% Mounted on
/dev/root       5.3G  3.8G  1.2G  76% /
devtmpfs        460M     0  460M   0% /dev
tmpfs           464M     0  464M   0% /dev/shm
tmpfs           464M   13M  452M   3% /run
tmpfs           5.0M  4.0K  5.0M   1% /run/lock
tmpfs           464M     0  464M   0% /sys/fs/cgroup
/dev/mmcblk0p6   68M   22M   47M  32% /boot
tmpfs            93M     0   93M   0% /run/user/1000
/dev/mmcblk0p8  488M  408K  452M   1% /media/pi/data
/dev/mmcblk0p5   30M  456K   28M   2% /media/pi/SETTINGS
/dev/sda1        30G   45M   28G   1% /home/pi/myFlash
pi@pi3plus:~$
```

Files.cpp

So, now that we have a filesystem to put them in and it's chowned to pi so that the pi account can write to it, let's go ahead and write a short C++ program to read and write some files. By now, you've done enough code projects that I don't really have to walk you through creating it, so we'll just go through the code. I'll explain things that don't seem obvious.

```
#include <iostream>
#include <fstream>
#include <string>
```

We need <iostream> for cout. <fstream> is our new library of the day, and it gives you the same kind of access to files that iostream gives you to stdio. The <string> library gives us std::strings, as always.

```
#define fullpath "/home/pi/myFlash/my_test_file.txt"
```

I'm hard-wiring the path here. You could ask the user for this and store it in a string, but I wanted to keep the program simple.

```
using namespace std;

int main(){
      string line;
      fstream file_object;
```

When we read from a file, it will go into the string line, declared previously. We also declare an fstream object called file_object. If it seems a lot like the sockets object we created previously, it is. The fstream object class is part of the <fstreams> library, so we don't have to make our own.

```
file_object.open(fullpath,ios::out);
if (file_object.is_open()){
```

Here, we tell file_object to open the file, using its open() method. fullpath is defined with our file path, and ios:: is a group of flags defined by <fstream> that tell the system which direction our file should be opened for. In our case we're opening it for output, so we can write to it. When you're talking about an fstream object, input and output are relative to your program, not the file. We're going to output to the file, so we open it with ios::out.

Once we're done trying to open the file, we check to see if it's really open using the file_object's is_open() method. is_open() returns logical true or false. If it's true, we go on. If not, we skip down to else, as shown here.

```
file_object << "This text goes into the file,";
file_object << " just like into cout."<<endl;
```

And here, we write to the file. It looks exactly like writing to cout. The truth, of course, is that cout looks exactly like writing to a file. The << operator moves the character strings into file_object exactly the same way it does with cout, save that the stream file_object is pointing at is a file, and not stdout.

```
cout <<"Wrote to the file."<<endl;
file_object.close();
```

Speaking of cout, we move the string "Wrote to the file." plus an endl to cout to tell the user we wrote to the file. Then we call the close() method of file_object to close the file.

```
}else{
        cout <<"Unable to open file to write. Exiting."<<endl;
        exit(1);
}
```

Remember that we were in an if() statement for these writes. If we did not get the file open, we don't try to write. We just tell the user and exit the program with error status. If this happens, check the permissions on your mount point directory and all the directories inside your added microSD card.

```
file_object.open(fullpath,ios::in);
if (file_object.is_open()){
```

Having closed the file from writing to it, we now open it to read from it. Again, we check to see if it opened successfully.

```
cout << "From the file, I read:"<<endl;
while (getline(file_object,line)){
        cout <<line <<endl;
}
```

We've used the getline directive before. It reads from the stream given (cin, socket streams, etc.) until it comes to the end of a line. If it succeeds, it returns true. If we run off the end of the file, the End Of File flag gets set, and getline fails and returns false. We loop until that happens, writing every line we read to cout. Effectively, we're just transferring data from one stream to another. A lot of programming comes down to that if you look at it hard enough.

```
file_object.clear();
cout <<"Cleared the EOF flag."<<endl;

file_object.seekg(0,ios::beg);

cout <<"Used seekg to go to the beginning of the file."<<endl;
```

But let's suppose we wanted to read the file again. We could close it and open it again, but there's another option. You can seek to a specific point in a file. This doesn't reset the End of File (EOF) flag, so we'll call the clear() method of file_object to clear EOF and all other flags on our file, then use the seekg method. seekg takes two parameters—an offset number of bytes, and a reference point to offset from. We are seekging to zero bytes from the beginning of the file, which we get from the definition ios::beg. Then, of course, we tell the user we did this, because this is a demo program.

```
while (getline(file_object,line)){
        cout <<line <<endl;
}
```

Read all the lines and print them again.

```
        file_object.close();
        //Close the file when we're done.
    }else{
        cout <<"Unable to open file to read. Exiting."<<endl;
        exit(1);
    }
```

Just like we did with Sockets.cpp, we close the file. It's particularly important to close the files, otherwise the data in the file can be corrupted.

```
    return(0);
};
```

And then we exit with no errors. Filesystem access is pretty straightforward. There are a number of ways to do it, but fstream objects are about as easy as it gets. You're not limited to text files, either, although you may need to use put() and get() instead of the stream operators << and >> to move data in and out if you're dealing with binary data. Go ahead and build the project. You don't even need to include wiringPi.h in the build instructions.

Test Run

This program is one of the least interactive programs in this book. It runs, prints some things to the screen, and exits. Here's what the run looks like.

```
Wrote to the file.
From the file, I read:
This text goes into the file, just like into cout.
Cleared the EOF flag.
Used seekg to go to the beginning of the file.
This text goes into the file, just like into cout.

------------------
(program exited with code: 0)
Press return to continue
```

If you do an ls on myFlash now, however, you'll see that it's written a file there. If you cat the file, you'll see that the Files.cpp program's output was telling the truth, that it wrote a file there, and about the contents of that file.

```
pi@pi3plus:~$ ls myFlash
lost+found  my_test_file.txt
pi@pi3plus:~$ cat ~/myFlash/my_test_file.txt
This text goes into the file, just like into cout.
pi@pi3plus:~$
```

Congratulations. In Linux, everything is a file. Now you can write programs that use them.

The Code

There are two pieces of code in this project—fstab, and the code for Files.cpp. Both are listed in this section.

/etc/fstab

```
proc            /proc             proc  defaults       0   0
/dev/mmcblk0p6  /boot             vfat  defaults       0   2
/dev/mmcblk0p7  /                 ext4  defaults,noatime  0   1
/dev/mmcblk2p1  /home/pi/myFlash  ext4  defaults,nofail   0   3
# a swapfile is not a swap partition, no line here
# use dphys-swapfile swap[on|off]   for that
```

Files.cpp

```cpp
/* Files.cpp
 * This program is free software; you can redistribute it and/or modify
 * it under the terms of the GNU General Public License as published by
 * the Free Software Foundation; either version 2 of the License, or
 * (at your option) any later version.
 *
 * This program is distributed in the hope that it will be useful,
 * but WITHOUT ANY WARRANTY; without even the implied warranty of
 * MERCHANTABILITY or FITNESS FOR A PARTICULAR PURPOSE.  See the
 * GNU General Public License for more details.
 *
 * You should have received a copy of the GNU General Public License
 * along with this program; if not, write to the Free Software
 * Foundation, Inc., 51 Franklin Street, Fifth Floor, Boston,
 * MA 02110-1301, USA.
 *
 */
/* Files.cpp
 * Copyright 2018 Jim Strickland <jrs@jamesrstrickland.com>
 *
 * This program is a simple demonstration of writing and reading a text file.
 * Binary files are done exactly the same way save that put and
 * get are used instead of the string formatted << and getline
 * directives.
 */

#include <iostream> //As always, we need iostream for cout.
#include <fstream>  //fstream gives us file streams.
#include <string>    //Since this is a text file demo, we need strings.
#define fullpath "/home/pi/myFlash/my_test_file.txt"
```

```
using namespace std; //As always, std:: namespace

int main(){
        string line; //data has to go somewhere when we read it.
        fstream file_object; //define the actual object

        file_object.open(fullpath,ios::out);
        //open the file for writing.

        if (file_object.is_open()){
        //Sanity check: is the file open?

                file_object << "This text goes into the file,";
                file_object << "just like into cout."<<endl;
                //If so, write to it...

                cout <<"Wrote to the file."<<endl;
                //...and tell the user...

                file_object.close();
                //...then close the file.

        }else{
                cout <<"Unable to open file to write. Exiting."<<endl;
                exit(1);
                //Otherwise something is horribly wrong. Exit.
                //(It's probably perms or ownership of the dir. on the SD card.)
        }

        file_object.open(fullpath,ios::in);
        //Reopen the file to read.

        if (file_object.is_open()){
        //Sanity check that it's open again.

                cout << "From the file, I read:"<<endl;
                //Tell the user.
                while (getline(file_object,line)){
                        cout <<line <<endl;
                }
                //Read while there are lines to read. When the EOF (end of file)
                //flag is raised, getline will return false.

                file_object.clear(); //clear the EOF flag. And all other flags.
                cout <<"Cleared the EOF flag."<<endl;

                file_object.seekg(0,ios::beg);
                //Seek to zero bytes from the beginning of the file.
                cout <<"Used seekg to go to the beginning of the file."<<endl;
```

```
            while (getline(file_object,line)){
                  cout <<line <<endl;
            }
            //Read while there are lines to read again.

            file_object.close();
            //Close the file when we're done.
      }else{
            cout <<"Unable to open file to read. Exiting."<<endl;
            exit(1);
      }

      return(0);
};
```

Conclusion

In this chapter, we connected a new flash device (drive) to the Pi's USB port. We created a filesystem on that device, then wrote a program that writes and reads a file to the filesystem on the device. In so doing, we learned about files and filesystems.

The next chapter's the last one, and it's about adding ICs to your breadboard to build an Arduino clone directly connected to the Pi. Yay! New hardware project!

CHAPTER 12

The Best of Both Worlds

So here we are in the second-to-last chapter of the book. We've dug into the Pi's hardware, we've learned a lot of WiringPi, and we've learned quite a lot of Linux system administration and programming. Hopefully you've seen the Pi's strengths (and weaknesses) as a platform for your gadget. I know, however, that some of you aren't convinced. What if, for example, you need more than one timer/counter? What if you need to be sure it doesn't skew its timing with the system clock? What if you've invested a lot of time and effort writing cycle-accurate AVR assembly for a particular project, but you want the extra compute power of the Pi, or Internet access? What if your circuit really needs 5v GPIOs? If you're one of those folks, this project is for you.

We're going to build our own Arduino-compatible, right on the breadboard, connected to the Pi, as shown in Figure 12-1. It will have a 5v ATmega328P-PU. It will run at 16MHz. It will not fry the Raspberry Pi. In all respects but the bootloader, it will be compatible with a traditional Arduino. We'll write sketches with the Arduino application right on the Pi, download them to our bare ATmega, over SPI, the ATmega's default programming interface. They'll run at full speed, and yes, at 5v. Truly, when we're done, we'll have the best of both worlds.

© James R. Strickland 2018
J. R. Strickland, *Raspberry Pi for Arduino Users*,
https://doi.org/10.1007/978-1-4842-3414-3_12

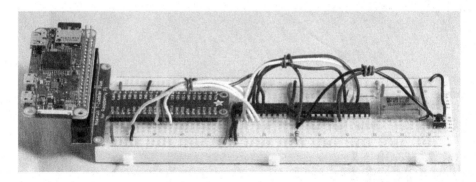

Figure 12-1. *Best of both worlds*

Bugs

We're digging into other people's code, and inevitably, there are at the time of this writing (late January, 2018) a couple of bugs.

I mentioned quite a while ago that WiringPi applications do not need to run as root. This is because the Pi foundation has extended access to the system components that drive the GPIO pins into user space (where our programs live). Unfortunately, in doing so, they introduced a bug. When a program requests access to the GPIO ports as a non-root user, it takes the system a certain amount of time to set things up. The request *should* block (remember blocking from our discussion on threads?), but it doesn't. The WiringPi library has delays built-in to take care of this. Unfortunately, the version of AVRDUDE available to the Pi with apt-get does not. There is a patch for AVRDUDE, but as of this writing, you have to build AVRDUDE from the source code to get it. We're not going to do that, because there's an easier workaround. We'll set AVRDUDE to run with root privileges when it runs, so that the mechanism's timing won't matter. It's a security risk, but a reasonable one, in my opinion, as you can always disable or uninstall AVRDUDE once you're happy with the sketch on the ATmega.

The Stuff You Need

- Your Raspberry Pi. Either model should work.

- ATmega328P-PU. As far as I know, these only come in 20MHz flavor, which works fine at 16MHz.

- 16MHz full can oscillator.

- The 74LVC245 octal bus transceiver. We'll use it as a level shifter, to shift 5v signals down to 3.3v.

- The generic LED, and a 220Ω dropping resistor for it.

- The tactile button and a 10kΩ pullup resistor for the ATmega's reset circuit.

- Hookup wire, as usual.

The Circuit

Figure 12-2 shows the schematic of the circuit we're building. Here's how it works. The Pi's 3.3v SPI signals are passed through the 74LVC245 where they remain at 3.3v, and are passed on to the ATmega. Even though the ATmega is running at 5v, its inputs are logical high at anything above 0.6v, so 3.3v is plenty. The ATmega will respond with 5v signals. These pass through the 74LVC245 and are lowered to the same level as the 74LVC245's Vcc, which is 3.3v. No signal pin on the Pi ever sees more than 3.3v, so the Pi is safe. We run all the signals through the level shifter, because the ATmega's SPI pins can become outputs running at 5v from program control. In fact, Blink, the program we're going to test the setup with, will do exactly that to SCK, aka Digital13.

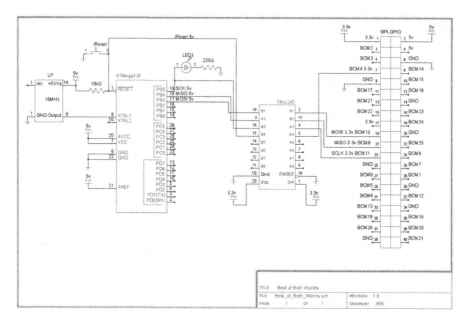

Figure 12-2. *Best of both worlds schematic*

The 16MHz full can oscillator runs on 5v and outputs a 16MHz clock for the ATmega. Breadboards can be tricky for higher frequency signals, but I've run full can oscillators up to 20MHz on one with no problems.

The reset circuit works just like the LEDs in the Larson scanner: the resistor holds the circuit logically high, keeping the ATmega from resetting, until something (the button, or a signal from the Pi) pulls it to the ground, when the resistor limits the current that the signal has to dissipate. Note the slash in front of the /Reset signal name. That, or a bar over the whole signal name, means the signal is active *low*.

I find it easiest to wire the power and ground lines for everything first, so wire the 3.3v line from pin 1 on the Pi to one positive rail on your breadboard, and wire the 5v line on pin 2 to the other one. It is critically important that you not mix these two rails up, or you'll be heading out to buy another Pi. To that end, I wired two grounds, even though they're connected together inside the Pi: one from pin 4 to the ground rail on the

398

5v side of the breadboard, and one from pin 9 to the ground rail on the 3.3v side. You can see this organization on the breadboard in Figure 12-1.

Once that's done, wire pin 20 of the 74LVC245 to the 3.3v rail of your breadboard and wire pin 10 to the ground. While we're wiring the 74LVC245, let's go ahead and hook pin 19 to the ground. This line is the /enable line, active low, that turns on the outputs of the 74LVC245. Likewise, connect pin 1, DIR, to 3.3v. This controls whether the 74LVC245 sends signals from its A pins to its B pins, or vice versa. Setting it high means signals go from A to B, which is what we want. Again, make doubly sure that all the connections between the 74LVC245 at this point are either to the 3.3v rail or to the ground.

We'll set up the ATmega next. It needs +5v on pin 7 (VCC) and on pin 20 (AVCC) and on pin 21 (AREF). The first two are for its power needs. The last is the line against which analog inputs are compared. If you have a good reason, AREF could be connected to 3.3v, but normal Arduinos have these connected to Vcc. The ATmega needs two ground circuits as well, one on pin 8 and one on pin 22. It will not work correctly unless both sets of power connections are hooked up.

The last IC to connect is the 16MHz full can oscillator. While it only has four pins, it's the same size as an 14-pin DIP and is often put in 14-pin sockets, so its pins are numbered as though it has 14 pins. Pin 1, the upper left, usually identified with a paint dot and by having the only square corner on the can, is not connected to anything. Pin 7 should connect to the ground rail. Pin 14 is connected to the 5v rail. The full can oscillator won't work correctly at 3.3v.

Let's do the /reset circuit next. Wire the 10kΩ resistor from the 5v rail to pin 1 on the ATmega. (It's shown wired to the 3.3v rail in Figure 12-2, which also works fine.) Then run a wire from pin 1 to some free space on the board, put your tactile button there, and connect the other side of that button to the ground. When you push the button, you'll short pin 1 to the ground for a moment, resetting the ATmega.

The LED circuit is the next one to do. Wire pin 19 of the ATmega to the cathode (+ side) of the LED. The anode of the LED gets connected to the 220Ω resistor, and through the resistor to the ground. This LED is active high.

All that's left now are the SPI circuits. Run a wire from the Pi's pin 19, aka BCM10, aka MOSI (remembering that this is a 3.3v signal) to pin 2, the A side of channel 1 of the 74LVC245. Then connect pin 18, the B side of the 74LVC245 to pin 17, aka MOSI (5v) on the ATmega. MOSI will come from the master (the Pi) through the 74LVC245's a channel, to the ATmega's MOSI pin.

The MISO pin is exactly the opposite of MOSI. Here I have to point out I did something a little unkind in the schematic. Look closely at pins 3 and 17 of the 74LVC245. You'll see that I flipped the A2 and B2 pins (and their numbers) to make the schematic easier to read. The MISO circuit originates at the ATmega's MISO (5v) pin, on pin 18, goes from the 74LVC245's A2 (pin 3) to B2 (pin 17) channel, where its voltage is lowered, and ends on the Pi's MISO pin, aka pin 21, aka BCM9 at 3.3v.

SCK/SCLK work the same as MOSI did. SCLK originates at the Pi (the clock circuit in SPI always comes from the master) at 3.3v, goes into pin 4 (channel 3's A side) of the 74LVC245, and emerges on pin 16, (channel 3's B side), where it connects to pin 19, aka SCK (5v), aka PB5, aka Digital 19 on the ATmega.

The reset circuit is next. For the ATmega to stop the running program and listen on SPI, it has to be reset at the right time, and we'll use BCM4 (pin 7 on the Pi's GPIO) for that job. It uses channel 4 of the 74LVC245 and is connected to the A side on pin 5, to emerge on pin 15, where it connects to the /reset circuit on pin 1 of the ATmega. When the Pi pulls BCM4 to the ground, the 74LVC245 will do likewise with the line to the ATmega, and whichever voltage (5v or 3.3v) we're feeding the reset circuit to hold it high will be shorted to the ground by the 74LVC245, causing a reset, just as though we'd pressed the button.

All that's left is the clock signal to the ATmega. Wire it from pin 14 of the full can oscillator (on the other side of the DIP from pin 1) to pin 9 (XTAL1) of the ATmega. We won't use XTAL2 at all.

Powering Up

Go ahead and plug your Pi in and turn on its power, but make sure to check the temperature of the full can oscillator and the ATmega very quickly afterward. Don't wait for the full boot up—the Pi's power supply rails go live as soon as you give the Pi power. If either of these chips gets hot (and be careful, they can get too hot to touch), or the Pi doesn't show signs of booting, disconnect the Pi's power *right now* and go over their wiring again. Something's not right. I've mixed up power connections on ATmegas many times, and once on a full can oscillator. If you're quick, these ICs will usually live through the experience.

The Software

You need two pieces of software: the Arduino application and AVRDUDE. You should have the Arduino package already. If not, flip back to Chapter 4 and download it now. Don't use the package you can get with apt-get. It's horribly out of date.

You may recall from our discussions in Chapter 4 that AVRDUDE is part of the Arduino distribution. It is, albeit a very old version. We're going to download a newer version that uses a driver that will talk to the GPIO port of the Pi. We'll also hack the files of the Arduino application to use it. Go ahead and type sudo apt-get install avrdude. Like so:

```
pi@PiOw:~$ sudo apt-get install avrdude
Reading package lists... Done
Building dependency tree
Reading state information... Done
```

Lots of stuff edited for brevity...

```
Preparing to unpack .../avrdude_6.3-2+rpi1_armhf.deb ...
Unpacking avrdude (6.3-2+rpi1) ...
Setting up avrdude (6.3-2+rpi1) ...
Processing triggers for man-db (2.7.6.1-2) ...
pi@PiOw:~$
```

Setting Up AVRDUDE

Now that we have AVRDUDE installed system-wide, we need to do a couple things to it. We need to set up a local configuration for the Pi account, and we need to change the permissions it runs at. To set a local configuration, we need to create a file, in /home/pi, called .avrduderc. Note the dot (.) in front of .avrduderc—this tells Bash that this file should be invisible to ls without passing ls the -a flag. Long ago, in the dinosaur UNIX days, this custom of making configuration files in your account invisible was probably to keep people from stepping on them and making their accounts unusable. This would be particularly true of brand new users. The tradition still continues to this day. Go ahead and edit /home/pi/.avrduderc in Geany, or your favorite editor.

In order to be as flexible as it is, AVRDUDE lets the user define the properties of the programming device it's expected to use. If you've poked around in the Arduino application and seen programmers like "Arduino as ISP" and so on, all of these and many others are possible, if AVRDUDE has code to drive them, and you tell AVRDUDE to use that interface and what to send on it. The version of AVRDUDE we just installed has an interface called linuxgpio, which is the standard Linux interface for talking to GPIO pins.

Local Configuration: .avrduderc

Here's what you put in your /home/pi/.avrduderc file.

```
programmer
  id    = "linuxgpio";
  desc  = "Use the Linux sysfs interface to bitbang GPIO lines";
  type  = "linuxgpio";
  reset = 4;
  sck   = 11;
  mosi  = 10;
  miso  = 9;
;
```

Declare the programmer id ("linuxgpio"), then provide a description so you know what you're looking at next year. The type is also "linuxgpio". The reset pin is on 4, sck is on 11, mosi is on 10, and miso is on 9. Be sure to close every line with a semicolon (;), as well as the entire file. AVRDUDE is very fussy about this.

Hardware versus Software SPI

The linuxgpio programmer uses software SPI, via sysfs. Instead of going through spidev0, it controls the GPIO pins just like we could from WiringPi to bang out the pulses that make up SPI, by turning individual pins on and off. In the old days, this was called bit-banging, and it still is in some circles. It works. It's not as fast, but the ATmega328P-PU only holds 32KiB of code, so it's less an issue here than it would have been in the last chapter.

The advantage to this method is simply this: it works. There is hardware SPI programmer code in AVRDUDE 6.3—the most recent version you can get as of this writing without building the code yourself—but it seems to have the same timing bug I mentioned earlier, and I couldn't find a good workaround for it. Software SPI will be fast enough. If you want your Pi to communicate with the ATmega via SPI (WiringPi has libraries for this), you may need to change the wiring slightly.

Fun with chmod

As mentioned, in order for AVRDUDE to do its job without being subject to the timing bug, it has to run with root privileges. While we could make it work with sudo, it would then want to use an .avrdude file in root's home directory, and in any case it wouldn't work with the Arduino application unless that too was running as root. And it touches the Internet. Bad idea. Instead, we'll set a special permissions flag on the AVRDUDE executable that lets it run with the permissions of its owner. That flag is called SETUID. We set it with chmod.

The AVRDUDE executable lives at /usr/bin/avrdude. If you didn't already know that, you could type which avrdude, and Linux would tell you. Then just type chmod u+s /usr/bin/avrdude. You can verify that it happened with ls -l /usr/bin/avrdude, and see the s flag set in the owner field. That's your setuid flag.

```
pi@PiOw:~$ which avrdude
/usr/bin/avrdude
pi@PiOw:~$ sudo chmod u+s /usr/bin/avrdude
pi@PiOw:~$ ls -l /usr/bin/avrdude
-rwsr-xr-x 1 root root 379432 Jun 12  2017 /usr/bin/avrdude
pi@PiOw:~$
```

Testing

Now, finally, we can test our build beyond "Is anything burning?" With AVRDUDE configured and set to run setuid, we can call it and ask it to say hello to the ATmega, and see if the ATmega answers. We do that with the avrdude command; pass it a -c and tell it to use the linuxgpio programmer that we just configured, then tell it the part number with -p. Here's the demo:

```
pi@Piow:~$ avrdude -c linuxgpio -p ATmega328P-PU

avrdude: AVR device initialized and ready to accept instructions

Reading | ################################################## | 100% 0.00s
```

```
avrdude: Device signature = 0x1e950f (probably m328p)
avrdude: safemode: Fuses OK (E:FF, H:D9, L:62)
avrdude done.  Thank you.
pi@PiOw:~$
```

Note particularly that it successfully read the ATmega, that it got a valid device signature (0x1e950f in hexadecimal), and that the fuses are okay. We'll get back to fuses shortly. If you don't get output similar to this (you can add the -v flag to get much more information), something's wrong. If, instead, you get an error that the device signature is different from the expected one, and the device's signature is actually 0x1e9514, you wound up with the ATmega328 instead of the ATmega328P-PU version, like I warned you about in Chapter 1. (I warned you about that so emphatically because I did it in preparation for this book. Buying the right IC is easier than hacking everything so an ATmega328 will work. If you did wind up with the wrong ATmega, this website has instructions for the aforementioned hacking: http://www.instructables.com/id/Bootload-an-ATmega328/.

If you get a message that the device is not responding, it's probably a wiring problem. If you get some other device ID, then you've got more complicated problems, and you need to make sure you're using the linuxgpio programmer and not linuxspi. I got that message a lot while trying to make linuxspi work.

Setting Up the Arduino Application

Now that we have a working version of AVRDUDE, we need to set the Arduino application up to use it. There are three things we need to do, and all of them involve diving inside the Arduino application's directories. Assuming your Arduino program is still in your Downloads directory like mine is (if you plan to use it regularly, you'll want to move it to its own directory and run its install.sh script), cd to /home/pi/Downloads/ arduino-1.8.5/hardware/tools/avr. Your Arduino version may change, and there's a chance they may reorganize things (they do that from time to time), but this is where you look. This directory is hardware specific things, tools for hardware, specifically for the AVR family, which our ATmega328P-PU is a member of. If you type ls, you'll see a number of directories that should make you suspicious, such as etc and bin. If you expect to find AVRDUDE itself in bin and avrdude.conf in etc, just as you'd find the system-wide AVRDUDE in /usr/bin and its configuration file in /etc/avrdude.conf, you're absolutely right. The Arduino application mimics those paths inside itself for its captive, antique version of AVRDUDE, among other things.

```
pi@PiOw:~/Downloads/arduino-1.8.5/hardware/tools/avr$ ls
armv7l-unknown-linux-gnueabihf  builtin_tools_versions.txt  lib
avr                             etc                         libexec
bin                             include                     share
pi@PiOw:~/Downloads/arduino-1.8.5/hardware/tools/avr$
```

We need to replace bin/avrdude with a symlink to the system's AVRDUDE that we've worked on, and etc/avrdude.conf with a symlink to the system's avrdude.conf. You can get the paths to the system versions by typing whereis avrdude.

```
pi@PiOw:~/Downloads/arduino-1.8.5/hardware/tools/avr$ whereis avrdude
avrdude: /usr/bin/avrdude /etc/avrdude.conf /usr/share/man/man1/avrdude.1.gz
pi@PiOw:~/Downloads/arduino-1.8.5/hardware/tools/avr$
```

Let's replace the Arduino version of AVRDUDE with the system version first. We'll do that using ln -s to make a symbolic link. Go into the bin directory (/home/pi/Downloads/arduino-1.8.5/hardware/tools/avr/bin) and remove the existing AVRDUDE. Then type ln -s /usr/bin/avrdude avrdude to create the symlink. The Arduino application will still call AVRDUDE in its own directory, but it'll get the system-wide one. A quick ls -l avrdude will show whether the link worked correctly. If not, check to make sure you have the parameters of ln -s in the right order. It's one of my

favorite mistakes to make. You can also verify it by typing ./avrdude to call
the AVRDUDE executable in this directory. You should get AVRDUDE 6.3
or higher. If you get version 5, you're still looking with the version that came
with the Arduino application, and it won't do what you want.

```
pi@PiOw:~/Downloads/arduino-1.8.5/hardware/tools/avr$ cd bin
pi@PiOw:~/Downloads/arduino-1.8.5/hardware/tools/avr/bin$ rm avrdude
pi@PiOw:~/Downloads/arduino-1.8.5/hardware/tools/avr/bin$ ln -s /usr/bin/
avrdude avrdude
pi@PiOw:~/Downloads/arduino-1.8.5/hardware/tools/avr/bin$ ls -l avrdude
lrwxrwxrwx 1 pi pi 16 Jan 31 16:44 avrdude -> /usr/bin/avrdude
pi@PiOw:~/Downloads/arduino-1.8.5/hardware/tools/avr/bin$ ./avrdude
Usage: avrdude [options]
```

Text deleted for brevity...

```
avrdude version 6.3, URL: <http://savannah.nongnu.org/projects/avrdude/>
pi@PiOw:~/Downloads/arduino-1.8.5/hardware/tools/avr/bin$
```

Next, we need to back out of the bin directory and do exactly the same
thing in the etc directory with avrdude.conf. So type cd ../etc. This will
take you up one level and then down into etc, all in one command. The,
just like before, type rm avrdude.conf and ln -s /etc/avrdude.conf
avrdude.conf. An ls -l avrdude.conf will verify that the link is where
you want it.

```
Testing pi@PiOw:~/Downloads/arduino-1.8.5/hardware/tools/avr/bin$ cd ../etc
pi@PiOw:~/Downloads/arduino-1.8.5/hardware/tools/avr/etc$ rm avrdude.conf
pi@PiOw:~/Downloads/arduino-1.8.5/hardware/tools/avr/etc$ ln -s /etc/avrdude.
conf avrdude.conf
pi@PiOw:~/Downloads/arduino-1.8.5/hardware/tools/avr/etc$ ls -l avrdude.conf
lrwxrwxrwx 1 pi pi 17 Jan 31 16:54 avrdude.conf -> /etc/avrdude.conf
pi@PiOw:~/Downloads/arduino-1.8.5/hardware/tools/avr/etc$
```

The last thing we need to do to get the Arduino application set up is
to add our new programmer, linuxgpio, to the programmer list in the
application. That file is in the directory (again, assuming your Arduino
application is still in Downloads) /home/pi/Downloads/arduino-1.8.5/

hardware/arduino/avr and unsurprisingly, it's called programmers.txt. Edit this file with your favorite Linux editor (Geany will work), scroll to the bottom, and add the following lines:

```
rpigpio.name=Pi GPIO
rpigpio.protocol=linuxgpio
rpigpio.program.tool=avrdude
```

Save the file. You're done tinkering with the guts of the Arduino application. Go ahead and start (or restart, as the case may be) the Arduino application. Select Tools ➤ Programmer, and Pi GPIO should show up in the list. Pick that. While you're here, select Tools ➤ Board ➤ Arduino Duemilanove or Diecimila, and make sure the processor is set to ATmega328P. This is the simplest Arduino that uses the ATmega328P.

Setting Up the ATmega328P-PU

There is, as Steve Jobs used to say, one more thing. Normally, if you were setting up a new ATmega328P-PU to be an Arduino-compatible, you'd have to find (or make) a bootloader. We're not going to. The bootloader really only does two things for you. It makes the Arduino listen for programs on its USART port and sets the fuses. If you try (or tried) to load a bootloader, you'd find that you get an error. Programmers are supposed to return a code when verifying a bootloader, but since our programmer is just a Linux device bit-banging SPI, it doesn't know about that. Fortunately, we don't actually need the bootloader at all. Since we're communicating with the ATmega via SPI, we can load programs to it directly, although it will mean we can't use Serial.print() in our programs meaningfully.

In fact, you could load programs into the ATmega right now, but if you did, you'd discover they run very, very slowly. To understand why, we need to talk about the fuses on the ATmega328P-PU.

Speed and Fuses

The fuses on the ATmega328P-PU are configuration settings. They're persistent, even when the power's turned off, and they determine how the microcontroller goes about its business. The whole listing is in the ATmega328P-PU's datasheet, but it's not one of the clearest parts of the datasheet. Instead, I suggest going here: `http://eleccelerator.com/fusecalc/fusecalc.php?chip=atmega328p`. Each fuse is called out by what it does, and if you click the right check boxes, you'll get the configuration you want.

You can configure a lot of options: what voltage to consider too low to operate, whether reset is enabled or not, and so forth, but the options we're interested in are the clock settings. By default, as the ATmega328P-PUs come from the factory, they're set up to use their internal clock, at 8MHz, and divide that clock by 8. From the factory, they want to run at 1MHz, and it's not an especially accurate clock. The Arduino software assumes we're going to run at 16MHz (you can configure this for custom hardware, but it's a big job). So uncheck the Divide Clock by 8 Internally option.

We also need to tell the ATmega328P-PU that we're using an external crystal oscillator, that it's faster than 8MHz, that it needs to wait 16K clock cycles on powerdown and reset before starting (to let the clock stabilize) and then 65ns (nanoseconds) beyond that. Or, if you scroll down further, check all the CKSEL (ClocK SELect) and SUT bits (Start Up Time) off. Note that like many things we've dealt with, ATmega configuration fuses are active low, so our resulting fuse bytes will have 1s for each bit we just set. The low-fuse byte should be (in hexadecimal) 0xFF (all bits high. inactive) the high-fuse byte should be 0xD9, and the extended fuse byte should be 0xFF. This would normally be in our bootloader. Since we don't have one, we'll just apply it by hand with AVRDUDE. It only needs to be set once. Type this:

```
avrdude -U lfuse:w:0xff:m -U hfuse:w:0xd9:m -U efuse:w:0xff:m -p
m328p -c linuxgpio
```

It calls AVRDUDE, tells AVRDUDE that we're going to specify a memory type (-U), specifies the memory type (lfuse, hfuse, and efuse, respectively), tells it to write, gives it the byte we want to set, and that this is a literal byte, not a filename or encoded in some way. It selects the part (m328p is the same as ATmega328P) and what programmer to use. You should get something like this:

```
pi@PiOw:~$ avrdude -U lfuse:w:0xff:m -U hfuse:w:0xd9:m -U efuse:w:0xff:m -p
m328p -c linuxgpio

avrdude: AVR device initialized and ready to accept instructions

Reading | ################################################## | 100% 0.00s

avrdude: Device signature = 0x1e950f (probably m328p)
avrdude: reading input file "0xff"
avrdude: writing lfuse (1 bytes):

Writing | ################################################## | 100% 0.00s

avrdude: 1 bytes of lfuse written
avrdude: verifying lfuse memory against 0xff:
avrdude: load data lfuse data from input file 0xff:
avrdude: input file 0xff contains 1 bytes
avrdude: reading on-chip lfuse data:

Reading | ################################################## | 100% 0.00s

avrdude: verifying ...
avrdude: 1 bytes of lfuse verified
```

AVRDUDE checked the device signature and wrote the low fuse, then verified that it was set correctly.

```
avrdude: reading input file "0xd9"
avrdude: writing hfuse (1 bytes):

Writing | ################################################## | 100% 0.00s

avrdude: 1 bytes of hfuse written
avrdude: verifying hfuse memory against 0xd9:
avrdude: load data hfuse data from input file 0xd9:
avrdude: input file 0xd9 contains 1 bytes
avrdude: reading on-chip hfuse data:
```

```
Reading | ############################################## | 100% 0.00s

avrdude: verifying ...
avrdude: 1 bytes of hfuse verified
```

Likewise, AVRDUDE set the high fuse, read it back, and verified it.

```
avrdude: reading input file "0xff"
avrdude: writing efuse (1 bytes):

Writing | ############################################## | 100% 0.00s

avrdude: 1 bytes of efuse written
avrdude: verifying efuse memory against 0xff:
avrdude: load data efuse data from input file 0xff:
avrdude: input file 0xff contains 1 bytes
avrdude: reading on-chip efuse data:

Reading | ############################################## | 100% 0.00s

avrdude: verifying ...
avrdude: 1 bytes of efuse verified
```

And once more, AVRDUDE set the extended fuse, read it back, and verified it.

```
avrdude: safemode: Fuses OK (E:FF, H:D9, L:FF)

avrdude done. Thank you.

pi@PiOw:~$
```

And we're done.

Blink

After all this, let's see if our handiwork actually works. Go to File ➤ Examples ➤ Basics ➤ Blink and select it. Don't click upload. It won't work. Choose Sketch ➤ Upload Using Programmer. Compiling will be slow, especially on a Raspberry Pi Zero W. After compiling the sketch, the Arduino application should call the system AVRDUDE, pick up the

411

Pi account's .avrduderc, upload the code and...the LED should flash. This is pretty much where we started with the Raspberry Pi, and now our Arduino-compatible is doing the job.

The Code

There isn't much code in this chapter—just one new configuration file and some additions to the existing configuration files. The code from here on out? That's up to you.

.avrduderc

```
programmer
  id    = "linuxgpio";
  desc  = "Use the Linux sysfs interface to bitbang GPIO lines";
  type  = "linuxgpio";
  reset = 4;
  sck   = 11;
  mosi  = 10;
  miso  = 9;
;
```

Modifications to programmers.txt

```
rpigpio.name=Pi GPIO
rpigpio.protocol=linuxgpio
rpigpio.program.tool=avrdude
```

Fuse Settings for the ATmega328P-PU

```
avrdude -U lfuse:w:0xff:m -U hfuse:w:0xd9:m -U efuse:w:0xff:m -p m328p -c
linuxgpio
```

Conclusion

In this chapter, we built an Arduino-compatible and connected it to the Pi via SPI. We hit bugs, specifically that the Pi's hardware SPI and AVRDUDE have a *race condition* (a place where timing matters and is not controlled) that means AVRDUDE can't write to the ATmega over hardware SPI. We took a different tack, using software SPI and modified AVRDUDE. We tampered with the innards of the Arduino application and produced a solution that lets the Pi upload Arduino code to the compatible.

You could, going further, set up SPI communications between the Pi and the Arduino-compatible using hardware SPI like we did in the last chapter, and then use WiringPi's SPI functions to communicate with the Arduino-compatible. If you need interrupts that take a known, predictable amount of time, this project would do the job for you. If you need to drive another Arduino project that requires 5v, this project would do that too. This chapter is all about adding to the flexibility of your Pi.

All that's left are some conclusions.

CHAPTER 13

Conclusions, Credits, and Parting Thoughts

When you write a book, any book, there's a temptation to look back at it as an epic journey. After all, it takes months to write one, to do all the projects (twice, sometimes more), research, and so on. It might not seem that way to readers. Nevertheless, we have been on an epic journey. We started out just buying the right parts and getting the Pi running. Here at the end, we've been through enough Linux to get things done, leveraging the C++ you already knew from Arduinos, learned the ins and outs of WiringPi, learned some system programming, and learned how to attach projects to the Pi so the whole operating system can see them. Finally, we came full circle and built our own Arduino compatible connected to the Pi, for those times when nothing else will do. It's been a journey. Hopefully, it's been fun. The projects have been simple, but that's because complexity just gets in the way when you're trying to learn new concepts. You can add the complexity. You can make the Pi do new and amazing things. I'm just here to give you the tools and to help you add the Raspberry Pi to your toolbox. Where you go from here is up to you.

If you've enjoyed this book, I should mention I have another book with Apress called *Junk Box Arduino, Ten Adventures in Upcycled Electronics*. It digs much deeper into the Arduino world, and into hooking up all kinds of old ICs that you might find in the electronics junk that are too good to throw away but not useful anymore.

© James R. Strickland 2018
J. R. Strickland, *Raspberry Pi for Arduino Users*,
https://doi.org/10.1007/978-1-4842-3414-3_13

Credit Where Credit Is Due

As I'm sure you're aware, it's really tough to come up with new projects for Raspberry Pis (or Arduinos). In most cases, someone, somewhere, has done it before you. That's a good thing. It's the advantage of having a community. As a result, however, I need to acknowledge a few sources.

For Chapter 12, I used ideas from Mark Williams' blog here: `http://ozzmaker.com/program-avr-using-raspberry-pi-gpio/` and Lukáš Lalinský's blog here: `https://oxygene.sk/2015/02/using-raspberry-pi-as-an-arduino-avr-programmer/`.

For all matters C++, I leaned heavily on this site: `http://www.cplusplus.com/doc/tutorial/files/` and various `stackoverflow.com` forums. If you ask a programming question in a Google search, Stackoverflow will probably have an answer. And perhaps a debate, minor flame war, and so on.

For socket programming, Eva M. Castro's "Porting Applications to IPv6" HowTo was a godsend, and ultimately it was her approach, ported to C++, that I used. See `http://long.ccaba.upc.edu/long/045Guidelines/eva/ipv6.html`.

Parting Thoughts

I have a few other thoughts, mostly hints and tips that came up during the writing of the previous chapters, but that just don't fit in the chapters. Instead, they're here, and in no particular order.

Be Patient

Pis are incredible little computers for their price and size, but we're spoiled by their desktop cousins that have many times more power. The Pi can do it. It just takes longer.

Label Your Pi

I can tell you from personal experience that almost nobody has just one Raspberry Pi. Label them, both in their configurations and preferably with a sticker or something on the hardware. Bonus points if you find a way to label the microSD cards. Does it sound like I had mixups? Reloaded the wrong microSD cards? Your ear has not failed you.

Use Terminal Applications When You Can

Most terminal apps hail from the bad old days when an entire campus might share a UNIX computer not much faster (except in disk I/O) than a Raspberry Pi. They're very, very fast, even on a Pi Zero W.

Get a Real Drive

It's entirely feasible to use your Pi as a backup desktop computer, but it's much, much less painful if you have it use a real drive instead of a microSD card for most of its jobs. We've connected additional flash filesystems to the USB ports, but with a cheap USB-SATA adapter, you can hang a laptop drive from the same port. There are a number of ways to connect this up (Google it), but the best is probably to configure the Pi's system chip to get *everything* from the USB drive. The Raspberry Pi 3 Model B (and presumably the modern Raspberry Pi 3 model B+) can apparently do this. I've done it the old way, where the kernel lives on the microSD card and mounts the external drive to the /root and /home filesystems. It works. Even a 5400RPM laptop drive is much faster.

Synergy

Right now, as I type this, there are three computers on my desk, including the Pi Zero W. I have room for one keyboard and one mouse (and expensive tastes in both). I've found the Synergy application to be incredibly useful for letting my Mac or my big Linux box serve this keyboard and mouse out to whatever Pi I have connected. I use the open source version, since the for-pay version does not support ARM platforms like the Pi. You can install a useable version on the Pi (1.4.16-2) with `apt-get`. Just turn encryption off. You can find more info here: `https://sourceforge.net/projects/synergy-stable-builds/`. Be advised that the open source version of Synergy is not considered secure.

Index

A

Acorn RISC Machine (ARM), 4

Apt-get package
    manager, 78–79

Arduino
    AVRDUDE, 133
    compiler, 129–130, 132
    IDE, 127–128
    IDE *vs.* Geany, 134, 137
    installation on
        Raspberry Pi, 123–126
    libraries, 132

ATmega328P-PU (IC), 408, 412

AVRDownloaderUploaDEr
    (AVRDUDE), 133

B

Best of both worlds
    application
    ATmega328P-PU, 408, 412
    AVRDUDE, 396, 401–402
    .avrduderc, 412
    Blink, 411
    bugs, 396
    circuit, 397–400
    configuration, 403
    downloads, 405–408

fuses configuration
        settings, 409–410
    hardware *vs.* software SPI, 403
    power supply, 401
    programmers.txt, 412
    setuid flag, 404
    test, 404–405

Bourne Again Shell (bash), 93

Bourne shell, 141

BSS segment, 262

Button_interrupt
    add #define, 225
    complete code, 230
    copy command, 224
    debouncing, 225–227
    INT_EDGE_BOTH, 229
    INT_EDGE_FALLING, 229
    INT_EDGE_RISING, 229
    ISR, 227–228
    variable types, 227
    wiringPiISR function, 228
    wiringPiSetupGpio(), 228

Button_polled
    code, 220
    create project, 218
    directory, 218
    main loop, 219
    pin, 218–219

© James R. Strickland 2018
J. R. Strickland, *Raspberry Pi for Arduino Users*,
https://doi.org/10.1007/978-1-4842-3414-3